INTERNATIONAL PERSPECTIVES IN SOCIAL JUSTICE PROGRAMS AT THE INSTITUTIONAL AND COMMUNITY LEVELS

INNOVATIONS IN HIGHER EDUCATION TEACHING AND LEARNING

Senior Series Editor: Patrick Blessinger, St. John's University and Higher Education Teaching and Learning Association, USA

Associate Series Editor: Enakshi Sengupta, Higher Education Teaching and Learning Association, USA

Published volumes:

INNOVATIONS IN HIGHER EDUCATION TEACHING AND LEARNING   VOLUME 37

INTERNATIONAL PERSPECTIVES IN SOCIAL JUSTICE PROGRAMS AT THE INSTITUTIONAL AND COMMUNITY LEVELS

EDITED BY

ENAKSHI SENGUPTA

Centre for Advanced Research in Higher Education, New York, USA
International HETL Association, New York, USA

PATRICK BLESSINGER

St. John's University, New York, USA
International HETL Association, New York, USA

Created in partnership with the
International Higher Education Teaching and Learning Association

https://www.hetl.org/

United Kingdom – North America – Japan
India – Malaysia – China

Emerald Publishing Limited
Howard House, Wagon Lane, Bingley BD16 1WA, UK

First edition 2021

Reprints and permissions service
Contact: permissions@emeraldinsight.com

British Library Cataloguing in Publication Data
A catalogue record for this book is available from the British Library

ISBN: 978-1-80043-489-9 (Print)
ISBN: 978-1-80043-488-2 (Online)
ISBN: 978-1-80043-490-5 (Epub)

ISSN: 2055-3641 (Series)

Printed and bound by CPI Group (UK) Ltd, Croydon, CR0 4YY

ISOQAR certified
Management System,
awarded to Emerald
for adherence to
Environmental
standard
ISO 14001:2004.

Certificate Number 1985
ISO 14001

INVESTOR IN PEOPLE

CONTENTS

LIST OF CONTRIBUTORS

Bruno F. Abrantes	Niels Brock Copenhagen Business College, Denmark
Wisdom Kwaku Agbevanu	University of Cape Coast, Cape Coast, Ghana
Francis Ansah	University of Cape Coast, Cape Coast, Ghana
Irene Antonopoulos	De Montfort University, Leicester, UK
Bridget Backhaus	Griffith University, Queensland, Australia
Paul Beehler	University of California at Riverside, USA
Patrick Blessinger	International Higher Education Teaching and Learning Association, New York, USA
Thomas D. Eatmon	Niels Brock Copenhagen Business College, Denmark
Charlotte Forsberg	De Montfort University, Leicester, UK
Omar Madhloom	University of Bristol, Bristol, UK
Erin McLaughlin	Cabrini University, Pennsylvania, USA
Rory Moore	University of California at Riverside, USA
Hope Pius Nudzor	University of Cape Coast, Cape Coast, Ghana
Kshama Pandey	MJP Rohilkhand University, Bareilly, India
Umesh Chandra Pandey	Indira Gandhi National Open University, Bhopal, India
Susan Jacques Pierson	Cabrini University, Pennsylvania, USA
Enakshi Sengupta	International Higher Education Teaching and Learning Association, New York, USA
Alia Sheety	Cabrini University, Pennsylvania, USA
Anil Shukla	MJP Rohilkhand University, Bareilly, India
Sharon Tao	Cambridge Education, Cambridge, UK
Faith Valencia-Forrester	Griffith University, Queensland, Australia
Alan Vogelfanger	University of Buenos Aires, Argentina

SERIES EDITORS' INTRODUCTION

The purpose of this series is to publish current research and scholarship on innovative teaching and learning practices in higher education. The series is developed around the premise that teaching and learning is more effective when instructors and students are actively and meaningfully engaged in the teaching–learning process.

The main objectives of this series are to:

1) present how innovative teaching and learning practices are being used in higher education institutions around the world across a wide variety of disciplines and countries;
2) present the latest models, theories, concepts, paradigms, and frameworks that educators should consider when adopting, implementing, assessing, and evaluating innovative teaching and learning practices; and
3) consider the implications of theory and practice on policy, strategy, and leadership.

This series will appeal to anyone in higher education who is involved in the teaching and learning process from any discipline, institutional type, or nationality. The volumes in this series will focus on a variety of authentic case studies and other empirical research that illustrates how educators from around the world are using innovative approaches to create more effective and meaningful learning environments.

Innovative teaching and learning is any approach, strategy, method, practice, or means that has been shown to improve, enhance, or transform the teaching–learning environment. Innovation involves doing things differently or in a novel way in order to improve outcomes. In short, innovation is a positive change. With respect to teaching and learning, innovation is the implementation of new or improved educational practices that result in improved educational and learning outcomes. This innovation can be any positive change related to teaching, curriculum, assessment, technology, or other tools, programs, policies, or processes that leads to improved educational and learning outcomes. Innovation can occur in institutional development, program development, professional development, or learning development.

The volumes in this series will not only highlight the benefits and theoretical frameworks of such innovations through authentic case studies and other empirical research but also look at the challenges and contexts associated with implementing and assessing innovative teaching and learning practices. The volumes represent all disciplines from a wide range of national, cultural, and organizational contexts. The volumes in this series will explore a wide variety of teaching and learning topics such as active learning, integrative learning, transformative learning, inquiry-based learning, problem-based learning, meaningful learning, blended learning, creative learning, experiential learning, lifelong and lifewide learning, global learning, learning assessment and analytics, student research, faculty and student learning communities, as well as other topics.

This series brings together distinguished scholars and educational practitioners from around the world to disseminate the latest knowledge on innovative teaching and learning scholarship and practices. The authors offer a range of disciplinary perspectives from different cultural contexts. This series provides a unique and valuable resource for instructors, administrators, and anyone interested in improving and transforming teaching and learning.

Patrick Blessinger
Founder, Executive Director, and Chief Research Scientist,
International HETL Association

Enakshi Sengupta
Associate Editor, International HETL Association

PART I

EDUCATION AS A FUNDAMENTAL RIGHT

CHAPTER 1

INTRODUCTION TO INTERNATIONAL PERSPECTIVES IN SOCIAL JUSTICE PROGRAMS AT THE INSTITUTIONAL AND COMMUNITY LEVELS

Enakshi Sengupta and Patrick Blessinger

ABSTRACT

The Sustainable Development Goals promoted by United Nations (UN) advocate that education is a fundamental right for human beings, and free universal primary education should be accessible to all regardless of gender or country of origin. Education on human rights aims to provide information on fundamental rights, equality and being non-discriminatory in nature by having its universal appeal. Learners should be exposed to human rights education and to relate it to their cultural context and build on real-life experience. Students should be encouraged to foster participation in creating a learning environment free from fear and upholds empowerment and human rights values. Universities and faculty members play a vital role in imparting education that helps build a strong foundation of society where people are respected and treated equally and gets equal opportunity for upward social mobility while protecting the dignity of such rights. This book addresses the role of education to uplift people out of poverty and oppression by imparting social justice education at the institution and the community level. Chapters are dedicated to human rights education which talks about fostering a sense of awareness among learners about the dignity of human life through various interventional programs. Such rights are

International Perspectives in Social Justice Programs at the Institutional and Community Levels
Innovations in Higher Education Teaching and Learning, Volume 37, 3–11
ISSN: 2055-3641/doi:10.1108/S2055-364120210000037001

discussed with respect to migrant workers, foster youth and prisoners in different
countries and how students from all levels can benefit from such education.

Keywords: Equality; non-discriminatory; accessibility; United Nations;
empowerment; social mobility; opportunity; social justice; awareness

INTRODUCTION

The United Nations (UN) advocates the need for human rights education (HRE)
for every student at the university level, arguing that a systematic change is
needed in the educational system in which HRE needs to be incorporated in a
more consistent manner (UN, 2006). In the present-day scenario, there is limited
knowledge on the presence of HRE in the curriculum how a complete course
can be evaluated and its value understood by both the learners and faculty members (Quennerstedt, 2015). Universal Declaration of Human rights (UN, 1948)
acknowledged that all individuals globally are universally entitled to free and
fair practice of their human rights. The Vienna Declaration and Programme of
Action, adopted by the World Conference on Human Rights, affirmed that

> States are duty-bound … to ensure that education is aimed at strengthening the respect of
> human rights and fundamental freedoms [and that] … this should be integrated into the edu-
> cational polices at the national as well as international levels. (UN General Assembly, 1993,
> Part I, para 33)

Following this declaration and in keeping with the policies, the UN Decade of
Human Rights Education (1995–2004) was launched (UN Commission on Human
Rights, 2000) and again in 2006, the UN World Program for Human Rights
Education (World Program) was presented (UN, 2006). The programs aimed to
encourage countries to develop their HRE curricula according to their cultural
context and social structure. The Decade of Human Rights Education (1995–2004)
gave guidelines and enumerated both processes and policy structures that the
nation could adopt. The scope for the World Program, was more encompassing and
broader. While it started in 2005, it defines HRE as "education, training and information aiming at building a universal culture of human rights through the sharing
of knowledge, imparting of skills and molding of attitudes" (UN, 2006, p. 1).

HRE recommended by the World Program was divided into three different
phases, and each had its own focus. The first phase that began in 2005 and continued till 2009 and was dedicated to integrate and inculcate HRE in the schools. It
was aimed at addressing and identifying gaps

> absence of explicit policies and detailed implementation strategies for human rights education
> and the lack of systematic approaches to the production of materials, the training of teachers
> and the promotion of a learning environment which fosters human rights values. (UN General
> Assembly, 2010, p. 295)

Once the gaps were identified, UN coordinating committee emphasized the
human rights framework, policies to develop teacher's training on human rights

and how these programs could be integrated into the teaching curriculum of the students.

The second phase from 2010 to 2014 was focused on developing HRE more on a higher education context and declared the access to HRE and adequate training both for educators and the students as a fundamental right. The Declaration highlights three critical dimensions of HRE:

- education about human rights, which includes providing knowledge and understanding of human rights norms and principles, the values that underpin them and the mechanisms for their protection;
- education through human rights, which includes learning and teaching in a way that respects the rights of both educators and learners; and
- education for human rights, which includes empowering persons to enjoy and exercise their rights and to respect the rights of others (UN General Assembly, 2011, Article 2).

The third and ongoing phases from 2015 to 2019 stressed the need to reengage and further strengthen the first two phases (UN General Assembly, 2014). The emphasis in this phase was to integrate HRE in the given curricula of the students and further research and investigate how this could be done seamlessly.

Empirical evidence on HRE research has shown that the subject had not been well integrated with the education system. The very first dimension of such programs is aimed at learning about human rights and then the second dimension is learning for human rights (Patel, 2007). Higher education needs to adopt the two phases to gain a comprehensive understanding of the subject and other components such as the existing structures, cultural context and the organizational framework is equally important in understanding and inculcating the subject in the existing curriculum of the students.

EDUCATION AS A HUMAN RIGHT

The modern human rights movement when traced back in history can be attributed to two key political revolutions in the late eighteenth century: the American Revolution and the French Revolution. The two key documents that owed its origin to these revolutions were the US Bill of Rights and the French Declaration of the Rights of Man and of the Citizen. Both documents emphasized political and civil rights.

The Universal Declaration of Human Rights or UDHR, Article 26, states that every individual has the right to education. Education shall be free, in the formative years of an individual and should be made compulsory by every nation. Technical and professional training shall be made generally available to all those who desire to access it, and higher education shall be equally accessible to all based on merit. Education should be designed in a manner that enhances the full development of the human personality and helps in strengthening of respect for human rights and fundamental freedoms. Education should aim at understanding, tolerance and friendship among all nations, racial or religious groups, and shall further the activities of the UN for the maintenance of peace. Parents have a prior right to choose the kind of education that shall be given to their children. These rights have enormous implications as to how each country allocates their resources, the roles of all parties engaged in the educational system and how all parties are treated within the educational system. Thus, understanding education as a human right forms the basis for moral and legal rights and inclusion of diversity in education.

The Dakar Framework of Action considers education as fundamental human rights as

> It is the key to sustainable development and peace and stability within and among countries, and thus an indispensable means for effective participation in the societies and economies of the 21st century, which are affected by rapid globalization. The basic learning needs of all can and must be met as a matter of urgency. (Dakar Framework of Action, 2000, Article 6)

Yet the truth has often been very different from the ideal state of being. Many children and adults remain deprived of educational opportunities and lead a life of abject poverty, and more so in the recent years with mass migration, war and pandemics. Normative instruments of the UN and United Nation Economic and Social Council Organization (UNESCO) have formulated the international legal obligations for the right to education. These instruments are meant to promote and develop the concept that every individual is entitled to enjoy access to education of good quality, without discrimination or exclusion.

It therefore becomes the duty of governments to fulfill their obligations, legally, politically and morally, to provide education for all and implement effective strategies toward education for all. Education is the primary tool for social mobility helping economically and socially marginalized adults and children to move out of poverty and lead a better life.

International agencies and universities working in this field have been appealing to widening participation by removing unnecessary access barriers and eliminating the monopolization of higher education by privileged groups and by improving practices in higher educational institutions that facilitate the free flow of higher education services across borders. As a result, over the last few generations, we have experienced, in many countries, a shift from elitist higher education systems toward mass and universal system of education.

Traditional boundaries for higher education institutions are increasingly melting giving way to online education and free access to resources as institutions are adapting to the rapidly changing conditions of an increasingly hyper-connected, globalized world. Higher education is entering a brave new era - an era where lifelong (and life-wide) learning is increasingly viewed as a fundamental human right. The notion of lifelong learning as a human right (and post-secondary education as a significant vehicle for delivering those lifelong learning opportunities) has started to gain more attention because of its growing importance in work and social lives of people.

CONCLUSION

Teaching human rights as a subject requires the democratization of the educational system and training of educators to be capable of imparting such education. Teaching of such a subject call for a multidisciplinary approach and a participatory mode of instruction. Faculty members must be sensitized to the need for HRE and the concept of justice, liberty, equality and dignity of individuals. Policymakers and influencers must understand the lack of accessibility of education and education being the only possible way toward upwards social mobility. Reorientation of teaching methods and curriculum will be required to incorporate new components into the existing syllabi.

CHAPTER OVERVIEWS

"Education in Human Rights: Changing the Way We Think and How We Feel," by Alan Vogelfanger, is about education as a fundamental right that can lift people out of poverty, empower women, safeguard children from exploitative labor and promote democracy. In this sense, the right to education, which is recognized in several treaties, cannot be separated from the right to an education in human rights. The latter is crucial to the realization of human rights and contributes significantly to achieving equality, tolerance and respect for the dignity of others. Plus, through education in human rights, people would not also become more sympathetic about our differences, but they would also be empowered to demand and exercise their own rights, which will certainly contribute to their observance and implementation. This chapter will explore why education in human rights is one of the most powerful tools to prevent atrocities and to guarantee every person a dignified life. Consequently, it will also argue that it is vital to integrate HRE into the curriculum and classroom. Furthermore, this chapter will consider the right to receive this kind of education and the State's obligation to guarantee it. Finally, it will analyze the best ways to teach human rights in higher education through active learning (simulations, discussions, role-play and moot-courts).

"Bridges to Zambia: Teaching Human Rights Through Immersion Experience," authored by Alia Sheety, Erin McLaughlin and Susan Jacques Pierson, talks about education as a fundamental factor of development, preparing the educated for a better tomorrow. Education serves to improve quality of life, is a means of enhancing the economic growth for individuals and nations and provides a way for marginalized children and adults to exchange lives of desperation, poverty and injustice for those illuminated with liberty, justice and self-determination. Education is declared by the UN as a human right. This chapter present one model to teach for human rights through experiential learning. It shares a unique experience of education and business students in their immersion trip to Zambia. The model used to develop the partnership is Integral Human Development (IHD). This chapter provides description of the model, how it was implemented and shares direct citations from students' reflection journals highlighting three themes: communication, reciprocity and self-exploration.

"What Next? Skill Development for Livelihood: A Study of Bangladeshi Immigrant Workers in Kurdistan," authored by Enakshi Sengupta, explores UN advocating compulsory and free education for all as specified in the Millennium Development Goal. Education is a right of every human being and it is the right to realize other rights. It is the right toward social mobility and to achieve an economic stability in life. Every year hundreds and thousands of people from the developing world leave their home in search of livelihood. They undertake perilous and life-threatening journey in search of jobs. Often, they are motivated with the desire to earn more and ensure a better livelihood for them and their families back home. At times they are driven by persecution, genocide or natural disasters. Bangladesh has been a source of immigrant workers who have been seeking employment mainly as unskilled workers outside their country. These workers working in construction sites, malls or as domestic helps have a "shelf life," which barely exceeds the age of 50 years. This study conducted in a province of Kurdistan region in northern Iraq explores the fear of losing their livelihood post 50 years of age. In most cases, these workers have not been educated and have not received any skill development training which would enable them to remain as the bread earner long after they have returned home. Both quantitative and qualitative studies were conducted with 149 workers from Bangladesh who have been staying and working in Duhok. The findings have been explained and suitable recommendations were provided in keeping with the data analysis.

"Prison Education Through Open and Distance Learning: Experiences From India," written by Umesh Chandra Pandey, begins by discussing the United Nation's Standard Minimum Rules for Treatment of Prisoners, popularly known as Nelson Mandela Rules categorically advocates for the Prison Education and its integration with the educational system of the country. Moreover, principles for the treatment of prisoners, adopted by United Nation in 1990, guarantees that prisoners retain the human rights and fundamental freedoms set out in Universal Declaration of Human Rights, which includes right to take part in education also. However, there is little sensitization about the rights of prisoners in many countries. The issue has gained prominence as several international organizations have now raised concern on these matters. Education of jail inmates has attracted the attention of Open and Distance Learning systems (ODL) in India. Among all the ODL institutions, Indira Gandhi National Open University (IGNOU) has been the major role player. Right from its first initiative to have a special study center in Tihar Jail in 1994, IGNOU's network for jail inmates has undergone significant expansion. University has now strong presence in the prisons. Under a special collaborative arrangement with Ministry of Home Affairs, IGNOU has started free education to jail inmates from 2010. This chapter gives a glimpse about the model being followed by IGNOU for providing education inside prisons, highlights its good practices, gaps in its functioning and makes recommendations for further strengthening of this network.

"Widening Participation in Service Learning," by Faith Valencia-Forrester and Bridget Backhaus, is about work-integrated learning (WIL) and service learning which are widespread approaches to experiential, practice-based learning in Australia. Both are associated with extensive bodies of research that support their benefits to students, industry and the community at large. What is less explored, however, is the accessibility of such experiences. In Australia, there are several groups of students that are at a disadvantage in terms of participation in WIL and service learning. When considering access to higher education as an emerging human right, the importance of addressing these inequalities becomes even more clear. This chapter draws on case studies of pedagogical and curriculum changes that challenge existing power structures from within the curriculum and improve the accessibility and inclusiveness of WIL. This includes a research project that informs redesigning WIL experiences to better suit the needs of students including, a pilot project to improve international student access to service learning, and the development of a Community Internship module that weaves First Peoples' knowledge and perspectives throughout. While by no means exhaustive, these cases represent the start of ensuring that all aspects of higher education, including experiential, practice-based aspects, are accessible to all students.

"Flux of Digital Activism to Leverage Peace and Human Rights," by Anil Shukla and Kshama Pandey, talks about Plato and contemporary thinkers including American philosopher Martha Nussbaum who have emphasized the need for political consciousness among the youth. *Cultivating Humanity: A Classical Defence of Reform in Liberal Education* authored by Nussbaum expressed that

> It would be catastrophic to become a nation of technically competent people who have lost the ability to think critically, to examine themselves, and to respect the humanity and diversity of others.

Ideologically, it has been proven that advancement in technology can shift social ethos if we use it intelligently and then technology can lead to activism. Digital activism can be defined as the use of electronic communication devices, for example, social media, Twitter, Facebook, YouTube, e-mail, e-blogging, microblogging and podcast for different forms of activism. It enables citizens to express ideology and spread information to a large audience regarding human rights. In this context, researchers have explored the level of digital activism among pupil teachers and found very little awareness regarding the same. Findings also reveal that the level of digital activism does not have any significant effect on attitude toward human rights and peace. Although findings reveal that attitude toward peace and human rights is positively correlated with each other. Therefore, on the basis of findings, an intervention program for digital activism has been suggested at the end of this chapter that can foster digital activism among them.

"Promoting International Human Rights Values Through Reflective Practice in Clinical Legal Education: A Perspective From England and Wales," written by Irene Antonopoulos and Omar Madhloom, is about the global Clinical Legal Education (CLE) movement transcending borders as law teachers worldwide try to inculcate law students and future legal practitioners with social justice values. One method of achieving this is through developing reflective practitioners. Kolb, finding common ground in the work of Lewin, Dewey and Piaget, formulated the four stages in the experiential development of concrete experience, reflective observation, abstract conceptualization and active experiment. Although Kolb's model is used in legal education literature, students may not be provided with the relevant conceptual tool required to engage in reflective practice. This often results in students providing subjective analysis of their work, which fails to fully contribute to their educational experience. One of the reasons for omitting analytical tools is that reflective practice suffers from a lack of conceptual clarity. According to Kinsella, the "concept remains elusive, is open to multiple interpretations, and is applied in a myriad of ways in educational and practice environments." A further issue hindering reflective practice relates to Donald Schön's critique of the positivist approach adopted by law schools. It is argued that the dominant positivist approach adopted by law schools in England and Wales is fundamental flaw in CLE which not only impacts on students but also vulnerable clients. This chapter will apply a human rights framework to CLE to develop reflective practitioners. The two main reasons for this are, first, human rights as formulated by the Universal Declaration on Human Rights are universal, interrelated and indivisible and, second, reflection based on these universal human rights values will benefit cross-jurisdictional societies in assisting vulnerable clients affected by emerging implied and direct human rights challenges.

"Bridging the Gap: The Case for Implementing Equity-Minded Academic and Mentoring Support Services for Foster Youth Within University Writing Programs," written by Paul Beehler and Rory Moore, explores their university and its writing program as a case study to interrogate established wraparound support systems for foster youth and the role that additional, faculty-led support services can play in retention and graduation rates. This chapter first provides research on college-going foster youth in the United States. Then, it considers the foster youth population and established support programs at the University of California, Riverside. Next, this chapter reviews the benefits of faculty-student mentoring and tutoring, specifically in composition studies, and how those benefits can contribute to a successful college-going experience. This chapter shifts to offering a model for those interested in establishing a similar program. Using business, communication, composition, education and psychosocial theory to ground the discussion, the authors provide a detailed account of the proposal, implementation and ongoing programmatic administration processes, including the rationale undergirding decision making. Ultimately, they show how equitable supplemental academic support led by composition faculty can bridge the gap between existing foster youth services and outstanding needs, an innovative approach that relies on the natural mentoring relationships which organically evolve from faculty-student interaction.

"Promoting Gender Equality in Colleges of Education in Ghana Using a Gender-Responsive Scorecard," by Wisdom Kwaku Agbevanu, Hope Pius Nudzor, Sharon Tao and Francis Ansah, presents the findings of a Gender and Leadership study on promoting gender responsiveness and equality in Ghanaian Colleges of Education (CoEs) conducted in 2017. Specifically, this chapter explores CoEs actors' perspectives on and experiences with using predetermined gender-responsive scorecard (GRS) as a strategy for promoting gender equality within the CoEs. Multiple-case study involving 10 CoEs selected purposively was used to explore the GRS implementation. Data collection and analysis methods included semi-structured interviews and "processual" analysis. The findings revealed a general contradiction among respondents regarding which gender actions/strategies had been implemented in the case study CoEs. Nonetheless, amid reported implementation challenges, there was general acknowledgment of the importance of the GRS in running gender-responsive CoEs in Ghana. The study concludes that the effective use and implementation of the GRS strategies appear imperative in promoting female success in CoEs, not only in Ghana but also in contexts where gender gap is an issue in teacher education.

"Ethical Issues and the Nordic Education Model: Learning-Driven Ecosystems Applied to International Cohorts," by Bruno F. Abrantes, Thomas D. Eatmon and Charlotte Forsberg, is about the societal role of universities (u-pillar) which has been a long-standing discussion dividing the education researchers worldwide. Entering the sphere of the eminent Nordic education model (NEM), the authors aim at grasping its contemporaneity with regard to social value creation (SVC) and to the promotion of equality in education (EiE). A theoretical review of literature revisits the foundations of the NEM in the light of the postmodern education challenges and the inherent governance practices of higher education institutions (HEIs) in the global eduscape. One of the oldest HEIs in Denmark, Niels Brock Copenhagen Business College (NBCBC), is here instrumentalized as the target case research. The latter exhibited a sophisticated educational design, oriented toward digital apprenticeship and cumulative proximity to the students' population of both national and international cohorts.

REFERENCES

Patel, J. V. (2007). *Human rights education.* Conference paper: UGC sponsored national seminar on human rights and values in education, at H.S. Shah College of Commerce, Modasa, Gujarat, Volume 1. Retrieved from https://www.researchgate.net/publication/274908579_Human_Rights_Education

Quennerstedt, A. (2015). Mänskliga rättigheter som värdefundament, kunskapsobjekt och inflytande: En läroplansanalys [Human rights as value base, object of knowledge and influence: A curriculum analysis]. *Utbildning & Demokrati, 24*(1), 5–27.

The Dakar Framework for Action. (2000). Education for all: Meeting our collective commitments adopted by the World Education Forum Dakar, Senegal, April 26–28. Retrieved from https://sustainabledevelopment.un.org/content/documents/1681Dakar%20Framework%20for%20Action.pdf

UN Commission on Human Rights. (2000). Retrieved from https://www.un.org/press/en/2000/20000317.hrcn979.doc.html. Accessed on April 3, 2020.

United Nations. (1948). Universal declaration on human rights. Retrieved from https://www.un.org/en/universal-declaration-human-rights/

United Nations. (2006). *World programme for human rights education first phase.* Geneva: United Nations.

United Nations General Assembly. (1993). Vienna declaration and programme of action, July 12, A/CONF.157/23. Retrieved from http://www.un-documents.net/ac157-23.htm

United Nations General Assembly. (2010). Final evaluation of the implementation of the first phase of the world programme for human rights education, August 24, A/65/322. Retrieved from https://documents-dds-ny.un.org/doc/UNDOC/GEN/N10/493/11/PDF/N1049311.pdf?

United Nations General Assembly. (2011). United Nations declaration on human rights education and training. General Assembly Resolution 66/137, December 19, U.N. Doc. A/RES/66/137.

United Nations General Assembly. (2014). Plan of action for the third phase (2015–2019) of the world programme for human rights education. General Assembly, August 4, U.N. Doc. A/HRC/27/28.

CHAPTER 2

EDUCATION IN HUMAN RIGHTS: CHANGING THE WAY WE THINK AND HOW WE FEEL

Alan Vogelfanger

ABSTRACT

Education is a fundamental right that can lift people out of poverty, empower women, safeguard children from exploitative labor and promote democracy. In this sense, the right to education, which is recognized in several treaties, cannot be separated from the right to an education in human rights. The latter is crucial to the realization of human rights and contributes significantly to achieving equality, tolerance and respect for the dignity of others. Plus, through education in human rights, people would also not become more sympathetic about our differences, but they would also be empowered to demand and exercise their own rights, which will certainly contribute to their observance and implementation. This introductory chapter will explore why education in human rights is one of the most powerful tools to prevent atrocities and to guarantee every person a dignified life. Consequently, it will also argue that it is vital to integrate human rights education into the curriculum and classroom. Furthermore, this chapter will consider the right to receive this kind of education and the State's obligation to guarantee it. Finally, it will analyze the best ways to teach human rights in higher education through active learning (simulations, discussions, role-play and moot courts).

Keywords: human rights; education; education in human rights; human rights education; UNESCO; 2030 agenda; Sustainable Development Goals

International Perspectives in Social Justice Programs at the Institutional and Community Levels
Innovations in Higher Education Teaching and Learning, Volume 37, 13–27
Copyright © 2021 by Emerald Publishing Limited
All rights of reproduction in any form reserved
ISSN: 2055-3641/doi:10.1108/S2055-364120210000037002

INTRODUCTION

Law is not enough. The persistent human rights violations across the world reflect that norms alone are insufficient to prevent atrocities or to guarantee every person a dignified life. Treaties, judgments and international standards represent only one element to ensure a complete satisfaction of our basic needs.

This chapter will argue that international human rights law is actually an over-developed tool. In other words, law is a couple of steps ahead of reality. Efforts should be destined to guarantee the application of this comprehensive body of law. Instead of trying to produce new treaties, "new human rights" or pushing for better standards, the main challenge now is to transform these norms from goals and hopes to actual changes.

This chapter will explore the education in human rights as one of the most powerful tools to prevent atrocities and to guarantee every person a dignified life. Consequently, it will also claim that it is vital to integrate human rights education into the curriculum and classroom. Cultural components are vital for major changes. Of course, formal education is just one tool and culture does not only mean educational institutions; it is also shaped by many other factors such as family, traditions, friends, media, etc. Nevertheless, formal education in human rights is still an area with a significant scope for improvement. Schools represent an important focus for the dissemination of human rights information and perspectives (Committee on the Elimination of Racial Discrimination (CERD), 2013). This chapter will consider the right to receive this kind of education and the State's obligation to guarantee it. Moreover, it will analyze its importance and the best ways to teach human rights in higher education.

THE RIGHT TO RECEIVE AN EDUCATION IN HUMAN RIGHTS AND ITS SIGNIFICANCE

Education is an empowerment right that can lift adults and children out of poverty, empower women and safeguard children from exploitative labor (Committee on Economic, Social and Cultural Rights (CESCR), 1999). It also enhances the enjoyment of other human rights and freedoms, yields significant development benefits, facilitates gender equality, boosts economic growth and increases the chances of having a healthy life (Committee on the Elimination of Discrimination against Women (CEDAW), 2017). Basically, "education is both a human right in itself and an indispensable means of realizing other human rights" (CESCR, 1999, p. 1).

Furthermore, education in human rights is also a tool to promote tolerance and respect:

> education in the twenty-first century needs above all to teach children what is arguably the single most vital skill for a flourishing multi-cultural society: the skill of living peacefully with other people (...) No country can hope to establish lasting foundations for peace unless it finds ways of building mutual trust between its citizens – and the place to start is in the classroom. (United Nations Educational, Scientific and Cultural Organization. (UNESCO), 2011, p. 3)

Indeed, children, youth and young adults are capable of playing a unique role in bridging many of the differences that have historically separated groups of people from one another (Committee on the Rights of the Child (CRC), 2001). However, sometimes schools perpetuate and reinforce stereotypes or social prejudices, often as a result of the poor implementation of policies by school governance bodies, teachers, principals or other school authorities (CEDAW, 2017). As the CERD (2013) explains, "because racism can be the product of indoctrination or inadequate education, especially effective antidotes to racist hate speech include education for tolerance" (p. 8). Of course, the nondiscrimination principle is a crucial part of human rights and a necessary component of human rights education.

What is more, through an appropriate education in human rights, people would also not become more sympathetic about our differences, but they would also be empowered to demand and exercise all of their rights, which will certainly contribute to their observance and implementation through pressure from "below." This is somewhat related to Paulo Freire's (2006) doctrine of liberating education. The current tendency of international human rights law is to include in this empowerment purpose some elements of pluralism and tolerance. Of course, they do not exclude each other. Since our rights can only be exercised in the framework of respect for the rights of others, the ultimate goal would be that the person is empowered to act as an agent of change within a context of diversity and inclusion. Furthermore, human rights education aims to develop the capacity of current and future government officials to meet their obligation to respect, protect and fulfill the human rights of those under their jurisdiction (Office of the United Nations High Commissioner for Human Rights & Equitas, 2011, p. 10).

Now, as the Danish Institute for Human Rights (DIHR, 2013) refers, "human rights are not just beautiful ideas floating in space; they are legal instruments based on strong human values that we have agreed upon internationally, regionally and nationally" (p. 15). Not only treaties but also other international instruments, such as recommendations and declarations that have political and moral force, have established a solid international normative framework for the right to education (UNESCO, 2015).

The right to receive an education in human rights is already enshrined in the Preamble of the Universal Declaration on Human Rights, adopted in 1948. The Preamble states that every individual and every organ of society shall strive by teaching and education to promote respect for the rights and freedoms guaranteed in the instrument. Moreover, article 26 of the Declaration explicitly recognizes the right to education. It establishes that

> education shall be directed to the full development of the human personality and to the strengthening of respect for human rights and fundamental freedoms. It shall promote understanding, tolerance and friendship among all nations, racial or religious groups.

A similar drafting to article 26 of the Declaration can be found in article 13 of the International Covenant on Economic, Social and Cultural Rights. This obligation to guarantee the human right to education (and to include an education in human rights) is also part of customary international law, so it is currently binding for every State (Villán Durán, 2006).

Furthermore, articles 28 and 29 of the Convention on the Rights of the Child also consider that the right to education must include (1) the development of respect for human rights and fundamental freedoms; (2) the development of respect for the children's own cultural identity, language and values; (3) respect for the national values of the country in which the child is living; (4) respect for the values of the country from which he or she may originate; (5) respect for civilizations different from his or her own; and (6) respect for the natural environment. In this sense, the CRC (2001) has interpreted that

> the education to which every child has a right is one designed to provide the child with life skills, to strengthen the child's capacity to enjoy the full range of human rights and to promote a culture which is infused by appropriate human rights values. (p. 1)

Of course, the rights of children are also an important part of human rights law. Finally, article 7 of the Convention on the Elimination of All Forms of Racial Discrimination requires States to

> adopt immediate and effective measures, particularly in the fields of teaching, education, culture and information, with a view to combating prejudices which lead to racial discrimination and to promoting understanding, tolerance and friendship among nations and racial or ethnical groups.

Article 24 of the Convention on the Rights of Persons with Disabilities establishes that States shall ensure an inclusive education system at all levels directed to the full development of human potential and sense of dignity, and the strengthening of respect for human rights. And article 10 of the Convention on the Elimination of All Forms of Discrimination against Women also refers to the appropriate measures States must take to eliminate discrimination against women in the field of education: guarantee access to the same curricula, teaching staff with qualifications of the same standard, same opportunities to benefit from scholarships and other study grants, elimination of stereotypes, etc.

To conclude, these are just some examples of sources that guarantee the right to receive an education in human rights, which of course includes elements of tolerance, respect and nondiscrimination. Before addressing the issue of how to implement this right and how to teach human rights, it is also important to analyze the efforts of the United Nations (UN) General Assembly in this matter.

THE WORK OF THE UN GENERAL ASSEMBLY

Between 1995 and 2004, the UN developed the Decade for Human Rights Education. In December 2004, in order to advance the implementation of human rights education programs in all sectors, the General Assembly proclaimed the World Program for Human Rights Education (2005–2019). Basically, the first phase of the program (2005–2009) focused on human rights education in the primary and secondary school systems. The second phase (2010–2014) focused on human rights education for higher education and on human rights training programs for teachers and educators, civil servants, law enforcement officials and military personnel. The third phase (2015–2019) focused on strengthening the implementation of the first two phases and on promoting human rights training for media professionals and journalists.

In its resolution regarding this World Program, the General Assembly (2004) explained that "human rights education is a long-term and lifelong process by which everyone learns tolerance and respect for the dignity of others" (p. 1). The General Assembly also reaffirmed that human rights education is essential to the realization of human rights and that it contributes significantly to promoting equality, preventing conflict and human rights violations, with a view to developing societies in which all human beings are valued and respected. In 2011, the General Assembly also adopted the Declaration on Human Rights Education and Training. The instrument defines education in human rights as:

> all educational, training, information, awareness-raising and learning activities aimed at promoting universal respect for and observance of all human rights and fundamental freedoms and thus contributing, *inter alia*, to the prevention of human rights violations and abuses by providing persons with knowledge, skills and understanding and developing their attitudes and behaviors, to empower them to contribute to the building and promotion of a universal culture of human rights. (UN General Assembly, 2012, p. 3)

The declaration also explains that human rights education includes (a) education about human rights (providing knowledge and understanding of human rights norms and principles); (b) education through human rights (teaching and learning in a way that respects the rights of both educators and learners); and (c) education for human rights (empowering persons to enjoy and exercise their rights and to respect and uphold the rights of others). In other words, there are three learning dimensions: knowledge, skills and attitudes/values because

> it is not enough that the learners know about human rights, they also need to be able to act upon that knowledge to defend their rights and those of others. (DIHR, 2013, p. 11)

Furthermore, one of the 17 Sustainable Development Goals (SDGs) adopted in 2015 is "Quality Education." One of its targets, 4.7, is to ensure, by 2030, that all learners acquire the knowledge and skills needed to promote sustainable development, including, among others, through education for human rights, gender equality, promotion of a culture of peace and nonviolence, global citizenship and appreciation of cultural diversity. The main indicators set to analyze the compliance with this objective are the extent to which (i) global citizenship education and (ii) education for sustainable development, including gender equality and human rights, are mainstreamed at all levels in (a) national education policies, (b) curricula, (c) teacher education, and (d) student assessment.

Also in 2015, UNESCO together with other agencies such as UNICEF, the World Bank, UNFPA, UNDP, UN Women and UNHCR organized a World Education Forum in Incheon, Republic of Korea, where the Education 2030 Framework for Action was adopted. The vision is to "transform lives through education, recognizing the important role of education as a main driver of development and in achieving the other proposed SDGs" (UNESCO, 2015, p. 7).

As it can be seen from the declarations, treaties, the interpretation of their supervisory bodies and the work of the UN General Assembly and other international agencies, the right to education cannot be separated from the right to an education in human rights. Therefore, the education to which everyone has the right to must necessarily include education in human rights. Or, put it differently, the right to education cannot be respected and guaranteed if it does not contemplate education in human rights.

Once again, this first part of this chapter provided some examples of binding treaties, customary international law and soft law that guarantee the right to receive an education in human rights. It is undisputed that States are obliged to guarantee the right to education and that they must introduce education in human rights in all learning levels, including higher education, private and public institutions, universities and schools of law (Villán Durán, 2006). However, this does not mean that, in practice, this obligation is strictly complied with (Inter-American Institute of Human Rights (IAIHR), 2007). In the next part, I will analyze the main challenges for the implementation of this obligation and the best ways to teach human rights.

THE CHALLENGE OF IMPLEMENTATION

Human rights law is necessary and important because it legitimizes and installs the issue in the agenda of States (IAIHR, 2013). Globally, 91% of children attend primary school and 84% are enrolled in secondary school (UN General Assembly, 2018). However, that still means that for millions of people, the enjoyment of the right to education remains a distant goal (CESCR, 1999): according to UNESCO (2016), 263 million children between the ages of 6 and 17 are still currently out of school. This organization also warns that "more than 220 million children, adolescents and youth will still be out of school in 2030" (UNESCO, 2019, p. 3).

Furthermore, in the national and international programs and policies on education, the elements embodied in article 29 of the Convention on the Rights of the Child "seem all too often to be either largely missing or present only as a cosmetic afterthought" (CRC, 2001, p. 2). For example, even if considerable progress has been made in the last years, only 50% of UNESCO's Member States indicate that they have integrated education for sustainable development into relevant policies (UNESCO, 2015). UNESCO (2019) also explains that monitoring progress on target 4.7 of the SDGs, which focuses on the content of education and includes education in human rights, remains challenging and that a methodology has not yet been adopted for the global indicator. In general, in order to monitor SDG 4 adequately US$280 million per year is needed, but, currently, the amount spent is an estimated US$148 million (UNESCO, 2019).

Basically, "the world is far off track on achieving international commitments to education" (UNESCO, 2019, p. 12). In this sense, it could be argued that what lawyers have done so far is to create a comprehensive body of law, knowledge and theory that is not reaching a lot of people and with not many practical consequences in the lives of every person (Mujica, 2002). Of course, this problem concerns the whole field of human rights, not just the right to education. A possible explanation is that, sometimes, the gap between aims and actions in the field of education is the product of long-standing historical distortions that encapsulate the contradictions and tensions of economic systems and patriarchal cultures. (United Nations Commission on Human Rights, 2004, p. 2)

HOW TO ADVANCE IN THE FULFILLMENT OF THE RIGHT TO RECEIVE AN EDUCATION IN HUMAN RIGHTS

As the DIHR (2013) argues:

> Human rights education is more challenging than teaching most academic subjects. It raises difficult and fundamental questions about human behavior, cultural diversity and insists on complex answers to why people have been denied their rights. Human rights deeply engage our values and involve our feelings and opinions, and can seriously challenge participants' world views and preconceptions. (p. 56)

Education in human rights is not just transmitting information: it means acquiring knowledge, abilities and values which are needed to understand and reaffirm our rights (IAIHR, 2013). However, sometimes the teaching of law is criticized because of its theoretical focus (Becerra Valdivia, 2018). In several occasions, it is difficult for educators to make the connection between human rights theory and its implementation in our everyday lives; even if teachers work with national jurisprudence, students usually still see these instruments as part of an abstract speech and not as the fulfillment of rights because they are lacking some kind of link with their own context (Becerra Valdivia, 2018). Of course, the strategies to promote human rights education will depend on the context of every country (Villán Durán, 2006). Nevertheless, there are some common components that should always be addressed.

The Crucial Need to Provide an Appropriate Budget

One first step to fulfill the right to receive an education in human rights and, consequently, to achieve a more tolerant society is to provide adequate economic, human and administrative resources. Currently, "only one third of all countries spend between 15% and 20% of total government expenditure on education, as recommended in the Education 2030 Framework for Action" (United Nations Economic and Social Council, 2019, p. 7). The CRC (2001) indicated that the "implementation of comprehensive national plans of action to enhance compliance with article 29.1 will require human and financial resources which should be available to the maximum extent possible" (p. 8). It also warned that "resource constraints cannot provide a justification for a State's failure to take any, or enough, of the measures that are required" (CRC, 2001, p. 8).

The Special Rapporteur on the right to education (UN General Assembly, 2019) insisted as well by stating that an essential condition for meeting SDG 4 is for States to allocate the maximum of their available resources to ensuring free, quality and public education for all. UNESCO (2019) also recently required from governments "finance efforts to analyze national curricula and textbooks to identify areas for improvement and alignment with the SDGs, from gender equality and human rights to skills for decent jobs" (p. 14).

In this sense, it is vital to tackle two frequent problems: (1) Education is sometimes considered more as a cost than an investment; and (2) When budget priorities are set, education is usually relegated to second or third place (United Nations Commission on Human Rights, 2004). Governments must understand that, in the long-term, "education is recognized as one of the best financial investments States can make" (CESCR, 1999, p. 1). Guaranteeing the right to universal, quality and inclusive education and training is the single most important policy investment that States can make to ensure the immediate and long-term development of adolescents (CRC, 2017). In particular, "the education of girls and women is considered to be one of the most effective investments for sustainable and inclusive development" (CEDAW, 2017, p. 1). Plus, as the CRC (2016) explained,

> in times of economic crisis, regressive measures may only be considered after assessing all other options and ensuring that children are the last to be affected, especially children in vulnerable situations. (p. 10)

In cases where financing is limited, an alternative to providing physical access to educational facilities, for example, is through the use of information and communications technologies (ICT): the use of mobile telephones, e-books, computers and portable devices has allowed young people to obtain a quality education in a safe and secure environment, taking part in eLearning programs that can be adjusted to the needs of the individual student (UN General Assembly, 2018). Such approaches provide distinct benefits for girls and women who are sometimes excluded owing to distance from school in rural areas, domestic work, parental responsibilities (child marriage and adolescent pregnancy) and on the basis of other social and cultural barriers (UN General Assembly, 2019).

Finally, in one of her last reports, the Special Rapporteur on the right to education (UN General Assembly, 2019) expressed her concern about the persistent underfunding of public education and the rapid growth of the involvement of private and commercial actors in education. States should be aware that this circumstance could threaten the implementation of the right to education for all if, as a consequence, quality education is only limited to wealthy people. The privatization of quality education would only perpetrate segregation and social inequality.

Preventing the Use of Cultural Differences to Deny Access to Education

Cultural differences should not serve as an excuse to refuse education in human rights. Specifically, States should "protect girls and women from being deprived of their right to education on the basis of patriarchal, religious or cultural norms and practices" (CEDAW, 2017, p. 14). There are plenty of universally recognized human rights that are being violated, and every country should at least start with education in those aspects. For example, the prohibition of torture; the prohibition of crimes against humanity, genocide or war crimes; and the nondiscrimination principle have reached such a huge consensus in the international community that they should be taught and learned everywhere, bearing in mind both the international standards and the local needs and beliefs of the targeted people.

Culture includes "a set of local truths which serve as a guide for life's many pursuits in a society" (Mutua, 2002, p. 22). However, culture itself is also "dynamic and alchemical" (Mutua, 2002, p. 22) which means that it can be influenced and changed, even if it takes a long time. Indeed, by definition, the human being is educable and transformable (Cussianovich, 2010, p. 115). The human rights movement attempts to guarantee minimum standards of human dignity for every person and there are universal core values that were accepted worldwide but are still being violated. Respect for local cultures cannot be used as an argument to defend and accept tortures, mutilations, racial discrimination, extrajudicial executions, impunity, oppression against women, etc. (Human Rights Committee, 2000). Certainly, human rights should serve as a limit to both State power and cultural practices. This does not mean that the human rights movement is trying to impose a new and unique culture, because culture is a "mix of many variables, including religion, philosophy, history, mythology, politics, environmental factors, language and economics" (Mutua, 2002, p. 22). Therefore, human rights law alone could not transform a whole culture.

In the end, the purpose of a universal education in human rights is to change those particular cultural aspects that contribute to persistent grave violations of human rights. At the same time, as it will be developed later, the local populations and its culture should be carefully considered while designing and implementing education in human rights. But the minimum standards of international law should be addressed, and this cannot be considered as a colonial imposition of an external culture. The idea is to ensure, on the one hand, that education acknowledges the key role that local conditions play in our everyday lives, and, on the other hand, that education builds awareness of heritage and diversity while emphasizing the importance of respect for human rights at the same time (UNESCO, 2015). The consequences of using cultural barriers to prevent education in human rights are far more dangerous than trying to incorporate some specific universally agreed values in the classroom. It is true that there are debatable areas within the human rights movement, but that does not mean that every State should not start disseminating the minimum core rights.

It is important not to fall under the naïve realism, basically defined as the unacknowledged assumption that one's cultural beliefs, values, attitudes or practices are natural and universally shared. Also, we should be aware of ethnocentrism; this is, the attitude that our beliefs, values or practices can be used to judge those of other cultures, or assuming that those who don't share our beliefs are inferior and that our culture is better. The point here is to understand, first, that there are some core universal values shared by almost every country in the world and, second, that trying to make everyone follow these minimum values does not mean an imperialist attempt to destroy other cultures.

The Importance of an Appropriate Curriculum

It is not within the scope of this chapter to analyze specifically which contents should be addressed through human rights education. The choice of curriculum could be a controversial and difficult issue and, of course, the topics would depend on each community and they should even be decided with a participatory approach. Still, there are some valid guidelines. For example, school curricula and teaching materials should be informed by and address human rights themes, seek to promote mutual respect among nations and endeavor to highlight the contribution of all racial, national, religious and ethnic groups to the social, economic and cultural enrichment of the national identity (CERD, 2013). Curricula for secondary education, for example, should be designed to equip adolescents for active participation, develop respect for human rights and promote civic engagement (CRC, 2017). Additionally, it is important for public authorities to review their national curriculum periodically in order to respond to emerging requirements and to ensure that textbooks in all schools – private or public – are in conformity with the values and objectives of education laid down in international human rights law (UN General Assembly, 2014).

The Demand for a Transversal and Participatory Approach

Human rights are a transversal issue and should not be limited to only one subject or course; instead, human rights should be integrated in almost every class and in the educational system itself (IAIHR, 2013; Medici, 2018). All the courses should be taught with a human rights-based approach (Ronconi, 2017), and this should serve as a prism through which we look to everything else. Thus, education in human rights is not only a matter of those professors who lecture specifically on human rights because it also includes every educator who is involved in teaching (Ronconi, 2017).

Sadly, only a few countries have a human rights office or direction inside their Ministry of Education, at least in Latin-America (IAIHR, 2007). Furthermore, as the Committee on the Rights of Persons with Disabilities (CRPD, 2016) explains regarding inclusive education, governments must ensure a comprehensive and transversal commitment. The objectives cannot be realized by education ministries in isolation. All relevant ministries and commissions must align their understanding of an inclusive education system in order to achieve an integrated approach and to work collaboratively toward a shared agenda (CRPD, 2016). In other words, while driven by education ministries, implementation of the education-related SDGs requires a "whole of government" approach to education (UNESCO, 2015). Professor Monica Pinto (2010) adds that "a multidimensional and complex object such as the knowledge in human rights needs also a complex approach, one that shows connections, implications, tensions and different angles" (p. 16).

Plus, increasing the participation of every actor involved in the field of education is also crucial; the challenge is to include not only the public officials that create public policies but also children, parents, teachers and schools (IAIHR, 2013). The CRC (2001) affirms that

> the participation of children in school life, the creation of school communities and student councils, peer education and peer counselling, and the involvement of children in school disciplinary proceedings should be promoted as part of the process of learning and experiencing the realization of rights. (p. 3)

As it happens with education in human rights, "participation is not only a right in itself but also a vital means to the realization of children's other rights"

(Hart, 2008, p. 407). Thus, a participatory approach is fundamental to the effective practice of human rights education (Office of the United Nations High Commissioner for Human Rights & Equitas, 2011).

Inclusive Education and Teacher Training

Moreover, "education must be ethnically, culturally and linguistically inclusive and no student should be made to feel excluded" (UN General Assembly, 2017, p. 22). As the Education 2030 Framework for Action mentions "inclusion and equity in and through education is the cornerstone of a transformative education agenda" (UNESCO, 2015, p. 7). Inclusive education implies that all learners, regardless of their linguistic and cultural backgrounds, physical and mental abilities or other personal characteristics, learn together in a welcoming and supportive environment (UN General Assembly, 2017). In this sense, inclusion "is central to achieving high-quality education for all learners, including those with disabilities, and for the development of inclusive, peaceful and fair societies" (CRPD, 2016, p. 1).

Consequently, it is crucial that teacher education includes a basic understanding of human diversity, growth and development, the human rights model of disability and inclusive pedagogy. This would enable teachers to identify students' functional abilities (strengths, abilities and learning styles) to ensure their participation in inclusive educational environments (CRPD, 2016). The Education 2030 Framework for Action also expresses the commitment to ensure that educators will be "empowered, adequately recruited, well-trained, professionally qualified, motivated and supported within well-resourced, efficient and effectively governed systems" (UNESCO, 2015, p. 8). Actually, target 4.c of SDG 4 requires to "substantially increase the supply of qualified teachers, including through international cooperation for teacher training in developing countries." Governments should make teaching an attractive, first-choice profession by improving teachers' professional status, working conditions and support, and States should also strengthen policy dialogue mechanisms with teacher organizations (UNESCO, 2015).

The Importance of Active Learning

People should learn about human rights "by seeing human rights standards implemented in practice, whether at home, in school, or within the community" (CRC, 2001, p. 6). Many social issues are not analyzed in association with human rights, even if they are closely related (e.g., migrations, displacements, poverty, sustainable development, sexual health); we still cannot build a perspective or an approach that focuses on human rights as a way to see and interpret our social reality (Rodino, 2014). Indeed,

> understanding human rights means to realize that they are present here and now, from our closest contexts to the most remotes: in our personal life as well as in our local community, in the problems of our country as well as in those of our region and the world; it means to recognize that through the defense and promotion of human rights, we are dealing with the life and happiness of the people. (Pinto, 2010, p. 16)

Regarding the best methods for teaching human rights and for connecting them with our everyday life, according to Edgar Dale's Cone of Experience, learners retain more information by doing than by listening or reading (Dale, 1946). As an old Chinese saying goes, "I hear it and I forget it, I see it and I remember it, I do it and I understand it." Therefore, simulations, moot courts or role-play activities should be predominant in human rights education. Moot courts consist on hypothetical cases provided to the students, who need to investigate and support a particular position before a "tribunal," first through a written "memorial" and then through an oral "pleading." Simulations and role-plays also allow students to represent a specific opinion and interact with "other stakeholders" with different positions, in different settings. A respectful exchange of contradictory arguments and using controversy as an educational method recognizes the value of critical pedagogy and reflects how life in society is more likely to be (Magendzo & Pavez, 2018).

Additionally, dialogue allows for active learning and helps to understand the coexistence with the other, so group discussions should be also a principal teaching method for human rights classes (Mujica, 2002). An adequate and organized debate may promote active listening, the respect for different points of view and an improvement of the ways people express their own opinions (DIHR, 2013). In the end, human rights education is about accepting different opinions and building the skills to discuss them (DIHR, 2013). Here, it is crucial to ensure "that the same people do not dominate discussions; that there is a pleasant atmosphere and that no one bullies or interrupts others" (DIHR, 2013, p. 52). The Case Method, working in small groups and participating in international competitions are also ideal to implement active learning (Noodt Taquela, 2016).

Finally, "learners are not only influenced by what you present, but how you present it" (DIHR, 2013, p. 14). Or, put it differently, the way human rights are taught and by whom is also a determinant factor that will affect the position that students will take toward them (Requesens Galnares, 2006). This is also why "teachers are the key to achieving all of the SDG4-Education 2030 agenda" (UNESCO, 2015, p. 54).

CONCLUSION

As Professors Hafner-Burton, Tsutsui, and Meyer (2008) explain, "the world human rights movement has been an enormous and surprising success in putting forward high standards for States and societies to follow" (p. 115). However, the question remains on how effective those standards are and why are they followed or disregarded. Sadly, "there are failures in the implementation of widely shared human rights norms, and human rights violations – often of the most extreme sorts – are found everywhere" (Hafner-Burton et al., 2008, p. 116).

Thus, the law, as important as it is, is not enough to prevent the grave violations of human rights and it is necessary to assume education as an effective mean to transmit and spread the content of the fundamental rights (Mujica, 2002). In this sense, the main purpose of this chapter is to provide an idea on how to shorten the distance between the law and the reality through, first, acknowledging education in human rights as a powerful tool to achieve a much-needed structural change and, second, by offering some elements to fulfill this right.

To sum up, education protects children from violence, exploitation, criminal activity and disease, and it can break the cycle of conflict, promote peace and reconciliation, teach tolerance and conflict resolution and help to build a better future for children and young people (UN General Assembly, 2018). In other words, "education is a fundamental human right and an enabling right" (UNESCO, 2015, p. 28).

Adolescents and young adults must be considered as agents of change with the potential to contribute positively to their families, communities and countries toward peace, human rights, environmental sustainability and climate justice (CRC, 2017). The experience of schooling "is highly influential in shaping young people's identities" (Ansell, 2005, p. 156) and the foundations laid down during adolescence in terms of emotional security, health, sexuality, education, skills, resilience and understanding of rights will have profound implications, not only for their individual optimum development but also for present and future social and economic development (CRC, 2017). Indeed, "it is through education that societies transmit to their new members the fundamental values that sustain their social structure and that guarantee their continuity" (González Contró, 2006, p. 135).

Plus, education in human rights would not only prevent private actions and omissions that could affect other individual's human rights but it would also raise awareness about the State's obligations, and it would put society in a better position to fight for compliance. In other words, people will be empowered to demand social, political and economic changes through pressure "from below." Still, as the former United Nations High Commissioner for Human Rights, Navanethem Pillay, highlighted:

> human rights education can contribute to its noble goals only if it is methodologically sound and fully relevant to the learners, so as to have a genuine empowering or sensitizing effect. (Office of the United Nations High Commissioner for Human Rights & Equitas, 2011, p. 4)

In this sense, we need, among others, (a) to pay close attention to all four stages of the public budget process – planning, enacting, executing and follow-up – (CRC, 2016); (b) to make use of ICT; (c) to eliminate cultural barriers that prevent the fulfillment of human rights; (d) an appropriate curricula; (e) a transversal human rights perspective through governmental offices and educational institutions; (f) a participatory approach; (g) adequate training for teachers; and (h) a proper application of the theoretical concepts to the people's everyday life through active learning, moot courts, role-play and debates: students usually learn better when they interact with the learning points, when they relate them to their own experiences and when they put this knowledge into practice (DIHR, 2013).

If human rights are just an interesting theory that does not transform our lives, modify the way we relate to each other and change how we feel or how we think, it is just an empty speech without practical consequences (Mujica, 2002). The education system is an area for transformation that, once achieved, can accelerate positive change in other areas (CEDAW, 2017). Supported by trained educators and adequately equipped schools, education in human rights can definitely make the world a better place.

REFERENCES

Ansell, N. (2005). *Children, youth and development*. London: Routledge Taylor & Francis Group.

Becerra Valdivia, K. (2018). El desarrollo de habilidades procedimentales en derechos humanos: Aporte de la metodología Aprendizaje-Servicio en estudiantes de Derecho. *Academia. Revista sobre enseñanza del Derecho*, *16*(31), 141–173. Retrieved from http://www.derecho.uba.ar/publicaciones/ rev_academia/revistas/31/el-desarrollo-de-habilidades-procedimentales-en-derechos-humanos.pdf

Committee on Economic, Social and Cultural Rights. (1999). *General comment no. 13: "The right to education."* E/C.12/1999/10. United Nations, Geneva.

Committee on the Elimination of Discrimination against Women. (2017). *General recommendation no. 36 on the right of girls and women to education*. CEDAW/C/GC/36. United Nations, Geneva.

Committee on the Elimination of Racial Discrimination. (2013). *General recommendation no. 35: Combating racist hate speech*. CERD/C/GC/35. United Nations, Geneva.

Committee on the Rights of Persons with Disabilities. (2016). *General comment no. 4 on the right to inclusive education*. CRPD/C/GC/4. United Nations, Geneva.

Committee on the Rights of the Child. (2001). *General comment no. 1: "Article 29(1): The aims of education."* CRC/GC/2001/1. United Nations, Geneva.

Committee on the Rights of the Child. (2016). *General comment no. 19 on public budgeting for the realization of children's rights (art. 4)*. CRC/C/GC/19. United Nations, Geneva.

Committee on the Rights of the Child. (2017). *General comment no. 20 on the implementation of the rights of the child during adolescence,* CRC/C/GC/20. United Nations, Geneva.

Cussianovich, A. (2010). *Aprender la condición humana: Ensayo sobre pedagogía de la ternura*. Lima: IFEJANT.

Dale, E. (1946). *Audio-visual methods in teaching*. New York, NY: Dryden Press.

Danish Institute for Human Rights. (2013). *The human rights education toolbox*. Denmark: Danish Institute for Human Rights. Retrieved from https://www.humanrights.dk/publications/the-human-rights-education-toolbox

Freire, P. (2006). *Pedagogy of the oppressed: 30th anniversary edition*. New York, NY: Continuum.

González Contró, M. (2006). La educación en derechos humanos como experiencia vital en la escuela, *Educación en Derechos Humanos* (pp. 135–144). México: Programa de Cooperación sobre Derechos Humanos México – Comisión Europea. Retrieved from https://archivos.juridicas. unam.mx/www/bjv/libros/5/2466/9.pdf

Hafner-Burton, E., Tsutsui, K., & Meyer, J. (2008). International human rights law and the politics of legitimation. *International Sociology*, *23*(1), 115–141. Retrieved from https://ssrn.com/ abstract=2698270

Hart, J. (2008). Children's participation and international development: Attending to the political. *International Journal of Children's Rights*, *16*(3), 407–418. https://doi.org/10.1163/157181808X311231

Human Rights Committee. (2000). *General comment no. 28: Equality of rights between men and women (article 3)*. CCPR/C/21/Rev.1/Add.10. United Nations, Geneva.

Inter-American Institute of Human Rights. (2007). *VI Informe Interamericano de la Educacion en Derechos Humanos*. San José de Costa Rica. Retrieved from https://www.iidh.ed.cr/multic/ UserFiles/Biblioteca/IIDH/3_2010/484ee56a-c4a5-4c7b-a29b-62f9ae2e651a.pdf

Inter-American Institute of Human Rights. (2013). *El Derecho a la Educacion en Derechos Humanos en las Americas*. San José de Costa Rica. Retrieved from https://www.iidh.ed.cr/IIDH/media/1517/ informe-interamericano-el-derecho-a-la-edh-2013.pdf

Magendzo, A., & Pavez, J. (2018). Educando en la Declaración Universal de los Derechos Humanos desde una mirada controversial. In A. Magendzo & P. Morales (Eds.), *Pedagogía y didáctica de la Declaración Universal de los Derechos Humanos a setenta años de su promulgación* (pp. 141–155). Chile: Ediciones Universidad Academia de Humanismo Cristiano.

Medici, A. (2018). Articulación de docencia-investigación-extensión para una práctica pedagógica crítica en la enseñanza de los Derechos Humanos. *Revista Derechos en Acción*, *7*(7), 126–145. https://doi.org/10.24215/25251678e147

Mujica, R. M. (2002). La metodologia de la educacion en derechos humanos. *Revista Interamericana de Derechos Humanos*, *36*, 341–364. Retrieved from http://www.corteidh.or.cr/tablas/R06835-13.pdf

Mutua, M. (2002). *Human rights: A political and cultural critique*. Philadelphia, PA: University of Pennsylvania Press.

Noodt Taquela, M. B. (2016). La participación en competencias internacionales como estrategia de enseñanza-aprendizaje del derecho y como un modo de iniciación en la investigación, *Academia. Revista sobre enseñanza del derecho, 14*(28), 157–170. Retrieved from http://www. derecho.uba.ar/publicaciones/rev_academia/revistas/28/la-participacion-en-competencias-internacionales-como-estrategia-de-ensenanza-aprendizaje-del-derecho-y-como-un-modo-de-iniciacion-en-la-investigacion.pdf

Pinto, M. (2010). La enseñanza de Derechos Humanos en la Universidad de Buenos Aires. *Academia: Revista sobre enseñanza del Derecho, 8*(16), 9–21. Retrieved from www.derecho. uba.ar/publicaciones/rev_academia/revistas/16/la-ensenanza-de-derechos-humanos-en-la-universidad-de-buenos-aires.pdf

Requesens Galnares, A. (2006). Retos a la educación en derechos humanos, *Educación en Derechos Humanos* (pp. 407–412), México: Programa de Cooperación sobre Derechos Humanos México – Comisión Europea. Retrieved from http://ru.juridicas.unam.mx/xmlui/handle/123456789/28222

Rodino, A. (2014). La institucionalización de la educación en derechos humanos en América Latina: Avances, desafíos y una propuesta de prioridades. *Sociedade e Cultura, 16*(2), 257–264. https:// doi.org/10.5216/sec.v16i2.32183

Ronconi, L. (2017). La enseñanza en derechos humanos en las Facultades de Derecho en Argentina: Desafíos pendientes. *Revista Pedagogía Universitaria y Didáctica del Derecho, 4*(1), 5–37. http:// dx.doi.org/10.5354/0719-5885.2017.46249

United Nations Commission on Human Rights. (2004). *Report submitted by the Special Rapporteur on the right to education*. E/CN.4/2005/50. United Nations, Geneva.

United Nations General Assembly. (2004). *Resolution adopted by the General Assembly on 10 December 2004*. A/RES/66/137. United Nations, New York, NY.

United Nations Economic and Social Council. (2019). *Special edition: Progress towards the sustainable development goals*. E/2019/68. United Nations, Geneva.

United Nations Educational, Scientific and Cultural Organization. (2011). *The hidden crisis: Armed conflict and education*. Paris: UNESCO Publishing. Retrieved from https://unesdoc.unesco.org/ ark:/48223/pf0000190743_eng

United Nations Educational, Scientific and Cultural Organization. (2015). *Education 2030: Incheon declaration and framework for action for the implementation of sustainable development goal 4*. Paris: UNESCO Publishing. Retrieved from https://unesdoc.unesco.org/ark:/48223/pf0000245656

United Nations Educational, Scientific and Cultural Organization. (2016). *Leaving no one behind: How far on the way to universal primary and secondary education?* Paris: UNESCO Publishing. Retrieved from https://unesdoc.unesco.org/ark:/48223/pf0000245238

United Nations Educational, Scientific and Cultural Organization. (2019). *Meeting commitments: Are countries on track to achieve SDG4?* Paris: UNESCO Publishing. Retrieved from https:// unesdoc.unesco.org/ark:/48223/pf0000369009

United Nations General Assembly. (2012). *Resolution adopted by the General Assembly on 19 December 2011*. A/RES/66/137. United Nations, New York, NY.

United Nations General Assembly. (2014). *Report of the Special Rapporteur on the right to education*. A/HRC/26/27. United Nations, Geneva.

United Nations General Assembly. (2017). *Report of the Special Rapporteur on the right to education*. A/72/496. United Nations, Geneva.

United Nations General Assembly. (2018). *Report of the Special Rapporteur on the right to education*. A/73/262. United Nations, Geneva.

United Nations General Assembly. (2019). *Report of the Special Rapporteur on the right to education*. A/HRC/41/37. United Nations, Geneva.

United Nations High Commissioner for Human Rights & Equitas. (2011). *Evaluating human rights training activities: A handbook for human rights educators*. Canada. Retrieved from https://www. ohchr.org/Documents/Publications/EvaluationHandbookPT18.pdf

Villán Durán, C. (2006). Las obligaciones de los Estados en materia de educación en derechos humanos, *Educación en Derechos Humanos* (pp. 23–39). México: Programa de Cooperación sobre Derechos Humanos México – Comisión Europea. Retrieved from https://archivos. juridicas.unam.mx/www/bjv/libros/5/2466/4.pdf

CHAPTER 3

BRIDGES TO ZAMBIA: TEACHING HUMAN RIGHTS THROUGH IMMERSION EXPERIENCE[1]

Alia Sheety, Erin McLaughlin and Susan Jacques Pierson

ABSTRACT

Education is a fundamental factor of development, preparing the educated for a better tomorrow. Education serves to improve quality of life, is a means of enhancing the economic growth for individuals and nations and provides a way for marginalized children and adults to exchange lives of desperation, poverty and injustice for those illuminated with liberty, justice and self-determination. Education is declared by the United Nations as a human right. This chapter presents one model to teach for human rights through experiential learning. It shares a unique experience of education and business students in their immersion trip to Zambia. The model used to develop the partnership is integral human development (IHD). This chapter provides description of the model, how it was implemented and shares direct citations from students' reflection journals highlighting three themes: communication, reciprocity and self-exploration.

Keywords: United States; integral human development framework; restorative approach; solidarity; reciprocity; self-exploration; interdisciplinary; education; United Nations

---

[1]All authors had equal contributions to this chapter.

International Perspectives in Social Justice Programs at the Institutional and Community Levels
Innovations in Higher Education Teaching and Learning, Volume 37, 29–44
Copyright © 2021 by Emerald Publishing Limited
All rights of reproduction in any form reserved
ISSN: 2055-3641/doi:10.1108/S2055-364120210000037003

INTRODUCTION

For a nation to flourish, it must protect and develop its human capital. Education is key to that development as is economic growth through income-generating, socially responsible and sustainable business ventures. Sadly, those who abuse power may withhold economic opportunity and education from others. When quality education is limited or denied, a nation's people may be indoctrinated and controlled by corrupt governments. The dominated others, or those Freire (1970) called the "oppressed," are, in this situation, represented as somehow inferior and deserving of domination, while the dominator is deserving of the benefits (Fields, 2016). As Apple (1990) reminds us that education is not neutral.

According to the 2016 report of the United Nations Educational, Scientific and Cultural Organization (UNESCO, 2016), illiteracy rates vary around the globe. Sub-Saharan Africa shares 27% of the world's illiterate people and is also plagued by extreme poverty and disparities in opportunity accorded to individuals depending on gender (UNESCO Institute of Statistics, 2017). The Declaration of the United Nations identifying education as a universal human right serves as a moral imperative for those with the tools and resources to provide access to quality education around the world. The struggle for human rights is a struggle against domination of body, mind and spirit and requires the development of societal structures and norms that ensure life, liberty and the pursuit of happiness for all people while promoting economic growth. Education equips people with the knowledge, skills and vision necessary to improve their lives and develop their nations. Providing legal legitimacy to the call for universal education is critical. All of us are called to champion the idea that education is not only necessary for the advancement of human rights but is itself an inalienable right of all people.

We, the authors of this chapter, teach in a mission-driven institution of higher education in northeastern Pennsylvania, United States of America. We strongly believe everyone has the right to education and that teaching others to recognize education as an integral human right not only promotes critical thinking about human rights around the globe but also serves as inspiration to work and advocate for social justice locally and internationally. This chapter provides a short review of the literature on human rights and the role of higher education in promoting understanding of important theoretical models including critical pedagogy and restorative practices. We also provide information about a model for teaching about and working for social justice that has been used at our mission-driven university. Finally, it introduces the newly developed partnership between our institution and nonprofits in Lusaka, Zambia, which included an immersion experience for undergraduate and graduate students from the United States to the nation of Zambia. The partnership supports our goal of teaching about and working for human rights in several ways. Because the immersion included working with teachers in Zambian schools to provide education for marginalized and vulnerable children, American students were able to see abstract concepts and the transformative power of education in action. Moreover, the infusion of new pedagogies and resources in Zambian classrooms helped enhance educational opportunities for vulnerable children. While in Zambia, students and faculty also facilitated development of a social business, designed to support the economic development of marginalized women and girls. Clearly, we are living in an increasingly interconnected world where the free flow of information, goods and services are the norm. Within that context, we share the story of how our students engaged in an international partnership that provided opportunities for them to understand more about working for social justice through education while preparing them to be engaged citizens of the world.

LITERATURE REVIEW

The United Nations Human Rights Office of the High Commissioner has defined Human Rights Education as educational training, information, awareness-raising and learning activities designed to promote universal respect for and observance for all human rights and fundamental freedoms, thus contributing to the prevention of human rights violations and abuses and promoting a universal culture of human rights. Moreover, human rights education includes education about human rights, education through human rights and education for human rights (United Nations Declaration on Human Rights Education and Training, 2011). Researchers and educators through the years struggled to agree on one definition of Human Rights. The study of Human Rights has proven to be challenging because educators focused on the historical facts associated with people and countries and struggled with the relationship between individual and cultural human rights. As Cranston (1989) pointed out, long lists of human rights may be too cumbersome to be taken seriously. Fields (2016) argued that for human rights to be of value they "need to be meaningful and/or effective, they must be circumscribed" (p. 69) As part of this holistic approach, Fields (2016) goes on to explain the importance of supporting both external and internal human development that occurs within cultural, economic and social relationships, through what he terms "co-and self-determination" (p. 70). Family, school, religious affiliation, friendship and even history play a role in this process.

According to Cortese (2003), "higher education institutions bear moral responsibility to increase awareness, knowledge, skills, and values needed to create a just and sustainable future" (p. 17). As higher education institutions train future teachers, they have a great influence on future generations of teachers and how they perceive the world. A shift toward increasing collaboration, forming partnerships with the local community and offering students opportunities to get involved and experience local injustices firsthand (Rademacher & Sheety, 2016) or integrating field experiences through international encounters (such as the current reported Bridges to Zambia) may create a powerful space for transformative learning.

Several models were developed to guide moving students from cultural awareness to cultural competence. For example, Hingson (2008), utilized what he calls a "Critical Pedagogy Approach," calling on students to become activists for social and political change by focusing on primary sources of data so that students understand the larger context. This approach forces us to confront the possibility that there is more than one "story" and that in order to truly understand and evolve, one must delve into those differing stories. Lucas (2009) argued that as educators teach about global injustice, they must help their students develop empathy. She used children's books to connect students to individual stories of those experiencing social injustice. Through these stories, readers were able to examine human rights issues and empathize with characters they could relate to.

DeLaet (2012) tries to "complicate" students' understanding and use of the word "they" in their discussion of important global issues. He focuses on developing understanding of a pluralistic world, one in which identity is characterized by diversity. Having students move away from "us" and "them" as a homogeneous group allows students to address their potential arrogance and naivety as they contemplate their understanding of global issues. This approach broadens students' thinking and forces them to disrupt what they are familiar with, by stepping outside of themselves and what they have been told and instead critically evaluating each element of the situation.

Others argue for the use of graphic novels with students (Carano & Clabough, 2016). They explain that this approach provides an excellent starting point for introducing questioning skills. Additionally, case studies, cross-cultural comparisons and experiential learning are important tools for improving the cultural competency of students (DeLaet, 2012). One pair of researchers, Sheety and Rademacher (2015), used inquiry-based learning (IBL) and reflective practices as they engaged their students in critical thinking and exploration of injustices around the globe.

Also relevant to human rights education are restorative practices which emerged from theories of restorative justice and encourage the concept of community, honoring both the individual and the group. According to Pranis (2001), restorative justice practices are "neither the rampant of individualism of modern western culture nor the mindless obedience of highly controlled cultures." Rather the practice of restorative justice within community "can provide fertile ground to raise and address social justice concerns" (p. 289). A core restorative principle is direct engagement of key stakeholders in decisions that affect them. Clearly, education plays an important role in this process, as it empowers individuals and groups to be active and engaged members of their community provides an opportunity for everyone to take a seat at the table and teaches the importance of working "with."

According to Bailie (2019), restorative practices scholarship is starting to provide a framework for the concept of human dignity that is communicable across cultures and disciplines. In Bolton's (2019) words, "restorative practices provide a simple framework to give people voice in a noisy world" (para. 20). And what a better way to ensure that than to ensure every person has access to education. Bailie (2019) suggests that "the desire to be treated with dignity is common to all human relationships" (p. 13). This desire manifests itself in three areas of human need: the need to belong, to have voice and to exercise agency in one's own affairs. Since research about restorative practices as the science of human dignity is still in its infancy, the main concept that restorative practices contribute is doing "with" instead of doing "for" or doing "to" (Wachtel, 2015). This coincides with Lamberty (2012, 2015) who emphasizes the shift from charity to solidarity when providing support to struggling communities. As educators teaching about human rights, it is our responsibility to help disrupts power relations by empowering students through allowing all voices to be heard as we work for educational access and equity (Brett, Mompoint-Gaillard, Salema, & Keating-Chetwynd, 2009; Lamberty, 2015; Olser, 2016; Parker, 2018; Pranis, 2001).

INTEGRAL HUMAN DEVELOPMENT (IHD) FRAMEWORK

Catholic Relief Services (CRS) has been serving the marginalized around the world since 1943. Since that time, they have worked internationally to advocate for human dignity for all. In 2002, CRS responded to requests from communities around the world to "guide programming," "find practical ways to incorporate the justice lens into our programs" and "develop a framework that links the justice lens with the food security framework and our relief and development goals." Their response to these requests was the development of IHD. The ultimate goal of IHD is to improve livelihood outcomes described by CRS as peace, justice and dignity. The IHD model provides a valuable framework for achieving social change through consideration of communities' assets, systems/structures in place and vulnerabilities. The model also provides for the development of mutually beneficial, sustainable relationships between struggling communities and those providing support. Another important element of the IHD model is that it offers a sustainable feedback loop, so that as assets and vulnerabilities shift, the dynamic model stands ready to adjust to consistently focus on the development and improvement of livelihood outcomes (Fig. 1). Use of this

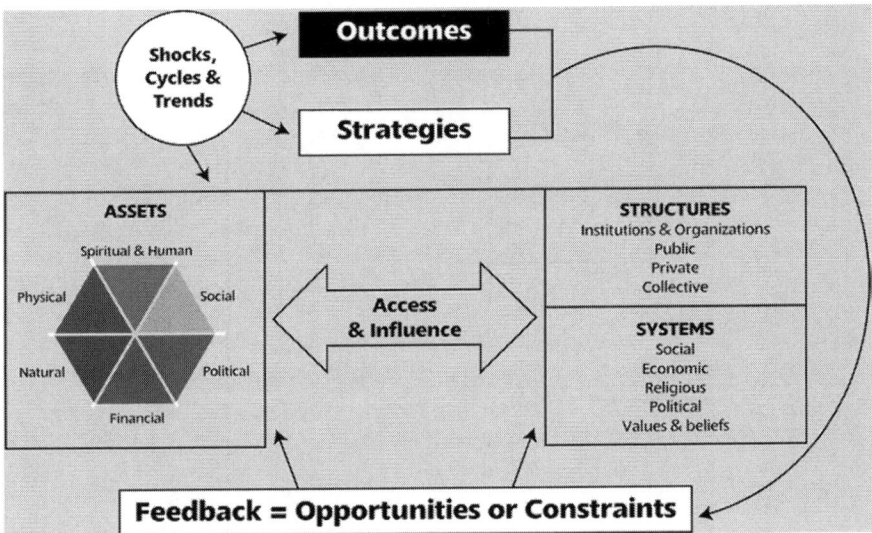

Fig. 1. Catholic Relief Services' Integral Human Development Model. Retrieved from: http://pqpublications.squarespace.com/IHD/

model helps students understand that they are not entering communities with the understanding of "helping" based on the past Western arrogance associated with the understanding that "we" can solve "their" problems. Instead, IHD focuses on students' understanding that they have created a mutually beneficial relationship, shifting from charity to solidarity (Lamberty, 2012).

HUMAN RIGHTS, SOCIAL JUSTICE AND CABRINI UNIVERSITY'S MISSION

In consideration of ongoing global events that impact the world, including the immigration crisis, climate change, war zones, poverty, etc., Cabrini, a small liberal arts institute of higher education that was founded for the "education of the heart" and whose mission is dedicated to "academic excellence, leadership development, and commitment to social justice" including "preparing students to become engaged citizens of the world," believes it has a moral responsibility to address various national and global issues related to social justice and human rights.

Cabrini University's faculty and administration recognize the importance of being intentional and systematic in providing opportunities to students in higher education to learn about injustices and to view education as a human right. This recognition led to the development of a core curriculum titled "Justice Matters." Faculty from different disciplines collaborated on the development of the curriculum and structured the courses called "Engagement with the Common Good" (ECG). The curriculum, through the various courses, approaches the Common Good through texts and community partnerships, exploring how power, privilege and difference affect solidarity, equality and dignity and helping students understand how to utilize their assets and the assets of community partners in the pursuit of social justice. One objective of the curriculum is to provide awareness of injustice through thought-provoking readings, classroom discussions of human rights violations around the world. Another important objective is for faculty and students, to explore means of addressing injustice by applying various pedagogical strategies including IBL, experimental learning, simulations and firsthand real-life experience, through immersion trips. The curriculum adapts a spiral model in which it contributes to build students' knowledge, skills, values and habits to benefit the Common Good. It starts with raising awareness and progresses toward advocacy and activism in a local and global context by inspiring informed actions.

Education of the Heart, according to Cabrini, can be achieved through the thoughtful implementation of various models, such as the Social Change (SC) model and the IHD model. Various opportunities in which the SC model (Francis & Colby, 2016; Rademacher & Sheety, 2016; Sheety & Rademacher, 2015) and the IHD model (Pierson, 2015) were effectively implemented and linked curricular and cocurricular experiences that amazed students and allowed them critically analyze their view of the world.

Some of the work that faculty at Cabrini initiated with their students is documented in various publications. For example, Francis and Colby (2016) reported how Cabrini faculty promoted the values of equity, social justice, collaboration, citizenship and service to foster transformative learning and group empowerment. As a result, "students came to see their shared humanity and responsibility to work together in service of others" (p. 43). Sheety and Rademacher (2015) sought to cultivate independent learning among students by making them partners in decision-making, concerning what they wanted to learn about and the strategies they would use to develop critical thinking skills while addressing the issues at hand. The process, although challenging and emotional, helped students exhibit leadership skills around a human right issue of their choice by utilizing IBL to better question and understand local and global injustices and seek methods of inquiry to address various questions. According to Sheety and Rademacher (2015), students' feedback and reflection journals indicated that

> they were hesitant at the beginning, expressing confusion at mid-point, and were positive toward the end when they realized how their inquiry gave rise to new insights and further questions into the various topics they studied[hunger, homelessness, honor killing, human trafficking] and how what they studied could be of service to others. (p. 133)

By developing a learning community, students were able to exchange knowledge and experiences with their topic, receive feedback from the rest of the students and the faculty and explore global issues. As one of Sheety and Rademacher's students reported:

> hearing the sisters [an international community of women religious] sharing their stories firsthand really challenged me to think about the impact that these women were having globally … and questioning my role. I firmly believe that this experience has shaped the way that I view things … this was the first real social justice experience that I had in college. (p. 131)

Pierson (2015), who led an immersion experience to Swaziland focused on preservice teachers, provided an example of collaboration between Cabrini and Swaziland teachers in planning and implementing strategies to support English Language Learners. The collaboration is a clear example of the shift from charity to solidarity, from doing "for" or "to" into doing "with." Pierson (2015) concluded by stating that:

> short term cultural immersion and field experience has clear benefits for pre-service teachers. In addition to unforgettable memories of a night spent on a homestead, participation in cattle drive and the smiles of new friends, our teacher candidates carried home new confidence in their abilities to meet the needs of culturally and linguistically diverse students, a deep understanding of the power of relationships, and an unshakable belief that those who work for social justice through education have the power to make a difference in their own lives and the lives of their students. (p. 182)

Previous literature related to the effects of overseas teaching experiences for teachers, including Doppen and Jing (2014) indicates that such experiences have significant effect and lasting effect on participants. Benefits reported include feeling more courageous, independent and confident. While acknowledging benefits of immersions is important to recognize that such powerful experiences can create cognitive dissonance. Cognitive dissonance is described as an uncomfortable internal state that takes place when new information conflicts or doesn't fit with commonly held beliefs (Festinger, 1957). Participation in courses that address social injustice challenges students by causing them to question what they think they already know and also to explore the unknown. While resulting in new learning, the experience takes students beyond their comfort zone, stirring powerful emotions. According to Rademacher and Sheety (2016), it is important for those teaching courses that embed sensitive topics, such as human rights and injustices that might trigger powerful emotional responses, to share with students early in the process some information on emotional intelligence, the amygdala and our body's defense system as well as provide a list of support centers for those who might need emotional support during the process.

In this chapter, we decided to share a recent immersion experience (Summer, 2019) that demanded deep emotional and physical commitment on the part of undergraduate and graduate Cabrini students from different disciplines (Education and Business) who spent one month working with partners in Zambia.

CABRINI UNIVERSITY (US) PARTNERS WITH ST. LAWRENCE SCHOOL AND VISION OF HOPE (VOH, ZAMBIA)

Zambia, a nation of approximately 15.5 million people, is a former British colony classified as a lower-middle-income country. Its official language (used in government and business) is English, but at least five major regional and 70 local languages are used by the Zambian people. Zambia is an exemplar of the challenges of a once-colonized nation that was severely destabilized during colonization and seeks change toward a more flourishing future. The International Labor Organization (2019) reported that 28% of children in Zambia work, 65% of children attend school and 6% of children die before the age of five. Additionally, 31% of girls marry before the age 18 and 58% of the population lives in extreme poverty.

Though only 65% of the children attend school, Zambians recognize the importance of education. The country's goal is to achieve middle-income status by 2030, and one important pathway to achieving that goal is its focus on continuing to improve the education of its young adult population. During the colonial period (as Northern Rhodesia), it was administered by the British South Africa Company (BSA), an entity which chose not to invest in the education of the country's children. When Zambia became independent in 1964, that lack of education was apparent in the dearth of educated citizens to lead and advance the country. The Zambian government thus formulated and implemented an education plan, but it was not until 2001, after education had not shown improvement, and in fact had declined, that the Zambian government committed significant resources to social policy development and education reform. In 2002, Free Basic Education (FBE) began, requiring nine years of basic education for all children, and the results have been positive. Most children receive a primary and a lower secondary education, although the percentage of children completing the nine years is higher in urban areas than it is in rural areas. The Zambian government has more recently focused on upper secondary education. The education priority for this age group is to equip students with technical education, vocational and entrepreneurship training and higher education. The challenge, however, is that in this age group, dropout rates are high, especially among adolescent females and adolescents in rural areas and the quality of education is questionable, especially in rural areas (Hall, 2019).

The co-directors of the Cabrini University initiative, Drs Pierson and McLaughlin, designed the "Bridges to Zambia" partnership to increase the cultural competency of US students and student-educators by focusing on the culture of Zambia through the lens of IHD, a principle of human dignity that centers on the human as a holistic entity with the responsibility to grow and maintain a global perspective. Along with the promotion of cultural competency, the co-directors set out to build a mutually beneficial relationship with two separate entities, St. Lawrence School and VoH. US students learned what it means to live in solidarity and work *with* and *alongside* in a mutually beneficial learning experience.

Bridges to Zambia participants from the US included seven preservice and in-service teachers (a mix of undergraduate juniors and seniors and graduate students in education who are pursuing teacher certification, master's in education degrees and also learning about theories and best practices for teaching English Learners) and five students focusing on the intersection of business administration and international business. The choice to integrate graduate and undergraduate as well as students from business, economy and education was intentional in order to make it possible for students to learn about the strong link between education and business and to view the value of collaboration that each could bring.

VoH, Zambia, is a rescue center for trafficked and exploited girls and young women. Because of the startling number of teenaged women on the streets of Lusaka, Zambia, many of whom have been trafficked or abandoned, VoH provides support and a safe place for the young women. These girls, as young as 11, need to know how to function productively in society. Ideally, they would be sent back to their families, but because of the social stigma – which often results in economic disruption – their families often do not want them back. Therefore, those young women need education and business skills to advance in life, become independent and get out of the poverty circle they live in. VoH provides a safe place where girls can live in a stable and protected environment while gaining access to resources such as medical care and educational support. Where possible, VoH strives to reunite girls with their families and reintegrate them into their communities. They guide girls through the process of reimagining their future, starting by providing a safe and secure environment for their rehabilitation and growth. The organization believes that all girls are a critical part of Zambia's future; educated girls have a lower risk of HIV infection and make a greater contribution to economic growth. VoH helps girls and young women realize their basic human rights and be a part of a stronger, healthier Zambia.

St. Lawrence School, Lusaka, Zambia, is a community school in Kamwala in Lusaka, Zambia. It is a school which educates more than 1,100 students – almost all from Misisi Township (one of the poorest townships in Zambia). Despite the challenges posed by the socioeconomic background of the school's student population it has achieved academic results beyond expectation. It is a school which strongly promotes gender equality and the promotion of girls and young women through education. The former Department of Education Secretary for Lusaka

Province – Mr Chimbuye (now DES for Chilange Province) – cites St. Lawrence School as an example of how a school in Zambia can achieve despite all the challenges. This is largely through inspirational leadership, community involvement and a long-standing partnership with Project Zambia (an Irish charity which is part of the Edmund Rice Network (formerly Christian Brothers) Developing World Immersion Program).

Bridges to Zambia Design

Bridges to Zambia was organized around three main concepts that were explored through the process:

1. *IHD*: A positive vision for people around the world, IHD centers on the idea that the dignity of the human person is expressed not only in work and economic activity but also in cultural richness, artistic creativity, religious belonging and spiritual practice. Most profoundly, human dignity is expressed in our relationships with and obligations to family, community and all of humanity around the globe. At Cabrini, IHD means more than passively listening; instead, it requires full engagement for a mutually beneficial, sustainable relationship to grow and be sustained in the long term. Bridges to Zambia participants immersed in Zambian culture, engaged with Zambians who taught them about the culture, art, food, religion, economics and history of Zambia and worked to form lasting, sustainable partnerships.
2. *Working for social justice through education*: This involves transitioning from the traditional model of charity to a restorative model that reflects awareness through the interchange between cultures and empowers both sides in the process. One aim of Bridges to Zambia was to establish strong and reciprocal relationships with teachers in Zambia for the benefit of both. Through their experience with Zambian teachers and students, Bridges to Zambia participants developed cultural competency and ESL teaching pedagogy that prepared them for their own diverse classrooms. We believe financial literacy education is also important. Those participants who knew more about developing financial plans shared that knowledge with our partners.
3. *Building a social business*: Through curriculum created to highlight meeting the needs of those VoH serves, participants explored the importance and benefit of building a social business, one that integrates a triple bottom line of people, planet and profit, meaning that the business concerns itself with the interconnected social, environmental and economic impacts of business decisions. Study of the triple bottom line included principles taken from the social sciences and the humanities (sociology, ethics, sustainability and others). The curriculum also taught participants the importance of identifying a mission and vision and building a social business around the mission. Participants came to understand trends in twenty-first-century business practices that focus on social responsibility, shared value and community impact.

To ensure that the learning experience would be comprehensive, we started a period of preparation (spring semester 2019). Students read and learned about

Zambia and studied human rights and social justice in theoretical frameworks. Then students applied their reading in developing plans for work with partners.

Faculty at Cabrini University understand the importance of building sustainable partnerships and made sure this was discussed in class and during special orientation sessions. To faculty participating in this project, this meant employing the principles of CRS' IHD. An important component of IHD is the understanding that a true partnership is mutually beneficial, and foundations are formed based on a holistic approach to helping people improve their livelihoods (CRS, 2017). IHD encourages us to focus on the assets, risks and systems and structures in place within a society. The foundation of these principles is based on performing a needs assessment. Listening to our partners as they shared *their* needs and wants was foremost in our strategic planning process, as we began building the partnerships with VoH and St. Lawrence School.

THE BUSINESS PLAN

More than a year before landing in Lusaka, Zambia, faculty worked with directors at VoH to determine foremost whether there was a need for an income-generating business. The question was quickly answered with a "Yes!" and "this is the kind of business we are looking for." Within a very short period of time, partners at VoH discussed with us all that they envisioned. The next step was for students to begin building the business plan based on the needs and wants of our partners. This step was accomplished in our Engagement for the Common Good, People, Planet and Profit class. Students remained in communication with VoH throughout the semester as they built the business plan, developed the branding and created an e-commerce website. All of the information was shared with and critiqued by VoH. Once in Lusaka, students worked with VoH to implement the plan. Students worked with directors at VoH to determine first steps. Once it was clear what VoH wanted, students worked to accomplish all that was asked and subsequently assisted with training VoH employees on the processes set in place. Upon return from Zambia, the work continues. Requests were made by VoH for assistance with website and US retail market access development. An important component to understand about IHD is that the partnership is based on peace, social justice and human dignity. For us, this translates to mean a sustainable, dynamic, long-lasting partnership. The partnership will continue long after the immersion experience ends. Future students will benefit from this experience as they will continue with the growth of the partnership remotely.

EDUCATION PARTNERSHIP WITH ST. LAWRENCE SCHOOL

It is important to remember that every school has strengths as well as needs and vulnerabilities. Therefore, before and during our immersion in Lusaka, graduate and undergraduate students were frequently reminded that our job was not to critique or to "fix" perceived deficiencies at St. Lawrence School but to walk alongside and accompany our new partners as they worked to meet the needs of their students [working *with*]. We knew the teachers at St. Lawrence School faced challenges and lacked resources, but we also recognized the many things that were going right and the things the teachers and staff were doing well.

Before we went to Zambia, we communicated with a representative of the faculty, providing a list of activities we were prepared to share once we arrived. This list included teaching reading/language arts through the use of Zambian and other African folktales, learning about and helping with human rights education and activities in social studies, facilitating writers' workshops, conducting interactive read-aloud using culturally relevant books and stories, conducting hands-on numeracy lessons and helping as students learned to use computer applications. Many of our lessons included the use of computer technology as we were able to bring laptops with us. One representative of the faculty and the head of the School, Sister Angela, created a schedule for us that included teaching at a variety of grade levels and encompassed many of the ideas we had suggested. In addition, we were asked to lead two professional development sessions, one for primary and the other for secondary teachers, sharing ideas for teaching reading/language arts, including reading in the content areas. The workshops were scheduled on our very first day in the school. We were understandably nervous, but knowing that this was important to our partners, worked hard to create and implement workshops that we believed would have relevance for the teachers and have an immediate impact upon classroom practice.

As was mentioned earlier, all students took part in a preparation program before they traveled. The Education students participated in a specially designed class the spring before the immersion experience. This class, Bridges to Zambia, emphasized learning about the history, culture, educational system, language and geography of the country. Students were also required to read books and stories that could be shared with children once we were in the school and to complete some simple lesson plans. Once the teaching schedule was in place, everyone worked in the evenings and on weekends to prepare for the next day's activities/lessons in the school. We were able to work individually or with teaching partners, and we also spent time reflecting on our work during discussions with the other educators in our group.

Although our time in the school was too short (one month was not nearly enough time to make a substantial impact), the experience was overwhelmingly positive. The teachers and heads of school remarked that our lessons and activities were enjoyable and also beneficial to the students. We received positive feedback about the professional development workshops too. In order to ensure continuity of our work, materials for teachers and students were placed online where they could be easily accessed even after our return to the United States. Plans are underway to create both a website and also file-sharing system that will facilitate continued communication and collaboration between our teaching partners in Lusaka and us. Of the seven preservice and in-service teachers who had the privilege to work with the students and teachers in Zambia, all are committed to continuing the partnership, remotely and face to face if we are able to obtain funding to return to Lusaka next summer.

STUDENTS' REFLECTIONS

Although the project comprehensive evaluation is still in progress, the profound impact this experience had on students is already clear. For this chapter, a qualitative coding was applied to the reflection papers that students wrote. The occurring themes were:

- Connection/relationship.
- Impact/reciprocity.
- Self-exploration/self-discovery.

Many of the students who took part in this experience shared the strong connection they have made with peoples in Zambia. As one undergraduate student majoring in business wrote: "I loved being able to connect with people from halfway across the world." One of the graduate students in education was touched by

the amazing kindness and love that was shown by almost everyone we encountered, even though their conditions and their poverty levels are so high ... I'm not sure if I have ever in my life been so intimately integrated with a group of people in such close quarters for such a long time. I think nothing can educate you on social interaction and various personalities more so than an experience like this.

An undergraduate education student described the interaction that led to building the community:

From the very first time the bus pulled into the lot, everyone at St. Lawrence has been nothing but welcoming. They truly were happy to see us and wanted to talk to us. Talking to the children and hearing what they have endured, you would have never guessed with the true happiness the children had. The smiles on their faces from being in the classroom with them and learning their games and dancing with them was amazing.

An undergraduate business student reflected on the impact of the experience by stating:

Yes, we may have helped create a business during our trip, but the even greater gift was what the people of Zambia did for me. They made me into a person that is culturally aware, one that does not judge by appearance, and one that is welcoming to all.

Another graduate student in education referred in her reflection to a quote from the book students had read during spring 2019, *Encountering God in the Margins* by Aidan Donaldson (2010). Peter Tembo, cited by Dr Donaldson provides this powerful reminder: "Remember, you cannot change the world; but together you can help us change our world." In his wonderful book based on experiences in Zambia, Donaldson goes on to say that

none of us are messiahs ... but change nevertheless relies on our efforts, no matter how small and imperfect they are. We can talk big and do nothing or we can accept our limitations and participate in working towards something truly remarkable.

And

we are, in fact, co-creators of the possible: We may never see the end results, but that is the difference between the master builder and the worker. We are workers, not master builders; ministers, not messiahs. We are prophets of a future not our own. (pp. 47–48)

The student continued,

I initially highlighted these words when I read the book for the first time. Being here though, in Zambia, amongst the people, learning and living in their world, this was when Aidan's words came alive for me and I truly felt it. I felt the impact that I can have on their world and I felt the impact that they can also have on mine. We have so much to learn from each other.

Other undergraduate students contributed these thoughts:

This entire immersion trip has been the most impactful trip and experience I have ever had. From leaving the Cabrini parking lot, to all our encounters in Zambia, each encounter has impacted me. This entire experience will be one that I will never forget.

Starting this immersion, I did not know how I would interact with the kids or even how much of an impact they would make on me.

This immersion trip to Zambia has impacted me in ways that I'm still trying to understand. In all honesty, I don't think I will be able to fully understand and see how this trip has changed me until I am home and acclimated. (Undergrad business student)

Two of the participating students, one from business and one from education, shared that through this immersion experience, they learned that they have chosen the right path with their major. They were able to see how they could make a difference with their future career. The Education student wrote:

This experience has impacted my life in many ways. The first way this trip has impacted my life is it allowed me to know that I 100% without a doubt want to be a teacher in life. When coming into college people say that students often change their mind on what career they want for themselves but after this trip, I know that teaching is where I am supposed to be! I absolutely love working with students and helping them achieve their goals in life.

The student from business wrote:

One thing that I am sure of is that I am enrolled in the right major. When I chose International Business as a major, I did not know all that entailed but after this amazing experience, I am so happy with my decision and I plan to continue in my pursuits.

Self-exploration is a powerful tool. It helps students reflect on human rights and injustices and question how they view the world. Those who are able to reflect on and challenge their own preconceptions and thinking have the potential to become engaged citizens and advocates for changing the dark sides of our world, as fighting for just causes including fair trade, eradicating human trafficking and advancing human rights. Some of the notes shared in the reflection papers that indicate self-exploration included:

Living in the United States has allowed me to live a privileged life and after experiencing this culture and life for the past month, I have grown to live a life that still uses everything that I have but I am now aware and I am not ignoring the fact that there are people who do not have everything handed to them on a silver platter. (Undergrad business student)

Some went further to reflect on sensitive and even threatening aspects of the immersion such as when one of the students shared:

While I don't feel as though I am a terribly judgmental person ordinarily anyway, I tried to take that to a new level here and not judge a person's statement, tone or attitude. I also really reflected on myself and my communication skills, actions and attitudes, and realized how I could be misinterpreted and tried to correct for future encounters. (Graduate student)

Another said:

> I learned a lot about people, personalities and myself as an individual … I think I gained some valuable insights that will be useful to me at home and really anywhere.

In one of the journals, a student summed up the three aspects discussed above – connection, impact and self-reflection in her closing statement:

> Our final time leaving St. Lawrence and Vision of hope yesterday was extremely sad. I was very emotional because for the past month we *made connections* with these children and they have made such *a lasting impact on me and my future teaching career*. I did not know how much these *kids would have an impact on us but I am forever grateful for those children and this immersion*. As it was a hard see you later not a goodbye, it makes me look forward to my next trip to Zambia. I know I will never forget my time here and everything I have learned. (Education student)

CONCLUSION

As we close this chapter, we think back to a special song the school choir greeted us with that later became our anthem:

> You're in the right place
>
> At the right time
>
> With the right people
>
> You'll never go back the same way you came.

The words to this song continue to resonate in our hearts, reminding us not only of the power of human rights education but also of the love we share. Although our efforts impacted the lives of our partners, accompanying them on their journey had an even more profound and transformative effect on each of us. Reciprocity and collaboration were in the heart of not only learning about human rights but also how to contribute to a more just world.

REFERENCES

Apple, M. (1990). *Ideology and curriculum* (2nd ed.). New York, NY: Routledge, Chapman, and Hall, Inc.

Bailie, J. W. (2019). A science of human dignity: Belonging, voice and agency as universal human needs. *IIRP Presidential Paper Series, 1,* 1–16. Retrieved from https://www.iirp.edu/restorative-practices/presidential-paper-series

Bolton, K. (2019). Restorative practices: A science of human dignity. In building a new reality. Retrieved from https://www.buildinganewreality.com/restorative-practices-a-science-of-human-dignity/

Brett, P., Mompoint-Gaillard, P., Salema, M. H., & Keating-Chetwynd, S. (2009). *How all teachers can support citizenship and human rights education: A framework for the development of competences.* France: Council of Europe.

Carano, K. T., & Clabough, J. (2016). Images of struggle: Teaching human rights with graphic novels. *The Social Studies, 107*(1), 14–18.

Cortese, A. D. (2003). The critical role of higher education in creating a sustainable future. *Planning for Higher Education, 31*(3), 15–22.

Cranston, M. (1989). Human rights real and supposed. In M. E. Winston (Ed.), *The philosophy of human rights* (pp. 121–128). Belmont, CA: Wadsworth.

DeLaet, D. (2012). Interrogating "they": A pedagogy of feminist pluralism in the international relations classroom. *International Studies Perspectives, 13*(3), 254–269.

Donaldson, A. (2010). *Encountering god in the margins.* Dublin: Veritas Publications.

Doppen, F., & Jing, A. (2014). Student teaching abroad: Enhancing global awareness. *International Education, 43*(2), 59–75.

Festinger, L. (1957). *A theory of cognitive dissonance.* Stanford, CA: Stanford University Press.

Fields, A. B. (2016). Human rights theory: Criteria, boundaries, and complexities. In N. K. Denzin & M. D. Giardina (Eds.), *Qualitative inquiry and human rights* (Vol. 5(1), pp. 174–184). New York, NY: Routledge. https://doi.org/10.4324/9781315421575

Francis, D. M., & Colbry, S. L. (2016). Campus community integration on a mission: Transformative learning for social change. In C. Wankel & L. Wankel (Eds.), *Integrating curricular and co-curricular endeavors to enhance student outcomes* (pp. 289–319). Bingley: Emerald Publishing Group.

Freire, P. (1970). *The pedagogy of the oppressed.* New York, NY: The Continuum Publishing Company.

Hall, S. (2019). *Dropping out? A participatory exploration of adolescent school journeys in Zambia.* Zambia: UNICEF.

Heinrich, G., Leege, D., & Miller, C. (2017). A User's Guide to Integral Human Development (IHD). Retrieved from https://www.crs.org/sites/default/files/tools-research/users-guide-to-integral-human-development

Hingson, J. (2008). Open veins, public transcripts: The national security archive as a tool for critical pedagogy in the college classroom. *Radical History Review, 2008*(102), 90–98. doi:https://doi.org/10.1215/01636545-2008-015

International Labor Organization. (2019). Child Labor and Forced Labor Reports. Retrieved from https://www.dol.gov/agencies/ilab/resources/reports/child-labor/zambia

Lamberty, K. (2012). Toward a spirituality of accompaniment in solidarity partnerships. *Missiology, 40*(2), 181-193.

Lamberty, K. (2015). The art of accompaniment. *Missiology: An International Review, 43*(3), 324–338.

Lucas, A. G. (2009). Teaching about human rights in the elementary classroom using the book *A Life Like Mine: How Children Live Around the World. The Social Studies, 100*(2), 79–84.

Olser, A. (2016). *Human rights and schooling: An ethical framework for teaching for social justice.* New York, NY: Teacher College Press.

Parker, W. C. (2018). Human rights education's curriculum problem. *Human Rights Education Review, 1*(1), 5–24. https://doi.org/10.7577/hrer.2450

Pierson, S. (2015). Crossing the Bridge to Swaziland: Results of a transformative field experience. *Journal of International Social Studies, 5*(1), 174–184.

Pranis, K. (2001). Restorative justice, social justice, and the empowerment of marginalized populations In G. Bazemore & M. Schiff (Eds.), *Restorative community justice: Repairing harm and transforming communities* (pp. 287–305). Cincinnati, OH: Anderson Publishing.

Rademacher, N., & Sheety, A. (2016). Enhancing learning through community-based partnership. In P. Blessinger & B. Cozza (Eds.), *University partnerships for international development.* Innovations in Higher Education and Learning (Vol.8, 191–205). London: Emerald Publishing. doi:10.1108/s2055-364120160000008018.

Sheety, A., & Rademacher, N. (2015). Inquiry-based learning as foundational tool for critical examination of social justice in theory and action. In P. Blessinger & J. Carfora (Eds.), *Inquiry-based learning for multidisciplinary programs: A conceptual and practical resource for educators.* Innovation in Higher Education Teaching and Learning (Vol. 3, 119–137). London: Emerald. doi:10.1108/s2055-364120150000003022

UNESCO. (2016). *Zambia education policy review: Paving the way for SDG 4 – Education 2030.* Zambia: UNESCO.

UNESCO Institute of Statistics. (2017). Retrieved from http://uis.unesco.org/. Accessed on September 29, 2019.

United Nations Human Rights. United Nations Declaration on Human Rights Education and Training. (2011). Retrieved from https://www.ohchr.org/EN/Issues/Education/Training/Compilation/Pages/UnitedNationsDeclarationonHumanRightsEducationandTraining(2011).aspx. Accessed on September 23, 2019.

Wachtel, T. (2015). Restorative practices and the life-world implications of a new social science. *Revista De Asistenta Sociala, 4*, 7–18.

CHAPTER 4

WHAT NEXT? SKILL DEVELOPMENT FOR LIVELIHOOD: A STUDY OF BANGLADESHI IMMIGRANT WORKERS IN KURDISTAN

Enakshi Sengupta

ABSTRACT

UN has been advocating compulsory and free education for all, as specified in the Millennium Development Goal. Education is a right of every human being, and it is the right to realize other rights. It is the right toward social mobility and achieves economic stability in life. Every year hundreds and thousands of people from the developing world leave their homes in search of livelihood. They undertake a perilous and life-threatening journey in search of jobs. Often, they are motivated with the desire to earn more and ensure a better livelihood for them and their families back home. At times they are driven by persecution, genocide, or natural disasters. Bangladesh has been a source of immigrant workers who have been seeking employment mainly as unskilled workers outside their country. These workers who work in construction sites, malls, or as domestic help have a "shelf life" which barely exceeds the age of 50 years. This study conducted in a province of Kurdistan in northern Iraq explores the fear of losing their livelihood post 50 years of age. In most cases, these workers have not been educated and have not received any skill development training, which would enable them to remain as the bread earner long after they have returned home. Both quantitative and qualitative studies were conducted with 149 workers from Bangladesh who has been staying and working in Duhok. The findings

International Perspectives in Social Justice Programs at the Institutional and Community Levels
Innovations in Higher Education Teaching and Learning, Volume 37, 45–55
Copyright © 2021 by Emerald Publishing Limited
ISSN: 2055-3641/doi:10.1108/S2055-364120210000037004

have been explained, and suitable recommendations were provided in keeping with the data analysis.

Keywords: Immigrant workers; social mobility; livelihood; unskilled; adult education; skill development; social cost; public good; accessibility; freedom

EDUCATION AS HUMAN RIGHTS

What is right? A right is "a justified claim on someone, or on some institution, for something which one is owed" (Orend, 2002, p. 17). An individual is entitled to claim the right to education, and the society expects that this claim is honored by other individuals who have the privilege over others to settle the right. This could be even purely contractual in nature. It means that if someone has paid to honor this right, it becomes the obligation of the receiver to provide education in return, as we see in the case of the schooling system. What happens if the individual is incapable of paying for his education? In that case, if the individual belongs to a democratic country whose rights are pronounced then, the individual can claim from the government its right to be educated. The right to education is then elevated from a purely conventional one to high moral ground as Orend (2002) referred to as,

> a high- priority claim or authoritative entitlement, justified by sufficient reasons, to a set of objects that are owed to each human person as a matter of minimally decent treatment. (p. 34)

The fact that education is a human right is established by theories of social welfare and fair distribution and access to public goods by all individuals who fall under the purview of this accessibility. Orend (2002) recommended, "we do not know the full scope of our human rights until we know that the duties correlative to them can be performed at a reasonable cost" (p. 139).

When we address education as a human right in most cases, we refer to children who need implementation of this basic right. Little thought is given to adult education and skill development of those who are unskilled, due to social context and social cost of implementation and scalability of the rights.

Education is an institution in itself and can be supported through social desires and supportive social institutions. The social dynamic of any country establishes the fact that education is the only way of ensuring social mobility. The more educated people are of that country, more prosperity is seen in abundance in that society. With this view in mind, education should be considered as a genuine public good that should be imparted first to the children and then to adult learners to ensure that they are not dependent on society but considered as valuable contributors. Various international bodies are working toward seamless distribution and accessibility of education like the International Covenant on Economic, Social and Cultural Rights (ICESCR) and the Convention on the Rights of the Child. The coded international laws found in these documents have implemented and provided the scope for an appropriate social structure that advocates the equitable distribution of educational opportunities. Article 13 (1) of the ICESCR, which stipulates:

> International bodies recognize the right of everyone to education. They agree that education shall be directed to the full development of the human personality and the sense of its dignity, and shall strengthen the respect for human rights and fundamental freedoms. They further agree that education shall enable all persons to participate effectively in a free society, promote understanding, tolerance and friendship among all nations and all racial, ethnic or religious groups, and further the activities of the United Nations for the maintenance of peace.

John Rawls (1996) argued that "that the major social institutions fit together into one system, and how they assign fundamental rights and duties and shape the division of advantages that arise through social cooperation" (p. 258).

> Social and economic inequalities are to satisfy two conditions: first they are to be attached to offices and positions open to all under conditions of fair equality of opportunity; and second, they are to be to the greatest benefit of the least-advantaged members of society.

According to Rawls, education is one of the primary social institutions that is an intrinsic part of a just society. He lays emphasis on children as the least-advantaged member. Yet, in this chapter, the author would like to posit that there are vulnerable sections among the adults who would need guidance to be a member of a just society where education is their only source of social mobility.

Defenders of education as a basic human right suggest that every country should respect the agenda of spreading education among those who are from the marginalized section of society. Individual countries should become a part of this effort coordinating and improving their own standards as per the international guidelines to provide maximum benefits to their citizens who are in need of personal and intellectual development through various forms of education from primary to vocational training in order to maximize the country's social and economic returns. Poverty alleviation is only possible when there is equitable distribution of education as a public good and its accessibility unrestricted among those who need the most.

MIGRATORY WORKERS

The migration of individuals in search of a better life and livelihood has become a central issue of discussion. Millions of people are leaving homes and crossing national borders in their quest for more security, safety, and a better lifestyle. Some are forcefully displaced by war, famine, violent conflict, persecution, and natural calamities and some wish to try their luck in an attempt to embrace prosperity. Access to global information, easier modes of transportation, and mushrooming agents luring them to promises in exchange of money has resulted in a greater number of people migrating from their own homeland to strange countries in search of livelihood. International migration is not an adverse phenomenon but can result in productivity and growth of a country. Unfortunately, international migration of labor is known for reasons other than economic prosperity and productivity. It is often associated with fraudulent scams, deplorable living conditions, inhuman treatment with almost no rights or policies to protect their vulnerabilities. International bodies are engaged in protecting illegal trafficking and formulating guidelines and policies to safeguard the interest of the migratory workers. Not many of them are implemented and most cases of abuse and violation of human rights go unnoticed. The policy-makers are prompting dialogues that can maximize their contribution toward the growth and development of such workers. There is a dearth of published information that inhibits the possibility of presenting a global picture and discusses the complexity of such issues, mainly in countries where governance capacities are restricted. These reports, while drawing guidelines of best practices, are often ignorant about the implementation of such practices owing to lack of data and transparency.

Migratory workers are a great source of inward foreign remittance for their countries. In 2016, migrants from developing countries sent home the estimated US$413 billion in remittances (World Bank, 2017). These remittances are the main source of household income for many and, at the same time, a greater contributor to health, sanitation, health care, education, housing, and infrastructure for their countries. The host countries benefit from addressing the labor gaps and even create jobs as entrepreneurs in those countries.

The period of 2000–2017 saw a surge in the rising number of migrant workers. Asia housed 30 million international migrants during this period, calculating to almost a net increase of about 1.8 million migrants per annum. Europe became the second largest home for international migrants between 2000 and 2017 (22 million), followed by Northern America (17 million) and Africa (10 million). Latin America and the Caribbean and Oceania added comparatively smaller numbers of migrants during this period (3 million in each of these regions). (International Migration Report, United Nations, 2017).

Women migrant workers are comparatively less in number, the proportion of women workers fell from 49.3% in 2000 to 48.4% in 2017 (International Migration Report, United Nations, 2017). There has been a slight growth in the median age of the migrant workers from 39.2 years in 2017, compared with 38.0 years in 2000. The age of migrant workers in middle-income countries is 37.3 years, and in low-income countries, the median is 29.8 years. International migrants living in Africa were the youngest, with a median age of 30.9 in 2017. The author, while collecting data from Bangladeshi immigrant workers, has found out that the age of the workers plays a significant role in determining their future, their economic prosperity, and the insecurity about their future.

The United Nations, Universal Declaration of Human Rights, adopted in 1948, states in clear terms that individuals, belonging to any race, color, sex, language, religion, political or other opinions, national or social origin, property, birth, or another status, are born free and should be treated equally in dignity and rights. There are several other instruments promoted by the United Nations that are relevant for protecting migrant workers from discrimination and exploitation on grounds other than their non-national status, including the International Convention on the Elimination of All Forms of Racial Discrimination (ICERD, 1965).

The ratification of the United Nations legal instruments related to international migrants and migration, while steadily increasing over time, remains uneven. The 1951 Refugee Convention and its 1967 Protocol have been ratified by 145 and 146 United Nations Member States, respectively. Likewise, 171 countries have ratified the protocol to combat human trafficking and 145 countries have ratified the protocol seeking to stem migrant smuggling. However, only 51 countries have ratified the 1990 International Convention on the Protection of the Rights of All Migrant Workers and Members of Their Families. As of September 2017, 37 Member States had ratified all five United Nations legal instruments related to international migration, while 13 Member States had ratified none of the relevant instruments. (International Labor Conference, 92nd Session, ILO, 2004, p. 85)

Issues pertaining to migrant labor can be sensitive in nature for any host country and they are related to social and political adjustments with implications to education, health and social welfare of a country. Governments cannot afford to merely look at gatekeeping issues anymore but find a more sustainable and human path toward integrating migration policies into mainstream planning.

BANGLADESHI MIGRANT WORKERS AND SKILL DEVELOPMENT

One of the most populous countries in the world is Bangladesh, sharing its borders with India and Myanmar. The population comprises mainly of youth in the age group of 15–49 years. A huge population of working age poses a serious threat to its government who is fraught with economic disparity, high rate of unemployment, poverty, lack of infrastructure, low wages, and a huge population of unskilled workers. This prompts a need among its youth to search for a better living in faraway lands and being untrained or unskilled makes their employment opportunity marginal. It is estimated (ILO report, 2004) that around 8.3 million Bangladeshi immigrant workers are engaged in 157 countries around the world. These workers can be categorized in largely four categories – professional, skilled, semi-skilled, and less skilled. While only 2.21% are professionals, the large number of them – 52.29% are less skilled workers (ILO report, 2004). These workers are also a source of foreign exchange for their country and have been contributing more than 13% of the gross domestic product (GDP) through foreign remittances.

The government of Bangladesh does realize that the earning expectancy of an immigrant worker is limited unless there is scalability in work, for which skill development of these workers becomes an integral part of their development. The 6th five-year plan of the government had given special emphasis on enhancing the skill base of the workers as well as that of the younger generation. Both public and private sectors have been involved in the skill development plan and capacity building along with non-governmental agencies. Technical and Vocational Education and Training (TVET) Reform Project is working toward the employability of Bangladeshi workers in the global market and thus reduce the overall poverty of the country through vocational education and facilitation of training. Two levels of vocational training have been introduced: (1) National Pre-Vocation Certificate 1 (NPVC 1) and (2) National Pre-Vocation Certificate

2 (NPVC 2) which were specially designed to help create training opportunities for the underprivileged and those who never had the opportunity to gain formal training toward skill development. The program aims to send more skilled workers abroad and focus on training under skilled workers into semi-skilled ones.

The migrant workers are classified by three Ds that is working in a condition that is dirty, demeaning, and dangerous. Their vulnerable situation makes them an easy victim of abuse and violations stripped of all kinds of human and labor rights. This job-oriented reality is faced much less by semi-skilled or skilled workers while working abroad (ILO report, 2004). The challenges of implementing such programs are many. The very first challenge is the extremely low awareness level. Enrollment in such vocational training institutes is as low as 1.8% of the total population. The women population is hardly noticeable in these enrollment figures. The quality assurance systems of these vocational training institutes are low. As a result, the recognition received for the certification of such programs is barely visible in foreign countries where these certificates are undervalued and are often not recognized. Skill gaps noticeable between Bangladesh and the host countries of these migrant workers must be appropriately defined using the quality assurance of the programs and common competency standards. To make overseas employment equitable for every Bangladeshi migrant worker, the government and non-governmental organizations (NGOs) must work toward a means to make their skills and qualifications recognizable.

Several kinds of training courses are delivered for immigrant workers. Certificates post completion of the courses are given from various sources, which are more or less recognized on a national level but not internationally. The quality assurance systems are not standardized. These training centers lack any coherent centralized policies. The curriculum and mode of delivery vary from center to center. The sector lacks accountability and lack of coordination, and no comparison can be drawn on the basis of certificates issued or courses delivered due to lack of a centralized apex body controlling the entire program. These centers often don't maintain a database of the students and they are not linked to overseas markets failing to understand the labor market demand in those countries. The duplication of course works, redundant course material, differences in curriculum and the actual delivery of module and training, and mismatch between the supply and the estimated demand and non-standardization of these courses result in a complete waste of effort and sponsor's resources.

Bureau of Manpower Employment and Training (BMET) in Bangladesh has been involved in creating a good governance system in the employability of Bangladeshi workers and ensuring that the overseas demands can be met along with the welfare of the migrant workers. BMET has been engaged in imparting training to the migrant workers for scalability. They have designed four-year diploma courses to six months of vocational training courses that include a variety of skill development opportunities for these migrant workers. Some of the common ones are mason, rod binders, shuttering, welding, fabrication, air conditioning, refrigerator mechanics, pipe fittings, electricians, auto mechanics, garment supervisors, and housekeeping. BMET works with NGOs who have pre-departure courses training the workers and answering their apprehensions.

Twenty-one-day housekeeping courses are offered to aspirant women migrant workers who would like to become potential housemaids in foreign countries. Usages of modern home appliances, culture, law and regulations, language, etiquette, manners, and safety and security are taught to these women migrant workers.

Fragmented databases and lack of any coherent policies have inhibited the growth of such programs. There is no control or accountability of pre-departure and post-return period of these migrant workers, and hence, in most cases, they land up working as menial laborers with no future prospect of employment on their return.

THE SURVEY

The author had access to immigrant workers from Bangladesh who were working in northern Iraq – Kurdistan region of Iraq in a city called Duhok. Most of these workers were working as cleaning agents in shopping malls, restaurants, and shops. A survey form written in Bengali was distributed among them, and the forms were collected back after a period of 10 days through one of the workers. Out of 165 forms that were distributed, 149 forms were returned duly filled in. Answers were written in Bengali, and almost all the questions were answered. Post which one-to-one interviews were organized with the workers in an informal manner. The interviews were conducted with 16 workers who worked in an adjacent shopping mall. The interviews were held in the food court of the shopping mall, where it was easier for them to come and talk to the interviewee during their tea break. Notes were taken during the interview, but no audio recording was done as the workers were not willing to record their voice as they feared that the owners who have hired them might not approve of such a gesture. Both quantitative and qualitative methods were used to collect data as the mixed method is more robust in nature, and the inner fears and despair of these workers cannot be expressed merely by quantitative questionnaire.

FINDINGS

The survey form gave certain demographic details. The average age of the workers was 36 years. The youngest of them was 24 years and the oldest being 52 years. Most of the other workers were in their late 30s and early 40s. These workers have been working outside Bangladesh for long. The average duration of working outside their home country was 16 years. Two of them have worked only for four years, whereas a couple of them have worked for more than 22 years. Their preferred destination of work has been Saudi Arabia, and they have worked in Iraq, UAE, Bahrain, Oman, Malaysia, and Singapore. According to these workers, the money earned in Malaysia and Singapore is less than that in Saudi Arabia and UAE, although the Southeast Asian countries are comfortable in weather and food habits. These workers are literate having studied till their school level, often in Madrasas. Most of them have not been able to qualify their board-level exam and some left their studies in classes 7 or 8. None of them had any special skill training certificate or attended any vocational courses.

The work done by them has been mainly cleaning in nature, stacking shelves in malls, cleaning dishes and plates in restaurants, working as a janitor, and as a helper in shops. They are used to lift weight, load cars, and trucks at times. The average hour of work is 12 hours, and lunch is generally provided to them. They preferred to cook their own dinner and breakfast and often took turns in helping the other Bangladeshi co-workers. Holidays were given once in every three years for two months and Eid is their preferred time of the holiday. Some workers did receive a one-way air ticket but most agreed that they are given bonus or air tickets when the economy of their host country is doing well and not otherwise.

All 149 workers agreed that they have a large family back in Bangladesh comprising their wife, children, elderly parents, unmarried sisters, and brothers. The salary is generally wired at the beginning of the month to take care of their families and to pay the loan which was borrowed to secure the overseas job through agents. These loans tend to be around 200,000 Bangladesh takas to 400,000 takas – an average of 2,500 dollars to 5,000 dollars paid to the agents as pre-departure fees.

When asked as to how long they wish to work in foreign soil, most of them answered as long as they are able-bodied to do so and can secure a job overseas. Once they retire, they wish to go back to their villages and start some kind of business. They have not given much thought to their future but want to start a restaurant or a grocery store to earn their living. All 149 participants agreed that they have never been exposed to any kind of training funded by the Bangladesh government and are not aware of the existence of any such training. They also agreed to the fact that no training is given to them on the job, and their job is usually hard labor and menial in nature and doesn't require any technical expertise.

THEMES

The qualitative interviews were analyzed to extract some common themes. Two main questions were posed to them – one about their retirement and the second one was about their future plans. Random notes were taken in Bengali which was later translated to form the themes. Some of the notes were discarded as the discussions were not relevant to the interviews and often bordered on ice-breaking and knowing each other well before divulging any of the information required for the survey.

The very first theme that was elicited was that of "uncertainty." The workers were aware of the fact that their current jobs were temporary in nature as no written contract or appointment letter was given to them. Although they had one year's visa which was to be renewed yearly, they were aware of the fact that the owner's whimsicality is ultimate in their kind of jobs.

> I don't know whether the owner will keep me tomorrow, if he gets angry with me for some reason I will be thrown overnight. It is difficult to get another job. The owners know each other, it is a small community here. (Participant 7)

I have paid a lot of money to come to Iraq and be in this job, I cannot afford to lose this job. What will I do after that? Getting a job is not easy. (Participant 11)

We have no job security, no terms and conditions. If we are asked to come at the middle of the night we have to. When there is a party or anything we work round the clock, managing to sleep for an hour or two in the early morning in our place of work. (Participant 8)

The next theme was that of "fear for the future." From uncertainty in their jobs had stemmed their fear for the future. These workers were not certain about their job prospect or their source of income. The have large families to support in Bangladesh, and they were also aware of the fact that job prospects in Bangladesh was very grim.

I cannot think what kind of calamity will strike me if I was to lose this job. Getting another overseas job is not easy, it requires a lot of money. I have not been able to pay of my loans to my agents. We will starve to death, me and my family. (Participant 3)

I am not very young, very soon I will not be considered as a suitable candidate for overseas travel, what will I do then? I cannot possibly take up a cleaning job in my country, they don't pay at all. My kids are still very young and I have daughters of marriageable age. Only God can help me. (Participant 5)

The next theme that emerged in continuation of the theme stated above was "fear of getting old" These immigrant workers have a shelf life, and the average age of workers preferred for unskilled menial jobs in foreign countries is less than 40 years. The nature of job, in most cases, being hard labor prefers young workers.

I am going to be 45, which means I cannot work for more than 5 to 6 years, and that is not enough for me to secure my kids future. (Participant 4)

No one wants to give visa if they see you are above 45 years, but we can still work and if we don't leave home what kind of work will get. After staying abroad for so long we have forgotten how to work in paddy fields … it is not for us anymore. (Participant 9)

Life doesn't finish when you are in your 40's. I have a two-year-old son and three other kids who are in school. I am always scared that in another 7 to 8 years the agents will consider me as redundant. What will I do then? I have not been able to save enough to start a shop, I wanted to start a garment and toy shop for kids. (Participant 13)

The workers were further asked whether they have undergone any skill development training in Bangladesh or while working overseas. The theme that emerged from the discussion was "unaware of any govt sponsored training." As was mentioned in this chapter earlier that lack of coordination, unclear policies have hindered the accessibility to skill development training and awareness among the migrant workers.

I am not aware of any training provided by the govt which is free of charge. The vocational schools in Dhaka charges a lot of money, I cannot afford that. Besides there is no guarantee of jobs after we have received the training. (Participant 14)

I stay in a remote village, I need three modes of transportation to reach home – air, bus and dingy boat – no govt or NGO comes to train us there. No nothing at the zila (district) level either – at least I have not heard about it. I don't expect the owners here to train us. They are paying us to work, not to study. (Participant 7)

We are poor and nobody cares about poor people. As long as we have the strength we will work and earn money and then we will be left to perish. No help is going to come to us from anyone, nobody cares, no one. (Participant 9)

Govt should have schemes that announces these training that you are talking about. It will surely help us in finding a livelihood post our return home. Govt should think of a way to reach us. It will be very helpful. (Participant 15)

DISCUSSION AND CONCLUSION

The research findings have revealed the fact that skill development and training for the underprivileged are slow in Bangladesh. Lack of effective partnerships to reach the remotest parts of the country along with unawareness of schemes has inhibited the growth of such a program minimizing its real impact on the ground. It is essential that the training providing bodies have an ongoing relationship with the industry, mainly the overseas markets and the recruiters. Activities to support the skill development program such as curriculum training and teacher training are undertaken at a very minimal level. Tie-ups with polytechnic colleges or district-level colleges are largely absent making accessibility to such programs an uphill task.

Bangladesh Bureau of Statistics maintains Labor Market Information System (LMIS) based on a periodic nationwide labor survey. These data should be adequate with job market information, skill and experience demand, and a regular cross-sector data analysis which can predict the employability of candidates and the unemployment structure. The analysis then again needs to percolate to the lowermost tier from where these immigrant workers arise. Informal workers have always learned their job informally while being at work. Thoughts must be given as to how these skills can be scaled with proper certification and recognition of the government so that they can be further used to seek better pastures. Incentive mechanisms should be provided to the grassroots-level training centers to track and build the data. The government can launch an online portal where data can be stored free of cost and analyzed at a macrolevel to find suitable curriculum and training needs. Upscaling the informal employees should be the basic strategy of the policy-makers to help develop an all-inclusive economic growth and help in mass-based poverty reduction.

Finally comes the question of educational boundaries and human rights. The basic right to education is viewed as the right of every child to get educated. It is somewhat lopsided where the need for adult education and education to earn one's livelihood is neglected to an extent. What is the right time to learn? Is it only our childhood? The new paradigm shift in education is looking at education as that of a whole life time and not just restricted to schooling.

Education, including formal education, public awareness and training, should be recognized as a process by which human beings and societies can reach their fullest potential. Education is critical for promoting sustainable development and improving the capacity of the people to address environment and development issues. While basic education provides the underpinning for any environmental and development education, the latter needs to be incorporated as an essential part of learning. Both formal education and non-formal education are indispensable to changing people's attitudes so that they have the capacity to assess and address their sustainable development concerns. (Agenda 21, 1992; UNESCO, 2000, p. 48)

Education should be viewed as lifelong education, coextensive with life and every individual should be given the opportunity to work toward the betterment of their lives.

In this chapter, the author had tried through the survey showcase the fear and anxiety of immigrant workers about their future economic prospects. In order to ensure sustainable growth and poverty reduction, it becomes the duty of every democratic nation to offer an equal opportunity of growth to its fellow citizens. The task is not easily burdened with an ever-growing population and lack of tracking and implementation of the programs. With the help of non-governmental and international bodies, the task is not unachievable. Careful planning and robust strategizing of such a program will benefit a whole new generation of immigrant workers.

REFERENCES

Agenda 21: Programme of Action for Sustainable Development. Rio Declaration on Environment and Development. Statement of Forest Principles. The final text of agreements negotiated by governments at the United Nations Conference on Environment and Development (UNCED), 3–14 June 1992, Rio de Janeiro, Brazil (p. 264). New York, NY: United Nations.

International Labor Office. (2004). *Towards a fair deal for migrant workers in the global economy.* International Labor Conference, 92nd Session, 2004. Geneva: ILO.

Orend, B. (2002). *Human rights: Concept and context.* Peterborough: Broadview Press.

Rawls, J. (1996). *Political liberalism.* New York, NY: Columbia University Press.

UNESCO. (2000). *The right to education towards education for all throughout life. World education report.* Paris: UNESCO Publishing.

United Nations. (2017). International migration report 2017. New York, NY: Department of Economic and Social Affairs, United Nations.

World Bank. (2017). *Migration and remittances: Recent developments and outlook. Special topic: Global compact on migration, migration and development brief no. 27.* Washington, DC: World Bank.

CHAPTER 5

PRISON EDUCATION THROUGH OPEN AND DISTANCE LEARNING: EXPERIENCES FROM INDIA

Umesh Chandra Pandey

ABSTRACT

United Nation's Standard Minimum Rules for Treatment of Prisoners, popularly known as Nelson Mandela Rules categorically advocates for the Prison Education and its integration with the educational system of the country. Moreover, principles for the treatment of prisoners, adopted by United Nation in 1990, guarantee that prisoners retain the human rights and fundamental freedoms set out in Universal Declaration of Human Rights, which includes right to take part in education also. However, there is little sensitization about the rights of prisoners in many countries. The issue has gained prominence as several international organizations have now raised concern on these matters.

Education of jail inmates has attracted the attention of Open and Distance Learning (ODL) systems in India. Among all the ODL institutions, Indira Gandhi National Open University (IGNOU) has been the major role player. Right from its first initiative to have a special study center in Tihar Jail in 1994, IGNOU's network for jail inmates has undergone significant expansion. The university has now strong presence in the prisons. Under a special collaborative arrangement with Ministry of Home Affairs, IGNOU has started free education to jail inmates from 2010. This chapter gives a glimpse about the model being followed by IGNOU for providing education inside prisons, highlights its good practices, gaps in its functioning and makes recommendations for further strengthening of this network.

International Perspectives in Social Justice Programs at the Institutional and Community Levels
Innovations in Higher Education Teaching and Learning, Volume 37, 57–76
ISSN: 2055-3641/doi:10.1108/S2055-364120210000037005

Keywords: Bachelor's Preparatory Program; distance learning; distance learning programs; higher education; human rights; IGNOU; *Making the Connection*; National Assessment and Accreditation Council; Nelson Mandela Rules; Open and Distance Learning

BACKGROUND

It is often said, citing both Churchill and Dostoevsky, that the state of a democracy is measured by the way it treats its prisoners (Muntingh, 2007, p. 5). The conditions prevailing in prisons not only have implications for the prisoners but also the entire community into which these prisoners will ultimately be released. United Nations Office on Drugs and Crimes (UNODC) specifies several reasons for prison reforms. Human rights have been central to the argument to promote such reforms (UNODC, 2015a). The issues concerning their education have been a cause of concern even in developed countries like United States of America (Centre for American Progress, 2018).

The issues concerning prisoners have also been highlighted in Sustainable Development Goals (SDGs) (UN, n.d.). Doha Declaration has at its center the understanding that the rule of law and sustainable development are interrelated and mutually reinforcing. The declaration, inter alia, seeks to enhance policies for prison inmates that focus on education, work, medical care, rehabilitation, social reintegration and the prevention of recidivism (UNODC, 2015b, p. 4). In this connection, prison education has attracted the renewed attention of planners across the world.

INDIAN SCENARIO

The human rights of the jail inmates have been a subject matter of Indian jurisprudence for quite some time. Supreme Court of India has shown its concern through several judgments. In its judgments on various aspects of prison administration, the apex court has laid down three broad principles regarding imprisonment and custody. First, a person in prison does not become a non-person; second, a person in prison is entitled to all the human rights within the limitation of imprisonment; and lastly, there is no justification for the suffering already inherent in the process of incarceration (Teji, n.d.). Though the rate of imprisonment in India is very low as compared to several other countries, Indian prisons are very overcrowded dominantly with under trial inmates within the age group of 18–50 years and most of them illiterate or school dropouts (~70%). A glimpse of Indian Prisons is given in Box 1.

Various committees, commissions and working groups were set up by the Government of India to study and make suggestions for improving the prison conditions and administration. An authentic account of such developments has been given in the letter written by the Joint Secretary, Ministry of Home to

---

Box 1. Prisons in Indian Jails, 2017: A Glimpse..

- As per the latest data on prisons published by National Crime Research Bureau (NCRB), 450,696 prisoners were lodged in various jails in India as on December 31, 2017 in 1,361 prisons of the country with actual capacity of 391,574.
- The number of convicts, under trial inmates and detenues were reported as 139,149, 308,718 and 2,136, respectively.
- The total budget for the financial year 2017–2018 for all prisons in the country was 5253.7 crore (1 crore = 10 million).
- Majority of these inmates (43.6%) belong to the age group of 30–50 years followed by the age group of 18–30 years (43.0%) of total prisoners.
- Further, most of them were school dropouts. As per latest report of NCRB, 40.2% prisoners were below class X, 20.5% were class X and above but below graduation, 6.1% were having a degree, 1.8% prisoners were postgraduates and 1.2 prisoners were technical diploma/degree holders. A total of 136,167 prisoners were illiterate.

Source: Compiled from National Crime Record Bureau (2017).

Principal Secretaries and Director Generals (DGs) of Prisons of all the State Governments (Ministry of Home, 2011). The objective of these committees was primarily to make prisons more conducive to the reformation and rehabilitation of prisoners. Some of the important committees are as follows:

- All India Jail Manual Committee (1957).
- Working Group on Prisons (1972).
- All India Prison Reforms Committee (1980–1983) known as Mulla Committee.
- All India Group on Prison Administration, Security and Discipline known as R.K. Kapoor Committee (1986).
- National Expert Committee on Women Prisoners known as Justice Krishna Iyer Committee (1987), etc.

In addition, Home Ministry of India showed special concern for promoting higher education (Ministry of Home, 2011) inside the prisons as a result of which several Indian universities (mostly open universities) have initiated collaborative ventures with department of prisons (National Crime Records Bureau, n.d., pp. 209–212).

Indira Gandhi National Open University (IGNOU) has been the biggest role player in the educational scenario of the country with a focus on inclusive education (Chaudhary, Khare, Gupta, & Garg, 2016). The university has been striving to enhance its reach among the socioeconomically disadvantaged sections of the society through several schemes and policies. Jail inmates have been a major target group for which IGNOU has initiated a scheme of free education. These free ships are available for several courses from certificate programs of six months' duration to postgraduate-level programs. During past several years, the university benefited the large segments of jail inmates. This chapter gives an account of IGNOU's initiatives to enhance the reach of higher education in Indian prisons. This chapter is divided into the following parts:

a) Part 1 "Issues in Prison Education" includes a rationale for prison educa-tion, different perceptions which sometimes lead to opposition for prison education and the problems in prison education.
b) Part 2 "Prison University Partnerships" explains the rationales for university–prison collaborations. It further explains how Open and Distance Learning (ODL) systems are advantageously placed to serve jail inmates.
c) Part 3 "Prison Education in IGNOU" gives an account of prison education through distance education in IGNOU.
d) The last part concludes this chapter.

ISSUES IN PRISON EDUCATION

Rationale for Prison Education

There has been a growing feeling that prisons should be developed as reform centers. It is in this context that prison education has come to forefront of prison reforms. Prisoners get cut off from mainstream while they remain inside the prisons, their opportunities for capacity building come to a standstill and they carry a stigma of being a criminal when they come out of prison. It is difficult for offenders to adapt with society, restart formal education and rebuild individual and social capital. They risk getting caught up in a vicious cycle of failed social integration, re-offending, reconviction and social rejection (UNODC, 2018, p. 3). Monotonous experiences inside the prisons have often been a source of frustration for inmates which raises the risk of injury for staff and other prisoners. It constrains their life options which makes it still harder to adjust in society and enhances their chances to again resort to crime. Prison education can improve their skills and education to make them more employable.

Several studies have concluded that learning in prison through educational programs have a positive impact on recidivism, reintegration and, more specifi-cally, employment outcomes upon release (UNHRC, 2009, p. 2). Education can significantly reduce possibilities of crime by raising earnings which increases opportunity cost of crime and time spent in the prison (Lochner & Moretti, 2004). Prisoners' engagement in education may help to alleviate security risk in prisons through relieving monotony. Furthermore, it reduces the occurrence of re-offend-ing by promoting critical thinking skills (Farley & Pike, 2016). International Covenant on Civil and Political Rights, General Assembly resolution 2200A

(XXI), Article 10(3) specifies the need for reformation and social rehabilitation in prisons (UNODC, 2017, p. 1). There is a widespread acceptance of the fact that imprisonment should not be limited to the deprivation of liberty alone. It should have a focus on reforms. There is an increasing realization to create opportunities of knowledge and skills to help them successfully integrate with society and desist from future offending. In this context, Nelson Mandela Rules (UNODC) are worth citing which strongly recommends for prison education and its integration with the country's educational system.

Nelson Mandela Rules: Rule 104

1. Provision shall be made for the further education of all prisoners capable of profiting thereby, including religious instruction in the countries where this is possible. The education of illiterate prisoners and of young prisoners shall be compulsory and special attention shall be paid to it by the prison administration.
2. So far as practicable, the education of prisoners shall be integrated with the educational system of the country so that after their release they may continue their education without difficulty. (UNODC, 2018, p. 34)

Several research studies have concluded that education can effectively bring down rates of recidivism (UNODC, 2017, p. 2; Vacca, 2004). It can have widespread benefits. One of the obvious benefits is the savings on the expenses of future prison sentences. The studies conducted in the context of UK conclude that every pound spent on prison education saves taxpayers more than two pounds. Similarly in the United States, the rate is four to five dollars saved for every dollar spent. Studies have compared the cost-effectiveness of both the crime control methods-educating prisoners and expanding prisons. It has been highlighted that correctional mechanisms through education are almost twice as cost-effective as crime control policy (Bazos & Hausman, 2004). In the context of Europe, Hawley, Murphy, and Souto-Otero (2013) highlight reduction in social costs of crime through education and training in Europe. The soaring expenditures on incarceration are putting ever-increasing burden on taxpayers to maintain prisons. Estimates show that it costs Australian taxpayers around $105,000 to accommodate one prisoner for one year which is further likely to increase to $3.17 billion each year (University of South Queensland (USQ), n.d.).

Though many research studies advocate for rehabilitation of prisoners and their reintegration into society, there have been very few instances where investments for prison education have attracted resistance from people. These arguments have often triggered academic debate, which seriously questions the benefits accrued by prison education program, rates of participation in such educational programs and success rates of those who participate in such programs (Chaudhary et al., 2016). Furthermore, there has been opposition to funding for prison education which has been viewed as waste of money. The initiation of educational interventions in prisons has often met with sharp criticism in the United States though such expenditures were much less than routine expenditures of prisons (Aalai, 2014).

Problems in Prison Education

Provisions of education for jail inmates are inherently complex and challenging due to a range of environmental, social, organizational and individual factors which are often insurmountable (UNHRC, 2009, paras 6 and 4). The prison environment is inherently hostile to liberating potential of education, brings down self-esteem and motivation and creates major challenges for the prison administration (UNHRC, 2009, para 6). Some of the major problems include staff and budget shortage, lack of educational expertise, infrastructure and transfers of the inmates between the prisons. Further, inmates are often found to be reluctant to participate due to several reasons, for example, their poor educational background, distrust in long-term solutions and embarrassment at their low literacy or sheer lack of interest in studies.

It's difficult to find teachers who are ready to go inside the prisons and teach prisoners which is a very challenging group in terms of diversity of age, educational level and employment history. Moreover, there are concerns of security which are much more important than teaching the prisoners (Tam, Herg, & Rose, 2007). It is difficult to provide them seamless access to net connectivity due to security concerns. The E-learning method which otherwise would have been a very powerful option does not satisfactorily work in jails.

UNIVERSITY PRISON PARTNERSHIPS

There is a convergence between what universities and the prisons try to achieve. Both of these institutions have a powerful role for individual and social transformation. They seek to capacitate and invest in people recognizing that social transformation is achieved through individual growth (Learning Together, 2016). It is in this context that there is a scope for educational partnerships between universities and prisons.

Several universities, in different contexts, have taken initiatives to collaborate with departments of prisons in their respective countries. Most of such universities give the prisoners opportunities to study along with other students while they are incarcerated and complete those courses once they are released. Besides, several universities have provisions for study centers inside the prisons where they can study along with other prisoners. Innovative applications of technology are also used by some universities to provide interactive academic support. There are separate models based on the specific needs of their countries. In several instances, universities have made special provisions to waive off fee for prisoners to motivate them to pursue these programs (IGNOU, n.d.; *Premium Times*, 2016).

Few such collaborative initiatives have been cited in research literature. For instance, the Prison to College Pipeline (P2CP) is a partnership between the New York State Department of Corrections and the City University of New York (UNODC, 2017, p. 34). Under this partnership, university's courses are provided in several liberal arts disciplines backed by full-scale developmental education program to build reading and writing skills, an academic counseling relationship and a wider program to address each individual's unique reentry needs, including housing, subsistence, health care, mental health or substance abuse treatment, social supports and compliance with criminal justice conditions of release (UNODC, 2017, p. 34). Learning Together initiative in the UK affords the opportunities to prisoners and students to study criminology courses together (Learning Together, 2016). University of Panama under a special partnership agreement developed a university extension in the Women's Rehabilitation Center which helped several women to get graduated (UNODC, 2017, p. 34).

Initiatives Through Open and Distance Education

With the emergence of post 2015 development agenda, the prison education has come up as a matter of concern. Increasing pretrial detentions are a major human right concern, and governments have an obligation to ensure educational opportunities for them. Curriculum, pedagogy and teaching learning of prisoners are the major issues to address their rehabilitation needs (Coates, 2016). The Open and Distance Education, due to its flexible and innovative work environment, suits the requirements of prison education. Several initiatives have been taken across the world to reach out to jail inmates through technology-aided means (European Prison Education Association, 2007). Procedural restrictions prohibiting prisoner access to the internet is major hassle to effectively use distance education methodologies for prisoners. However, innovative initiatives have been tried in several countries to allow greater access of the self-paced higher levels of education. The E-learning projects for inmates in the UK and Australia are well documented (Farley & Pike, 2016). Under these initiatives, efforts have been made to equip prisoners with digital literacy skills in spite of the lack of internet access.

Main idea behind such initiatives is to provide access for Open University courses via a "walled garden." The "Walled Garden" is a secure version of the Open University's learning management system (Pike & Adams, 2012). Prisoners can communicate with their university tutors through secure messaging services. Such secure learning management system enables students to interact with the Open University's learning materials. However, they are prevented from accessing other websites (Pike & Adams, 2012). Such a restricted learning environment prevents any possibility of security lapse and at the same time provides students to have a feel of being part of wider students' community. Moreover, it will help them to relate to wider student community once they are released (Pike, 2015, p. 288).

Under an almost similar E-learning project, USQ (n.d.) initiated a *Making the Connection* under which USQ's researchers developed a simulated online study environment inside the prison. They developed sophisticated, secure learning platforms and introduced notebook computers and onsite servers to house learning materials. The initiative has evoked encouraging response. However, still there are significant challenges for the incarcerated students to take benefit of E-learning programs primarily because of their digital exclusion. It is difficult for the prison authorities to balance between institutional prison priorities such as order and security against digital learning experiences to be afforded to incarcerated students (Hopkins & Farley, 2015).

Despite the apparent usefulness of Distance Learning Programs in prison, it has also been a subject of intense criticism. Quite often, there is a feeling among those who practice prison education that incarcerated students do not have access to educational experiences similar to their non-incarcerated peers. While analyzing the most essential components of a high-quality in-prison higher education program, the Prison University Project carried out by the Alliance has observed that distance learning programs (whether online or correspondence) fail to facilitate meaningful, sustained contact between students and a fully qualified instructor; provide a rigorous, comprehensive curriculum; include opportunities for individualized feedback, tutoring, mentoring and advising; or facilitate communication between students (Erzen, Gould, & Lewen, 2019, p. 8).

PRISON EDUCATION THROUGH IGNOU

Motivations at Policy Level: Initial Developments

The concerns for vocational and educational programs for prisoners have been shown by several committees on prison reforms in India (Ministry of Home Affairs, n.d.). The major motivational factors for such reforms were their social rehabilitation and also to enable them to earn livelihood once they are released from prisons. The model code of prison prepared by Government of India in 2003 had specifically mentioned about education and vocational training and shows strong concerns to protect their human rights. The Supreme Court of India came strongly in favor of judicial scrutiny and intervention whenever the rights of prisoners in detention or custody were found to have been infringed upon (Ministry of Home, GoI, 2003). The concerns for prison education have been consistent.

It has been strongly felt by almost all the committees that educational interventions are required for the social rehabilitation of jail inmates and to enable them to earn their livelihoods once they are released from jails. Government has prepared a Model Prison Manual which has provisioned for vocational and educational training for the jail inmates. The need for education is clearly spelt out as below:

> [...] Education in prisons has to be pursued as an important means of reformative treatment. It not only implies providing literacy but also inculcating values among prisoners as are considered conducive to their social mainstream. Therefore, education personnel have to offer a comprehensive programme of education to prisoners in which various educational functionaries will perform their specific duties ... (Model Prison Manual, Bureau of Police Research, Ministry of Home, GoI, 2003)

The manual also emphasizes that prisons should establish liaison with the Department of Education/NOS/IGNOU and other approved educational institutions for obtaining educational material and other help. Further, the Parliamentary Standing Committee on Modernization of Prisons in its 142th report submitted in 2009 has also made following recommendations.

> [...] There should be an effort to achieve total literacy among prisoners across the country. It has therefore recommended that there should be facility of correspondence courses in vocational

disciplines in the prisons and degrees/diplomas should be awarded to the prisoners after successful completion of their courses so that they can lead a normal life in the mainstream of society after their release. The committee had also desired that the Government may consider opening of ITI like institutions within Jail premises to impart industrial training in various disciplines to the inmates which would go a long way in rehabilitating them after their release. In this context, the state authorities can also consider converting existing prison workshops in to ITIs. (Parliamentary Standing Committee on Modernization of Prisons in its 142th report submitted in 2009)

The need for educating jail inmates is therefore well realized and understood. There is significant level of sensitization among policy-makers, and initiatives taken so far led to satisfactory results. Government of India has made major initiatives for the prison education at several levels. These initiatives have been made at the level of school education, higher education and other isolated short-term educational programs through non-governmental organizations (NGOs) at various places. Jail inmates are one of the most disadvantaged categories of people for whom ODL systems have shown special concern. These initiatives have brought a large number of jail inmates to the fold of education. For school education, National Institute of Open Schooling which is the largest network of school education through distance mode had established its study centers across the country. However for interventions for higher education required much more flexible and innovative educational set up. IGNOU's academic programs are innovative and capable of linking school dropouts directly to higher education.

As far the higher education is concerned, IGNOU and several other State Open Universities (e.g., Nalanda State Open University, Karnataka State Open University, etc.) are offering academic programs inside the prisons in India. However, the network of IGNOU is biggest. It is perhaps the only university in the world which has created extensive network of exclusive study centers for jail inmates (IGNOU, 2014). The National Assessment and Accreditation Council (NAAC) of India have shown special concerns for prison education. The sensitivity of open universities for prison education is viewed by NAAC as an important institutional value and social responsibility. It is included in the yardsticks for assessment and accreditation of open universities in India (NAAC, 2019).

Tihar Jail: IGNOU's Educational Intervention in Prison

Initially commissioned during British period as Delhi jail in 1937, Tihar Jail is considered the biggest jail in Asia, the most notorious and overcrowded jails in India. As per the latest statistics displayed on the website, it consists of 16 different jails with a total capacity of 10,026 against which 17,534 inmates are accommodated with more than 50% of them belonging to the age group 20–30 years (Tihar Jail, 2019). Recidivism among the prisoners was around 23.89% during 2018. Most of the inmates (around 66%) are school dropouts having education below class X. Further, most of the inmates (around 78.90%) belong to lower income strata with monthly income less than Rs. 8,000 and 49.79% of the prison population comprises of people who earn an annual income below Rs. 50,000 at the time of their arrest which indicates a linkage between educational standard, poverty and criminality (Tihar Jail, 2019). Very few inmates (~7%) bear higher educational qualifications.

This kind of educational profile of the jail inmates has been nearly uniform for past several years. IGNOU started a study center in Tihar Jail in early 1990s. It was the first such initiative of any university in India to create opportunities of higher education inside the jail. The IGNOU's intervention was well taken primarily because of its innovative and flexible ways of imparting higher education. The university had a unique scheme, named as Bachelor's Preparatory Program (BPP) specially designed to link school dropouts to higher education. The school dropouts who have minimum of 18 years of age are directly given admission in BPP. Once they complete this program, they become eligible to pursue degrees and diplomas of IGNOU. The scheme attracted a large number of inmates in higher education program. The study center in Tihar Jail has now grown to the biggest study center for jail inmates in India. The center has facility to pursue a range of programs from certificate to degree-level programs. For spreading the Gandhian philosophy, a Gandhi Centre has been established by Gandhi Smriti and Darshan Samiti, Government of India, at IGNOU ward. More than 500 books on Gandhian philosophy were added to the library. The successful initiative inside Tihar Jail attracted the attention of several other jails in India where study centers were established. In most of the other places also, jail inmates showed interest in BPP.

Expansion to Other Prisons

After having established its first center in Tihar, IGNOU subsequently established a study center at Sabarmati Jail Ahmadabad in 1995. This process continued and in the course of time IGNOU's study centers spread over several central jails across the country (Toms & Reddy, 2018, pp. 126–127). However, the response from jail inmates till 2010 was not very encouraging. Till 2010, IGNOU had already been operating 52 study centers with total enrollment of about 1,500. Such study centers were working in those places where the local administration had shown proactive initiatives. Such initiatives were largely dependent upon individual initiatives of prison administration, situational leaderships at the level of regional directors and the response of prisoners. Further, since the inmates were expected to pay fee for these programs, it was difficult to generate enrollment. Only in those pockets where prisoners could afford paying fee, the enrollment could be generated. Hence, such provision for distance education programs inside prisons had limited penetration in prison system.

In view of the recommendations of various committees, Ministry of Home, Government of India, had consultations with the IGNOU HQs in 2010 to explore the possibilities of providing educational opportunities to jail inmates. The consultative meeting of IGNOU and Ministry of Home looked into possibilities in diverse areas like Agriculture, Insurance, Business Process Outsourcing, Computer and Information Sciences, Security, Tourism, Retail, etc. After the initial negotiations between the authorities of IGNOU and Ministry of Home, it was decided that IGNOU will take up the initiative further and set up study centers in large number of jails across the country. It was felt that the setting up of study centers should be expedited both at the level of departments of prisons in different states and IGNOU. It was decided that expeditious processing of the proposals will require a state-level nodal officer of senior rank. Ministry of Home Affairs sent a letter to all the state governments asking them to expeditiously process the proposals for creation of IGNOU's centers in identified jails. Ministry also issued directives to all the state-level DG (Prisons) asking them to nominate the nodal officers and initiate action to set up a special study center (SSC) for jail inmates in identified jails, to motivate jail inmates to take admissions in IGNOU's programs and liaise with IGNOU's officials to arrange academic support services for admitted inmates. The most important feature of the collaboration was that IGNOU will not charge any tuition fee/other expenses from enrolled inmates. Everything including the prospectus cost, admission fee and examination fee was exempted from jail inmates. It was the most revolutionary step in the field of educational interventions in the jails of India. As a result, the network expanded to a nationwide network of 177 SSCs across India.

Modus Operandi for Study Centers in Prisons

Creation of academic activities inside the prison where normally the entries of outsiders are strictly prohibited is a challenge. IGNOU has worked out an arrangement with the approval of Home Ministry of the country. Under this arrangement, there is a provision of study center to be managed by part-time staffs who are supposed to perform the responsibilities for the study center in addition to their normal responsibilities for prison. The responsibilities of various activities are clearly divided between the prison authorities and IGNOU. The operating procedure is as follows:

a) *Administrative supervision of prison activities*

Keeping in view of the sensitivity of the prison administrative coordination between the prison department and IGNOU is regulated through a memorandum of understanding (MOU). As per the standard procedure, the study center is headed by a coordinator. The activities to be performed are well defined and norms are laid down by IGNOU. Normally, the activities are organization of academic counseling services for jail inmates, assignment evaluation, conduct of examinations, etc. The jail superintendent is appointed as the in charge of the study center. In case s/he is not available due to any other commitments than any other employee nominated by the competent authority can act as coordinator of the study center. Under such cases, a penal of proposed employees is submitted to vice chancellor of IGNOU for approval. The coordinators have to perform such responsibilities in addition to their normal duties and commitments for prison. Hence, functioning timings are well defined. Normally, they have to perform responsibilities for IGNOU's activities for 20 hours a week.

b) *Identification of counselors/mentors: a major concern*

Due to several security concerns, it's difficult to allow easy access for the external experts for organizing academic counseling. It is therefore difficult for the prison authorities to find out suitable academic counselors who can take counseling sessions for the inmates. The technology-enabled ways of interaction have limited scope keeping in view the security issues. Hence, availability of academic counselors has been a serious constraint for the functioning of study centers inside the prisons. IGNOU has made a special provision to identify inmates as counselor (in case they bear requisite qualifications). Administrative approvals in such cases remain a prerogative of IGNOU. Involvement of inmates in academic delivery makes IGNOU's interventions unique.

c) *Availability of physical space*
Availability of physical space inside the prison for exclusive use of IGNOU's activities has been a big challenge. Indian prisons are already overcrowded which makes it even more difficult. Therefore, allocating space for IGNOU's activities is a major constraint. As per standard MOU between prisons and IGNOU, one or two rooms with a space of approximately 500–800 sq. ft. for exclusive use of IGNOU has to be allocated by prison authorities for exclusive use of activities of IGNOU's including the office of coordinator, SSC (Prisons). This is considered to be the minimum space needed for IGNOU's study center in prisons. The space is utilized for workplace of coordinators, a small library and office space. Besides, prison authorities have to agree for arranging halls/rooms available for holding counseling, practical, term-end examinations, extend library, computer and laboratory facilities, etc., as per the requirements of the programs being offered. The prison authorities have to plan out schedules of counseling services and accordingly arrange the services inside the prison. The IGNOU is the monitoring body and its representatives can make surprise checks to ensure quality of services. IGNOU also provide the required self-instructional and audio-video materials pertaining to the program(s) being offered.

IGNOU can also consider providing the study center additional facilities like a computer, a TV set and dish antenna to watch IGNOU educational programs, if there are more than 150 learners at any such center. The most unique part of the collaboration is that IGNOU does not charge any tuition fee/other expenses from enrolled inmates of the host institution. The officials of IGNOU make regular visits to prisons to sensitize the inmates about educational opportunities, the counseling to motivate them and assist the coordinator, if necessary, in the process of admissions/examinations.

The jail superintendents are also remunerated by IGNOU at Rs. 6,000 per month as remuneration. Further, university also bear all the recurring expenditure toward stationary, postal and photocopying as per actual and pay the counselors (inmates or external) as per IGNOU norms and expenditure toward assignment/project evaluation. The IGNOU also conducts examinations in the jail, makes surprise visits during exams and makes payments for the conduct of examination. In cities where IGNOU has a regional center, the SSC (Prisons) is attached to it for administrative purposes and at other locations to the nearest regular study center. IGNOU is the monitoring body for all the activities inside the prison and has the right to shift or close the SSC

(Prisons) if it finds that support services are not being provided, as per the requirements of the university.

Issues and Challenges

a) *To conduct sensitization programs*

Such sensitization programs were immediately needed primarily because the jail inmates did not have sufficient initial level of motivation. The idea of taking education was not a lucrative idea for the under trials. They were psychologically not prepared to invest time and energy in a long-term activity. Education was not perceived as something which could address immediate issues of priority in their lives. Crime breeds in the society primarily due to failed system of education. Their perceptions were quite understandable as they had practically no faith in the system of education. As most of the jail inmates were school dropouts, the BPP – a bridge program of six months duration, which gives the school dropouts an easy access to higher education could be useful. Such a unique opportunity to pursue higher education created some enthusiasm among school dropouts. However, such an enthusiasm was not sufficient to motivate them to enroll with IGNOU. Despite the fact that programs were absolutely free, it was difficult for them to overcome the low psychological state of most of the jail inmates. IGNOU's authorities and the jail administration had to do extensive exercise of sensitization of jail inmates. The IGNOU regional center's officials started visiting various jails where group meetings were conducted with jail inmates. The meetings were followed by interaction on specific issues. Hence, with extensive motivational exercises the jail inmates started showing interest to get enrolled.

b) *To deal with administrative constraints*

It was decided that only jail inmates (Indian citizens) be allowed to take admission. Jail inmates can be enrolled only at the SSC located in the jail where they are housed. In other words, if a particular jail does not have an SSC of IGNOU, the inmates of that jail cannot take admission in IGNOU. Inmates of one jail are not allowed to take admission in IGNOU at an SSC located in another jail. It was not possible to launch all the programs at every location. Admission in programs having practical/workshop/ extended contact programmes (ECP) component could not be given unless facilities for conduct of workshop/practical/ECP are available within the jail and jail authorities were willing to extend the facility. It was also decided that if a jail inmate enrolled in a program is released, she/he may be treated like other students. Under such circumstances she/he would be charged fees as applicable. Change of study center from a jail center to an outside center was not permissible under normal circumstances. It was felt that such requests would be entertained only on the basis of a certificate issued by the jail authorities.

c) *To identify academic counselors*

Most of the jails did not have required level of academic expertise to give academic counseling to jail inmates. The academic counselors are expected to have prescribed educational qualifications. It was a major challenge for the officials of jail administration to arrange the academics who fulfilled required educational qualifications and were ready to go inside the jail premises to give academic counseling to inmates. Very few of such resource persons were mentally prepared. It required an extensive exercise of interorganizational coordination.

d) *Low pass out rates*

The prison inmates in most of the jails in India come from economically poorer segments of the society. They are mostly school dropouts and therefore have difficulty while pursuing programs of higher education. The bridge program of six months' duration offered by IGNOU can afford them to take admission in IGNOU's programs. However, they find it difficult to pursue the degree-level programs. The pass out rates in degree programs mostly for jail inmates are therefore very low. Though very few studies have taken up the underlying reasons, a chart which shows the pass out rates is given below. There is a need to carry out in-depth studies in this regard.

Some Good Practices

IGNOU announced its "Free Education for Prisoners" initiative in the 2010 academic session and waived off fees for all jail inmates across the country who wish to pursue the university's programs. The university has projected its initiative of free education as one of its achievement. Several good practices have been noticed in the implementation of scheme at Nagpur, Ahmadabad and Delhi. Details about such initiatives have been displayed by the university (IGNOU, 2016). IGNOU's SSCs for jail centers in some of the places have done exceedingly well and achieved laurels.

a) *Holding placement drive*

As per the information available through the website of IGNOU, campus placement activities are regularly organized in Tihar and Ahmadabad jails of the country. Tihar Jail had organized such placement activities based on the following criteria.

- Whether inmates had faultless conduct inside the jail where they utilized their time to gain education and vocational skills.
- Whether they were expected to be released within a year or so.
- Whether they were keen to rehabilitate themselves and lead a new life.

The first drive for job placement was organized on February 25, 2011. As reported by Singh (2013, p. 41), in the first round, 45 inmates participated and 15 companies came forward. In the second round, 18 companies showed interest in participating in the program, of which 15 companies turned up. A total of 74 inmates were selected from 100 inmates. It has also been reported that until year 2013, a total of 357 prisoners had been given job offers by different corporations. A placement cell has been constituted which consistently holds such drives to ensure that a maximum number of inmates can be benefited. Further, inmates are consistently motivated to participate in such drives, improve their behavior, conduct and academic credentials (Singh, 2013, p. 41). It is one of the major reformative and rehabilitative moves which has generated tremendous enthusiasm among the inmates for taking admission in IGNOU's programs. There are several success stories of placement drives in IGNOU, which have attracted media attention in India (IGNOU, 2011).

b) *Using radio broadcasts for providing educational support*

Technological interventions inside the prisons are not freely allowed inside the prisons primarily due to security reasons. This is a major handicap for the Open University which strongly relies on the technology-enabled methods to provide educational support to its learners. The IGNOU's regional center in Nagpur (India) utilized radio broadcast for involving jail inmates in live interactive teaching learning processes which were found very useful by inmates (Box 2).

Box 2. Nagpur Experiment for Radio Live Counseling for Jail Inmates..

Some successful initiatives for using radio have been reported from different parts of the world, for example, the Prison Radio Project in San Francisco; Prison Radio Association (PRA) in the UK, Radio Focus in Israel; and Community Radio in Pune, Mumbai and the Central Jails of Maharashtra, India (Ansari as cited in Sivaswaroop, 2020). Live broadcast for giving live interactive academic support to jail inmates was experimented by Gyan Vani Educational Radio Station in Nagpur (India). The main feature of the Nagpur Radio Experiment is that prisoners are involved in a "live" broadcast on public radio where they can ask their questions.

With the joint efforts of prison authorities and IGNOU, a space was earmarked where student prisoners could sit and participate in the live programs. However, in order to ensure the jail's security provision, inmates were not allowed to directly access the phone. They were instead informed about scheduled sessions about a week in advance and were asked to keep their questions ready to be dealt during the live programs. The inmates were asked to submit their queries, doubts, questions and clarifications on the relevant topic to the coordinator of the jail study center well in time. Such live sessions were scheduled keeping in view the convenience of inmates and allotted time schedules of their duties (generally 9 a.m. to 10 a.m.). Most of such students were generally undergraduate students, and the average number of questions asked by them per session was three and sometimes went up to six. The organizers of this program have claimed encouraging response from jail inmates.

Source: Sivaswaroop (2020, pp. 191–192).

---

c) *Popularizing BPP for involving school dropouts*

Most of the jail inmates in India are school dropouts. They lack the basic eligibility (10 + 2-level qualification) to directly enter in to conventional degree-level program. However, IGNOU's specially designed program called **BPP** has proved handy for such school dropouts. BPP is a bridge program of six months' duration. Anybody who is minimum 18 years of age and intends to pursue a degree-level program can take admission in this program. Such students get two years to complete this bridge course. Once they complete this program, they become eligible to take admission in bachelor's degree-level programs and a range of certificate and diploma-level programs. IGNOU publicized this program in a big way through sensitization programs in prisons, as a result of which a big number of jail inmates took admissions.

CONCLUSIONS AND ROAD AHEAD

Prison education has now picked up at level of basic literacy programs, secondary school, vocational education and tertiary education level. In addition, several other activities such as rehabilitation programs, physical education and arts and craft also became part of prison education activities. Such initiatives are mostly provided, managed and funded with governmental control though there have been instances when the inmates were also required to pay for such capacity-building programs. In most of the countries, educational ventures inside the prisons have been implemented by governments through collaborative efforts with educational institutions. A range of challenges, quite often insurmountable, has hindered the development of prison education programs.

Though several countries have initiated programs on prison education, prisoners are afforded such programs as privileges rather than as matter of right. There is yet to be a strong philosophical basis for rights of education to prisoners. Some major issues in prison education especially in Indian context are given below:

a) *Prison education: a matter of right*

According to the United Nations Special Rapporteur on the right to education, education for people in detention should be guaranteed and entrenched in constitutional and/or other legislative instruments (UNHRC, 2009, para 90). However, it is generally felt that a thorough and robust articulation of the justification of the right to education in prison is absent. This is perhaps one reason why the right is not as secure and consistently upheld in practice as it ought to be (Vorhaus, 2014, p. 172).

Despite the fact that provisions for prison education have been created in most of the prisons, most of correctional institutions view it as part of prison management. Such facilities are generally provided as an opportunity rather than treating education as fundamental rights for prisoners (UNHRC, 2009). Report brought out by UN Human Rights lists out several lacunas in delivery of courses in prisons which shows lack of sensitivity about their human rights. For example:

> courses interrupted or terminated on the personal whims of prison administrators; the absence of libraries; waiting lists of up to three years for programmes; limited or no access to training in information technology; vocational courses that are dated paths to nowhere; indifference to needs associated with specific disabilities; and the withdrawal of educational "privileges" as a punitive measure. (UNHRC, 2009, para 32)

There is a need for a strong philosophical basis for prison education and a complete change of mindsets of those who manage such prison education programs. The prison education should be taken up as a right of prisoners and not just a privilege granted to them.

b) *Need of sharing of experiences*
   Initiatives for prison education have led to encouraging results in several prisons. However, most of the knowledge and experiences created through such experiments has remained localized. There is a need to share the experiences for replication of good practices. It will help the prison administration to take benefits of successful initiatives in other prisons and improve the delivery of academic services.

c) *Innovative applications of technology*
   It is absolutely necessary to enhance access to prisoners through technology-enabled means, make them feel part of wider students' community and extend them facility of placement services. However, the technological interventions in prisons have so far been confined to developed countries. Initiatives in such countries have been quite successful, and developing nations should replicate them.

   The initiatives taken by the Open University and Queensland University have made innovative applications of digital technologies to provide cost-effective education to inmates. Technology can significantly reduce cost, compensate for the lack of infrastructure or academic expertise available inside the prisons and create far-reaching learning experiences for inmates. As far as concerns, apprehension about security breaches, innovative secure learning management systems can be created. IGNOU's initiatives for technological interventions inside prison are still in their infancy. Though there are some innovative initiatives taken through radio, security concerns are the major apprehensions to utilize interactive technologies inside prisons (Sivaswaroop, 2020). The prison education in India can learn from the technology-enabled initiatives taken in developed countries and suitably contextualize them in Indian prisons.

d) *Involve qualified inmates as teachers*
   It has been observed, quite often, that good quality academic expertise is not ready to go inside the prisons for giving academic services to prisoners. There are varieties of reasons because of which jail administration is hesitant to allow outsiders inside the jail. This is one of the reasons why prison education has been suffering from such lack of academic expertise. However, little has been done to utilize the expertise among the prisoners to participate in such academic support services. If these options can be sufficiently explored, then

it will help to create a more meaningful academic activity inside the prisons. The provision of involving qualified jail inmates as Academic Counselors is a welcome initiative taken by IGNOU. Though very few such inmates have so far been involved by the University for Academic Delivery in prisons, such an initiative can have far-reaching impact.

e) *Linking them to job opportunities*

The prison education should be predominantly job oriented. The reintegration of prisoners can be effectively carried out if they have income-generating opportunities available to them, once they are released from prisons. It will give them a sense of self-worth, enhance their self-esteem and help to explore productive roles in the society. However, very few universities seem to have explored such possibilities. IGNOU's initiatives to hold campus interviews for the prisoners within jail premises are a positive step in this regard.

Though IGNOU has taken several pioneering initiatives in India to bring about meaningful change in the life of jail inmates, there is a need to enhance employability of inmates, utilize technology in a much bigger way and create infrastructure for effective student support services inside prisons. Further, jail inmates need to be offered skill-oriented and short-term programs rather than general degree programs. Educational activities in jails are absolutely a welcome initiative, but such initiatives have so far been taken only by the Open Universities. The conventional universities have largely not ventured in these activities. In very few places, conventional universities have taken such isolated initiatives, for example, Guru Nanak Dev University, Amritsar (India). There is also a need of voluntary participation of welfare organizations and NGOs which will help to safeguard prison education as a human right.

REFERENCES

Aalai, A. (2014). Access to education for prisoners: A key to reforms. *Psychology Today.* Retrieved from https://www.psychologytoday.com/intl/blog/the-first-impression/201404/access-education-prisoners-key-reform. Accessed on December 10, 2019.

Bazos, A., & Hausman, J. (2004). *Correctional education as a crime control program* (pp. 34). Los Angeles, CA: National Institute of Corrections.

Centre for American Progress. (2018). Education opportunities in prison are a key to reducing crime. Retrieved from https://www.americanprogress.org/issues/education-k-12/news/2018/03/02/447321/education-opportunities-prison-key-reducing-crime/. Accessed on December 19, 2019.

Chaudhary, S. V. S., Khare, K., Gupta, S., & Garg, S. (2016). Towards inclusive education: A case study of IGNOU. *Journal of Learning for Development, 3*(3), 43–59. Retrieved from https://jl4d.org/index.php/ejl4d/article/view/143/158. Accessed on December 20, 2019.

Coates, D. S. (2016). *Unlocking potential: A review of education in prisons.* Ministry of Justice. Retrieved from https://assets.publishing.service.gov.uk/government/uploads/system/uploads/attachment_data/file/524013/education-review-report.pdf. Accessed on April 14, 2020.

Erzen, T., Gould, M. R., Lewen, J. (2019). Equity and Excellence in Practice: A Guide for Higher Education in Prison. In St. Louis (Ed.), MO: Alliance for Higher Education in Prison and San Quentin. CA: Prison University. Retrieved from the Alliance for Higher Education in Prison website,equity-and-excellence-in-practice.pdf (luminafoundation.org). Accessed on December 4, 2020.

European Prison Education Association. (2007). Education, audiovisual and culture executive agency, "Eliminating languages barriers in European prisons through open and distance education technology: progress report 2007." Retrieved from http://eacea.ec.europa.eu/; and FORINER project: www.foriner.com/.

Farley, H., & Pike, A. (2016). Engaging prisoners in education: Reducing risk and recidivism. *Advancing Corrections: Journal of the International Corrections and Prisons Association, 1*, 65–73.

Hawley, J., Murphy, I., & Souto-Otero, M. (2013). *Prison education and training in Europe: Current state-of-play and challenges*. Brussels: European Commission. Retrieved from http://ec.europa.eu/education/library/study/2013/prison_en.pdf. Accessed on December 10, 2019.

Hopkins, S., & Farley, H. (2015). eLearning incarcerated. *The International Journal of Humanities Education, 12*, 37–45. doi:10.18848/2327-0063/CGP/v13i02/43833

IGNOU. (2011). A second coming for IGNOU students in Tihar Jail. Retrieved from http://www.ignou.ac.in/ignou/bulletinboard/news/latest/detail/A_second_coming_for_IGNOU_students_at_Tihar_Jail-174. Accessed on December 18, 2019.

IGNOU. (2014). IGNOU educates jail inmates. Retrieved from http://www.ignou.ac.in/ignou/bulletinboard/news/latest/detail/IGNOU_educates_Jail_Inmates-594. Accessed on December 17, 2019.

IGNOU. (2016). Media releases on the website of IGNOU. Retrieved from http://www.ignou.ac.in/ignou/bulletinboard/news/latest. Accessed on January 30, 2016.

IGNOU. (n.d.). Waiver of IGNOU's Programme Fee for Jail inmates. Retrieved from IGNOU web site, IGNOU - Student Registration Division (SRD) - Waiver of IGNOU programme fee for Jail Inmates . Accessed on December 4, 2020.

Learning Together. (2016). Educational partnerships between universities and prisons: How learning together can be individually, socially and institutionally transformative. *Prison Service Journal,* 9–17. Retrieved from https://www.researchgate.net/publication/304252348_Educational_Partnerships_Between_Universities_and_Prisons_How_Learning_Together_can_be_Individually_Socially_and_Institutionally_Transformative. Accessed on December 18, 2019.

Lochner, L., & Moretti, E. (2004). The effect of education on crime: Evidence from prison inmates, arrests, and self-reports. Retrieved from https://eml.berkeley.edu/~moretti/lm46.pdf. Accessed on April 14, 2020.

Ministry of Home. (2011). Advisory issues by Ministry of Home regarding guidelines for educational programme for prison inmates (15th June 2011). Retrieved from https://www.mha.gov.in/sites/default/files/AdvEducationProg15062011.pdf . Accessed on December 4, 2020.

Ministry of Home Affairs. (n.d.). Prison reforms. Retrieved from https://mha.gov.in/Division_of_MHA/Women_Safety_Division/prison-reforms. Accessed on December 15, 2019.

Ministry of Home, GoI. (2003). Model prison manual for superintendence and management of prisons in India. Retrieved from http://bprd.nic.in/WriteReadData/userfiles/file/5230647148-Model%20Prison%20Manual.pdf. Accessed on December 15, 2019.

Muntingh. (2007). Prisons in South Africa's Constitutional Democracy. *CSVR*, October. Retrieved from https://www.csvr.org.za/docs/correctional/prisonsinsa.pdf. Accessed on December 12, 2019.

NAAC. (2019). Institutional accreditation manual, self study report of open universities. Retrieved from http://www.naac.gov.in/images/docs/Manuals/ODL-Manual-22_04_2019.pdf. Accessed on April 14, 2020.

National Crime Record Bureau. (2017). Prison statistics – India. Retrieved from http://ncrb.gov.in/StatPublications/PSI/Prison2017/Executive%20Summary-2017.pdf. Accessed on December 19, 2019.

National Crime Records Bureau. (n.d.). *Rehabilitation and welfare of prisoners* (pp. 209–212). Retrieved from https://ncrb.gov.in/sites/default/files/psi_table_and_chapter_report/CHAPTER-10_0.pdf

Pike, A. (2015). *Prison-based transformative learning and its role in life after release*. PhD thesis. The Open University. Retrieved from http://oro.open.ac.uk/61452/1/13834868.pdf. Accessed on December 11, 2019.

Pike, A., & Adams, A. (2012). Digital exclusion or learning exclusion? An ethnographic study of adult male distance learners in English prisons. *Research in Learning Technology, 20*(4), 363–376. Retrieved from https://www.learntechlib.org/p/167807/. Accessed on December 11, 2019.

Premium Times. (2016). Nigeria Open University waives fees for prison inmates. *Premium Times,* May 5.

Singh, K. P. (2013, September). Reaching the unreached: IGNOU's intervention in Tihar Central Jail. *AAOU, 8*(2), 33–43. Retrieved from https://www.emerald.com/insight/content/doi/10.1108/AAOUJ-08-02-2013-B003/full/pdf. Accessed on December 17, 2019.

Sivaswaroop, P. (2020). Innovative phone-in radio program for prisoners enrolled as students at Indira Gandhi National Open University. *Journal of Prison Education and Reentry, 6*(2). Retrieved from https://scholarscompass.vcu.edu/jper/vol6/iss2/8/. Accessed on April 10, 2020.

Tam, K. Y., Herg, M. A., & Rose, D. (2007). Voices from correctional educators and young offenders in Singapore: A preliminary needs assessment study of the Kaki Bukit Centre Prison School. *Journal of Correctional Education, 58*(2), 129–144.

Teji, R. P. S. (n.d.). The prison, objects and reforms. Retrieved from https://delhidistrictcourts.nic.in/ejournals/RPS%20TEJI%20-%20PRISON%20OBJECT%20REFORMS.pdf. Accessed on December 19, 2019.

Tihar Jail. (2019). Website of government of NCT Delhi-India (updated on March 19, 2020). Retrieved from http://tte.delhigovt.nic.in/wps/wcm/connect/lib_centraljail/Central+Jail/Home/Prisoner+Profile. Accessed on April 14, 2020.

Toms, B., & Reddy, V. V. (2018, December). IGNOU's educational interventions for the imprisoned. *Asian Journal of Education and e-Learning, 6*(6), 126–127.

UNHRC. (2009). *Right of education for persons in detention. Report of the Special Rapporteur on the Right to Education.* Geneva: United Nations Human Rights Council. Retrieved from https://www2.ohchr.org/english/bodies/hrcouncil/docs/11session/A.HRC.11.8_en.pdf. Accessed on December 11, 2019.

United Nations. (n.d.). SDG16 – Promote just, peaceful and inclusive societies. Retrieved from https://www.un.org/sustainabledevelopment/peace-justice/. Accessed on December 10, 2019.

University of South Queensland. (n.d.). Making the connection. Retrieved from https://www.usq.edu.au/making-the-connection. Accessed on December 11, 2019.

UNODC. (2015a). United Nations' standard minimum rules for prisoners. Retrieved from https://www.unodc.org/documents/justice-and-prison-reform/GA-RESOLUTION/E_ebook.pdf. Accessed on December 10, 2019.

UNODC. (2015b). The Doha Declaration. Retrieved from https://www.unodc.org/documents/congress//Declaration/V1504151_English.pdf. Accessed on December 10, 2019.

UNODC. (2017). Roadmap for the development of prison based rehabilitation programs. *Criminal Justice Handbook Series.* Retrieved from https://www.unodc.org/documents/middleeastandnorthafrica/2018/Roadmap_for_the_Development_of_Prison-based_Rehabilitation_Programmes_ENG.pdf. Accessed on December 10, 2019.

UNODC. (2018). Introductory handbook on the prevention of recidivism and social reintegration of offenders. *Criminal Justice Handbook Series.* Retrieved from https://www.unodc.org/documents/justice-and-prison-reform/18-02303_ebook.pdf. Accessed on December 10, 2019.

Vacca, J. S. (2004). Educated prisoners are less likely to return to prison. *Journal of Correctional Education, 55*(4), 297–305.

Vorhaus, J. (2014, July). Prisoners' right to education: A philosophical survey. *London Review of Education, 12*(2), 162–174. Retrieved from https://files.eric.ed.gov/fulltext/EJ1160353.pdf. Accessed on December 12, 2019.

CHAPTER 6

WIDENING PARTICIPATION IN SERVICE LEARNING

Faith Valencia-Forrester and Bridget Backhaus

ABSTRACT

Work-integrated learning (WIL) and service learning are widespread approaches to experiential, practice-based learning in Australia. Both are associated with extensive bodies of research that support their benefits to students, industry, and the community at large. What is less explored, however, is the accessibility of such experiences. In Australia, there are several groups of students that are at a disadvantage in terms of participation in WIL and service learning. When considering access to higher education as an emerging human right, the importance of addressing these inequalities becomes even more clear.

This chapter draws on case studies of pedagogical and curriculum changes that challenge existing power structures from within the curriculum and improve the accessibility and inclusiveness of WIL. This includes a research project that informs redesigning WIL experiences to better suit the needs of students including, a pilot project to improve international student access to service learning, and the development of a Community Internship module that weaves First Peoples' knowledge and perspectives throughout. While by no means exhaustive, these cases represent the start of ensuring that all aspects of higher education, including experiential, practice-based aspects, are accessible to all students.

Keywords: Human rights; accessibility; community; education; employability; development; First People; cultural; development; higher education

International Perspectives in Social Justice Programs at the Institutional and Community Levels
Innovations in Higher Education Teaching and Learning, Volume 37, 77–88
ISSN: 2055-3641/doi:10.1108/S2055-364120210000037006

INTRODUCTION

Work-integrated learning (WIL) represents a widely accepted approach to experiential, practice-based learning in Australia. WIL refers to any programs or initiatives that integrate formal academic learning with work-based practice to help tertiary student develop workplace skills and prepare them for their transition to the workforce (Jackson, 2015; Patrick et al., 2009). Service learning represents a more community-oriented form of WIL that aims to instill a sense of citizenship within students. Morgan and Streb (2001) argue that it is imperative that citizens develop the following civic values: political engagement, connectedness with community, tolerance, and a belief that individuals are able to affect change. Taking a more holistic view of university education, service learning aims to give graduates not only academic and professional skills but also a sense of civic values and responsibility (Mabry, 1998). This requires a careful course design that places equal emphasis on the learning and the service provision, so that both service providers and recipients benefit equally (Furco, 1996). While service learning is relatively underdeveloped as a pedagogical approach in Australia, there is a significant body of work that details the benefits of service learning for students, most notably the far-reaching review of Eyler, Giles, Stenson, and Gray (2001) who found that service learning is associated with increased graduate employability, cultural competence, and a stronger sense of civic responsibility.

Service learning provides an opportunity for students to have a hands-on, practical experience with human rights. Teaching human rights in Western universities can sometimes lack the nuance and understanding needed to impress the importance of human rights issues upon privileged students. Australian states and territories are increasingly introducing legislation formalizing the recognition and value of human rights. As such, an understanding of human rights is rapidly becoming an important graduate attribute. Teaching human rights requires freedom, respect, equality, and diversity.

While both service learning and WIL, more broadly, are associated with extensive bodies of research that support their benefits to students, industry, and the community at large. What is less explored, however, is the accessibility of such experiences. In Australia, there were several groups of students that were susceptible to issues of equity and access including "international, employed students/ students with family responsibilities, students from lower socioeconomic backgrounds, those with a disability, Indigenous students, and those from regional and remote areas" (Patrick et al., 2009, p. 24). When considering access to higher education as an emerging human right, the importance of addressing these inequalities becomes even more clear.

This chapter details case studies of pedagogical and curriculum changes put in place to challenge existing power structures from within the curriculum and improve the accessibility and inclusiveness of WIL for groups that have historically been excluded. This includes a research pilot project designed to improve international student access to service learning and the development of a Community Internship (CI) module that weaves First Peoples' knowledge and perspectives throughout. While, by no means exhaustive, these cases represent the start of ensuring that all aspects of higher education, including experiential, practice-based aspects, are accessible to all students without discrimination or exclusion.

WIL AND SERVICE LEARNING IN AUSTRALIA

Practice-based education, commonly referred to as WIL, is a stalwart of the curriculum across a range of disciplines and institutions within the Australian higher education sector. Though WIL is widely utilized as a pedagogical approach, definitions vary across disciplines and even within schools. Given the definitional difficulties surrounding WIL, there is some consensus in the literature that it is best engaged as an"umbrella" term for programs that integrate student academic and workplace knowledge (Patrick et al., 2009). In summation, Orrell (2011) refers to WIL as intentionally integrating theory with practice knowledge.

Considering WIL as an umbrella term covering a wide range of experiential learning activities, service learning sits firmly underneath. Service learning is based on the premise that a university education should produce graduates with a strong sense of citizenship, alongside the requisite professional skills and academic knowledge (Mabry, 1998). Berry (1987) suggests that universities should aim to produce"fully developed human beings" and argues that a sense of citizenship is essential to this process (p. 77). Service learning aims to instill such values by providing experiential learning experiences that place equal value on the provision of service and learning and equal benefits to both the providers and recipients of said service (Furco, 1996). Simply imparting academic knowledge and professional know-how limits tertiary education and overlooks the formative nature of the diverse experiences that students encounter at university. In contrast, service learning creates a space for students to develop a sense of citizenship, alongside more traditional graduate attributes.

INTEGRATING SERVICE LEARNING AND HUMAN RIGHTS INTO THE CURRICULUM

WIL has long been a feature of university programs in Australia and Griffith University is no different. There has, however, been a recent refocus on the provision of centrally offered internships to incorporate aspects of service learning, community engagement, and human rights. The CI course at Griffith University is available to both undergraduate- and master's-level students. A multidisciplinary course, all students at the institution are eligible to enroll in the course. It is offered as a free-choice elective, and in a small number of programs, the CI course is listed as a core component. The majority of students enrolled in the CI course have chosen to complete the course as a free-choice elective. Composed of two interrelated components, the course comprises academic lectures, workshops, and assessments combined with a voluntary internship of 50-80 hours of community work with a community partner. The course is pedagogically structured to scaffold and develop reflective student learning as the internship progresses alongside the academic component. This allows students to learn in a dialogically reflexive environment providing multiple opportunities for student understanding to be assessed and reinforced.

The academic components of this service learning course allow students to consider significant social issues within the context of a human rights framework. Students are encouraged to consider human rights issues and how they impact their local communities, nationally and globally. Students are required to consider their own privilege and how their activities can impact the rights of others and what actions they can take to contribute to a more equitable society while considering the environmental impact of humankind. These underlying principles were fundamental to the design of the CI course.

Students learn about the ongoing issues affecting human rights continue to impact modern society globally. Students confront issues they would not come across in some of their courses. Students also learn how much of the development of human rights over the past half a century in Australia and internationally have been related to and informed by the demands of First Peoples. Within an Australian context, human rights issues are also examined in relation to our own historical abuses of human rights. Students learn about the forcible removal of Aboriginal and Torres Strait Islander children from the parents according to governmental attitudes and policies from the early 1900s up until quite recently. This era in Australian history is known as the Stolen Generation and has had a monumental impact not only on those involved but also on the wider Aboriginal and Torres Strait Islander community. Progress on Indigenous rights is slow in Australia and First Peoples continue to face many issues today in asserting their rights as Indigenous people and overcoming the legacies of colonization. This approach highlights the importance of a human rights framework and encourages privileged students, who are the majority in tertiary education in Australia, to challenge their preconceived notions and their own layers of privilege.

CASE STUDIES

The CI course places a strong emphasis on service learning and human rights. The course consistently attracts strong enrollments and positive student feedback. The challenge that remains though is to ensure that this course is accessible and meaningful to all students. This chapter details two case studies from the CI course of different approaches to increasing accessibility and participation in service learning through the CI course ranging from research, to curriculum development, to the provision of standalone, tailored experiences. The first case study details an intervention to increase international student participation in service learning. The final case study explores the efforts to closely interweave First Peoples' knowledge throughout the CI curriculum.

International Student Service Learning Project

International students represent an important group within the Australian higher education sector. Australia attracts the third-largest number of students from overseas, behind the United States and United Kingdom (Hare, 2018), and has the largest per capita number of international students of any country in the world (Babones, 2019). These numbers have significant financial implications, with the international student market in Australia worth A$34 billion in 2018 (Ross, 2018). The importance of maintaining this market and ensuring Australia remains an attractive destination for international students is paramount in the increasingly globalizing higher education sector.

Despite these numbers and the implied popularity of Australia as a study destination, international students are questioning the return on investment of studying in Australia. A recent survey found mixed perceptions in that regard and argued that Australian higher education providers must do more to ensure international graduate outcomes (Hare, 2018). Glass (2012) emphasizes these findings, observing that"just because a student attends a foreign institution does not mean he or she necessarily has a meaningful international experience" (p. 244). Therein lies the potential value of WIL and service learning for international students, particularly given the aforementioned benefits in terms of graduate outcomes.

Despite this potential, research suggests that international students face challenges in fully participating in WIL and service learning. Satisfaction with WIL experiences is significantly lower among international students and they were often frustrated by the lack of opportunities compared to domestic students (Patrick et al., 2009). International students may be prevented from gaining mainstream experience by being relegated to the"ethnic sector" (Harrison & Regine, 2013). International students are distinctly disadvantaged when it comes to fully participating in WIL and service learning experiences, thus a specialized program was designed in order to facilitate this.

The international student program was designed as a pilot study to give international students the opportunity to participate in a tailored service learning experience. Participants would benefit from developing the transferable skills necessary for a more formal service learning placement and would also learn about and engage with Australian social issues. The program was designed and incorporated as part of the CI course but specifically targeted international students from across a range of schools and disciplines.

The program saw international students enrolled in the CI course engage with three local community organizations over the course of the study period. The organizations were selected based on their ongoing relationships with the university and their willingness to accommodate a different approach to service learning. Each organization was focused on a different social issue and, as such, students were exposed to topics including environmental sustainability, inequality, poverty, and homelessness. Students engaged with the organizations in three phases: introductory visits, fundraising, and service delivery. Introductory visits were aimed at building relationships and confidence, as well as teamwork among the cohort of students through structured group activities and learning. The second phase of the program saw students work in groups to fundraise for the Christmas programs of two of the organizations. Students met and consulted with community stakeholders, then raised funds to purchase presents for underprivileged or homeless young people. The final stage of the project was the delivery and distribution of the Christmas presents.

The international student program broadly followed the CI course model with a series of lectures and workshops supplementing the practice experience. Course content included case studies of successful fundraising campaigns as well as the use of design software to produce marketing collateral. Students were supported by two staff facilitators and a peer mentor who had previously completed the CI course. This represents significant additional support as students in the general CI course are usually supported by one academic advisor. However, Harrison and Regine (2013) note that domestic students who undertake overseas placements are not held to the stringent language standards imposed on international students in Australia and are often supported by translators. In this context, the extra support offered to international students in this course was not excessive and was very well received by the students involved.

While the international student project represents a small pilot study, the initial results were promising. Students were surveyed throughout the experience and were also interviewed at the end. Student participants reported increased confidence and improved communication skills resulting from their involvement in the program. Communication skills were identified as particularly important, not only through initial student surveys but also in the literature. Communication skills have been identified by several authors as a key barrier to international student engagement with WIL (Harrison & Regine, 2013; Patrick et al., 2009; Pham, Bao, Saito, & Chowdhury, 2018; Safipour, Wenneberg, & Hadziabdic, 2017). Issues of confidence and communication led to the program activities being carefully scaffolded. Students first interacted with each other and facilitators through group activities and then worked closely with their peer mentor, before finally engaging with community partners and the broader student community. One of the staff facilitators discussed the profound changes in the students over the course of the study period, drawing on an example of one student who was initially too shy to participate but eventually took on a leadership role in fundraising. Creating supportive spaces to gradually build confidence and communicative skills was in direct response to the expressed needs of international students and, as such, contributed to developing an inclusive program that they were able to benefit from.

The international student service learning project achieved overwhelmingly positive feedback from the students involved. The emphasis on soft skill development and the scaffolded, supportive environment were greatly appreciated by students, who reported improved communication skills and increased confidence in their own abilities. Further, students demonstrated increased understanding of the social issues facing Australian society and reflected on how they might apply their increased knowledge and empathy to their own home countries. This pilot project has since been successfully replicated and now forms an important part of improving the service learning experiences of international students from within the CI course.

Weaving First Peoples' Knowledge into the Curriculum

Indigenous peoples are internationally recognized as being the most marginalized vulnerable populations (Australian Human Rights Commission, 2019). Given the multidisciplinary nature of the course, engagement with communities and its focus on human rights, it was appropriate that the course include the knowledge and perspectives of Australia's First Peoples' as a formal component of study. Drawing on the history of First Peoples being marginalized and excluded, it was decided to include and recognize the important contributions of First Peoples based both on their own traditions and cultures and through this experience of marginalization and exclusion (Kwaymullina, 2016; McKnight, 2016; Mignolo, 1999, 2011; Nakata, 2007b). It was important that the students understood that First Peoples have their own legitimate worldviews and terms of reference that represent legitimate ways of knowing, being and doing and to include it in course content for this reason, rather than any need to overcome any specific or general social-justice concerns.

The CI course structure and delivery allowed for inclusion of First Peoples' theoretical frameworks to be integrated throughout the course delivery as opposed to simply"adding" First Peoples' content as a one-off topic that would tick a box. The First Peoples' knowledge and perspectives were woven throughout the course program, providing students with an opportunity to engage with First Peoples' knowledge and perspectives in an ongoing reflexive practice as they moved through the course. Further, the assessment was designed to include the place-based knowledge, and students were guided in the development of practical understandings of relational being.

Given the criticism of previous attempts at"Indigenising" or"decolonising" course content (Collins-Gearing & Smith, 2016; Nakata, Nakata, Keech, & Bolt, 2012), it was appropriate to embed First Peoples' knowledge and perspectives in a way that was authored and guided by First Peoples. A First Peoples' Reference Committee, consisting of traditional owners, members of the University Council of Elders and other Indigenous academic staff, was established as a way of creating space for First Peoples to authorize and lead the decision-making process beyond inclusion. This approach ensured First Peoples' knowledge and perspectives integrated throughout the course utilized First Peoples' methodologies to inform course design itself. Space within the curriculum was also made for an independent standalone module developed and included according to First Peoples' terms of reference. It was important to not only teach First Peoples' content but also to do so according to a First Peoples' pedagogy.

There is a growing appreciation and consideration of First Peoples' knowledge within the Western academy. Within higher education, Martin Nakata (2007b) describes complex places where different knowledge systems intersect as"contested knowledge spaces." Russell (2005) suggests Western and Indigenous knowledges are considered separate and incompatible. While acknowledging the differences inherent to both knowledge systems, Nakata (2007b) suggests that the complexity of the two systems is"not clearly black or white, Indigenous or Western" (p. 9).

From a human rights perspective, an important aspect of introducing students to First Peoples' perspectives and experiences was how these experiences impacted the lives of individuals and communities (Battiste & Henderson, 2009; Nakata, Nakata, Keech, & Bolt, 2014). What is important with the inclusion of Indigenous knowledge and experience however isn't necessarily the content that is taught, but ensuring the practice and process of teaching incorporated First Peoples' ways of knowing and learning (Nakata et al., 2014; Rigney, 2012). Traditionally, this has been a challenge for universities and institutions more familiar with Western knowledge systems, so it was considered important that the CI course countered the role institutions have historically played in the exclusion and denial of Indigenous peoples (Rigney, 2012; Pridham, Martin, Walker, Rossengren, & Wadley, 2015). Additionally, rather than limit educational possibilities by tokenistic inclusion of Indigenous content (Nakata et al., 2014), the course viewed the inclusion of First Peoples knowledge and perspectives as an opportunity to enhance them. Giovanangeli and Snepvangers (2016) suggest non-Indigenous Australian educators have limited desire and ability to engage with Indigenous topics. Including First Peoples content within the course went beyond situating "Western" philosophies and worldviews against "Indigenous" but attempted to factually address traditional knowledge and power relationships between Indigenous peoples and educational institutions (Carey, 2015; Carlson & McGloin, 2013; Nakata et al., 2014).

This approach was also based on developing the deeper connections and relational nature of First Peoples' cultures and traditions (Black, 2011; Graham, 2008, 2014; Grieves, 2008; Hollinsworth, 2013). The process of including First Peoples' knowledge and perspectives acknowledged that

> it [was] not possible to bring in Indigenous knowledge and plonk it in the curriculum unproblematically as if it is another data set for Western knowledge to discipline and test. (Nakata, 2007, p. 8)

The course designers purposefully did not try to fit First Peoples' culture into Western pedagogies and curricula (Riley, Howard-Wagner, & Mooney, 2015) because the literature strongly criticized the incorporation of First Peoples and knowledges into Western institutions, especially within education institutions, that support this (Nakata, 2007a; Rigney, 2012; Smith, 2012; Watson, 2014). The process of including First Peoples' knowledge and perspectives involved reviewing the nature and form of Indigenous content and knowledge in Indigenous studies program areas and more broadly across the university curriculum (Battiste & Henderson, 2009; de Oliveira Andreotti, Stein, Ahenakew, & Hunt, 2015; Gilbert & Tillman, 2017; Henderson, 2005; Smith, 2012) and the method of the delivery of Indigenous content across Indigenous studies programs and the university curriculum. It was established at the outset that content was not just included, but rather situated and made available in ways that enable First Nations theoretical frameworks (Carey, 2015; Gilbert & Tillman, 2017; Heckenberg, 2015).

The content developed for students emphasized that in order to understand First Peoples' theoretical frameworks, it is important to understand the relational links between law, land, and people (Kwaymullina, 2005; Kwaymullina & Kwaymullina, 2010; Maduro, 2012). As in the majority of cultures and traditions, First Peoples' theoretical frameworks are informed by the way that First Peoples produce and understand knowledge about themselves and the world that they live in through "Ways of Knowing, Ways of Being and Ways of Doing"

(Martin & Mirraboopa, 2003, p. 208). These ways of knowing, being, and doing are informed by creation stories and dreaming and embedded in the land and waters that First Peoples coexist in relation with.

First People teaching staff share"Aboriginal philosophy" with students in an effort to help students gain a deeper understanding the complex relational systems as described by Aboriginal scholars Ambelin Kwaymullina and Blaze Kwaymullina (2010) as being"a pattern comprised of other patterns, of systems inside systems" (p. 196). Emphasis is placed on understanding that everything in these systems is"interrelated and interdependent" and the interrelated nature of"place" - often described as country - and"being" from a First Peoples' point of view (Graham, 2008, 2014; Heckenberg, 2015).

Prior to participating in the course, 75% of students rated their awareness of First Peoples as either"Low" or"Neutral." Data collected following completion of the course suggest the course content and delivery was well received and contributed to students being more culturally capable when working with First Australians. Three quarters of the students responding to the post survey agreed that First Peoples' content should form part of their program of study irrespective of their discipline. While more research is needed, these promising results indicate an appreciation and identified need for more cohesive First Peoples' content woven throughout the broader curriculum.

CONCLUSION

In conclusion, service learning and WIL, more broadly, are invaluable educational experiences for students when it comes to developing citizenship and an understanding of human rights. The CI course at Griffith University offers service learning experiences firmly entrenched within a human rights framework. The academic components encourage students to engage with and reflect on human rights issues and how they impact communities locally, globally, and internationally. The practical aspects of this course see students undertake service learning experiences within the community in order to operationalize their theoretical learnings.

The value of these experiences serves to emphasize the importance of ensuring that service learning and WIL are accessible to all members of the student body. Research suggests that there are groups of students who have been unable to fully participate in WIL and service learning, including students with disability, international students, and First Nations students. Thus, this chapter has detailed two different case studies aimed at improving the accessibility of service learning experiences for all students. Research strongly suggests that students benefit from participating in WIL and service learning, therefore it is imperative to continue to find out more about their experiences so as to design more accessible programs. Similarly, international students have been disadvantaged when it comes to fully participating in WIL. The international student service learning project developed a tailor-made program targeted specifically at international students. By scaffolding learning, focusing on soft skill development, and providing additional layers of support, international students were able to greatly benefit from participating in service learning. Finally, making a concerted effort to interweave First Peoples' knowledge throughout the curriculum, as opposed to simply adding on a standalone topic, increases student engagement and understanding of First Peoples, particularly against a backdrop of human rights.

To conclude, service learning has immense value as a way of teaching and supporting students toward engaging with human rights. There are, however, issues of accessibility that cannot be overlooked. What this chapter has demonstrated though is that with concerted effort to engage the entire student body in all its diversity, service learning and practical human rights education can be accessible to all students.

REFERENCES

Australian Human Rights Commission. (2019). Indigenous international rights. Retrieved from https://www.humanrights.gov.au/our-work/aboriginal-and-torres-strait-islander-social-justice/indigenous-international-rights. Accessed on November 8, 2019.

Babones, S. (2019). *The China student boom and the risks it poses to Australian universities.* Sydney: Centre for Independent Studies. Retrieved from https://www.cis.org.au/app/uploads/2019/08/ap5.pdf

Battiste, M., & Henderson, J. Y. (2009). Naturalizing indigenous knowledge in eurocentric education. *Canadian Journal of Native Education, 32*(1), 5.

Berry, W. (1987). *The loss of the university. Home economics.* San Francisco, CA: North Point Press.

Black, C. F. (2011). *The land is the source of the law: A dialogic encounter with indigenous jurisprudence.* London: Routledge Cavendish.

Carey, M. (2015). The limits of cultural competence: An indigenous studies perspective. *Higher Education Research & Development, 34*(5), 828–840.

Carlson, B., & McGloin, C. (2013). Indigenous studies and the politics of language. *Journal of University Teaching & Learning, 10*(1), 1–10.

Collins-Gearing, B., & Smith, R. (2016). Burning off: Indigenising the discipline of English. *The Australian Journal of Indigenous Education, 45*(2), 159–169.

de Oliveira Andreotti, V., Stein, S., Ahenakew, C., & Hunt, D. (2015). Mapping interpretations of decolonization in the context of higher education. *Decolonization: Indigeneity, Education & Society, 4*(1), 21–40.

Eyler, J. S., Giles, D. E., Jr, Stenson, C. M., & Gray, C. J. (2001). At a glance: What we know about the effects of service-learning on college students, faculty, institutions and communities, 1993–2000. *Higher Education.* Paper 139. Retrieved from http://digitalcommons.unomaha.edu/slcehighered/139

Furco, A. (1996). Service-learning: A balanced approach to experiential education. In A. Furco (Ed.), *Expanding boundaries: Serving and learning.* Washington, DC: Corporation for National Service.

Gilbert, S., & Tillman, G. (2017). Teaching practise utilising embedded indigenous cultural standards. *The Australian Journal of Indigenous Education, 46*(2), 173–181.

Giovanangeli, A., & Snepvangers, K. (2016). Spaces of multiplicity: Rethinking indigenous perspectives in Australian tertiary education through altering teacher beliefs and practices. *Commonwealth Essays and Studies, 38*(2), 39.

Glass, C. R. (2012). Educational experiences associated with international students' learning, development, and positive perceptions of campus climate. *Journal of Studies in International Education, 16*(3), 228–251.

Graham, M. (2008). Some thoughts about the philosophical underpinnings of aboriginal worldviews. *Australian Humanities Review, 45*(45), 181–193.

Graham, M. (2014). Aboriginal notions of relationality and positionalism: A reply to Weber. *Global Discourse, 4*(1), 17–22.

Grieves, V. (2008). Aboriginal spirituality: A baseline for indigenous knowledge's development in Australia. *The Canadian Journal of Native Studies, 28*(2), 363–398.

Hare, J. (2018). It's still worth it for overseas students to study in Australia, but universities could be doing more. *The Conversation,* November 22. Retrieved from https://theconversation.com/its-still-worth-it-for-overseas-students-to-study-in-australia-but-universities-could-be-doing-more-107180

Harrison, G., & Regine, I. (2013). Extending the terrain of inclusive education in the classroom to the field: International students on placement. *Social Work Education, 32*(2), 230–243.

Heckenberg, R. (2015). Learning in place, cultural mapping and sustainable values on the Millawa Billa (Murray River). *The Australian Journal of Indigenous Education, 45*(1), 1–10.

Henderson, J. H. (2005). Insights on First Nations humanities. *The Australian Journal of Indigenous Education, 34*, 143–151.

Hollinsworth, D. (2013). Forget cultural competence; ask for an autobiography. *Social Work Education, 32*(8), 1048–1060.

Jackson, D. (2015). Employability skill development in work-integrated learning: Barriers and best practice. *Studies in Higher Education, 40*(2), 350–367.

Kwaymullina, A. (2005). Seeing the light: Aboriginal law, learning and sustainable living in country. *Indigenous Law Bulletin, 6*(11), 12–15.

Kwaymullina, A. (2016). Research, ethics and indigenous peoples. *AlterNative, 12*(4), 437–449.

Kwaymullina, A., & Kwaymullina, B. (2010). Learning to read the signs: Law in an Indigenous reality. *Journal of Australian Studies, 34*(2), 195–208.

Mabry, J. B. (1998). Pedagogical variations in service-learning and student outcomes: How time, contact, and reflection matter. *Michigan Journal of Community Service Learning, 5*, 32–47.

Maduro, O. (2012). An (Other) invitation to epistemological humility: Notes toward a self-critical approach to counter-knowledges. In A. M. Isasi-Daz & E. Mendieta (Eds.), *Decolonizing epistemologies: Latina/o theology and philosophy* (pp. 87–106). New York, NY: Fordham University Press.

Martin, K., & Mirraboopa, B. (2003). Ways of knowing, being and doing: A theoretical framework and methods for indigenous and indigenist research. *Journal of Australian Studies, 27*(76), 203–214.

McKnight, A. (2016). Meeting country and self to initiate an embodiment of knowledge: Embedding a process for Aboriginal perspectives. *The Australian Journal of Indigenous Education, 45*(1), 11–22.

Mignolo, W. D. (1999). I am where I think: Epistemology and the colonial difference. *Journal of Latin American Cultural Studies, 8*(2), 235–245.

Mignolo, W. D. (2011). Decolonizing western epistemology/building decolonial epistemologies. In A. M. Isasi-Daz & E. Mendieta (Eds.), *Decolonizing epistemologies: Latina/o theology and philosophy* (pp. 19–43). New York, NY: Fordham University Press.

Morgan, W., & Streb, M. (2001). Building citizenship: How student voice in service learning develops civic values. *Social Science Quarterly, 82*(1), 154–169.

Nakata, M. (2007a). *Disciplining the savages, savaging the disciplines.* Canberra: Aboriginal Studies Press.

Nakata, M. (2007b). The cultural interface. *The Australian Journal of Indigenous Education, 36*(S1), 7–14.

Nakata, M., Nakata, V., Keech, S., & Bolt, R. (2012). Decolonial goals and pedagogies for Indigenous studies. *Decolonization: Indigeneity, Education & Society, 1*(1), 120–140.

Nakata, M., Nakata, V., Keech, S., & Bolt, R. (2014). Rethinking majors in Australian indigenous studies. *The Australian Journal of Indigenous Education, 43*(1), 8–20.

Orrell, J., (2011). *Good practice report: Work-integrated learning,* ALTC: Strawberry Hills.

Patrick, C.-J., Peach, D., Pocknee, C., Webb, F., Fletcher, M., & Pretto, G. (2009). *The WIL (Work Integrated Learning) report: A national scoping study.* Australian Learning and Teaching Council (ALTC). Retrieved from http://catalogue.nla.gov.au/Record/4584343http://www.acen.edu.au/resources/docs/WIL-Report-grants-project-jan09.pdf

Pham, T., Bao, D., Saito, E., & Chowdhury, R. (2018). Employability of international students: Strategies to enhance their experience on work-integrated learning (WIL) programs. *Journal of Teaching and Learning for Graduate Employability, 9*(1), 62–83.

Pridham, B., Martin, D., Walker, K., Rossengren, R., & Wadley, D. (2015). Culturally inclusive curriculum in higher education. *The Australian Journal of Indigenous Education, 44*(1), 94–105.

Rigney, L. I. (2012). *Review of indigenous higher education consultancy: Indigenous higher education reform and indigenous knowledges*. Report commissioned for the Review of Higher Education Access and Outcomes for Aboriginal and Torres Strait Islander People. Retrieved from https://docs.education.gov.au/documents/indigenous-higher-education-reform-and-indigenous-knowledges

Riley, L., Howard-Wagner, D., & Mooney, J. (2015). Kinship online: Engaging 'Cultural praxis' in a teaching and learning framework for cultural competence. *The Australian Journal of Indigenous Education, 44*(1), 70–84.

Ross, J. (2018). Australian international education earnings reach A$34 billion. *Times Higher Education*, November 1. Retrieved from https://www.timeshighereducation.com/news/australian-international-education-earnings-reach-a34-billion

Russell, L. (2005). Indigenous knowledge and archives: Accessing hidden history and understandings. *Australian Academic & Research Libraries, 36*(2), 161–171.

Safipour, J., Wenneberg, S., & Hadziabdic, E. (2017). Experience of education in the international classroom – A systematic literature review. *Journal of International Students, 7*(3), 806–824.

Smith, L. T. (2012). *Decolonizing methodologies: Research and indigenous peoples*. London: Zed Books.

Watson, I. (2014). *Raw law: Aboriginal peoples, colonisation and international law*. London: Routledge.

PART II

PROMOTING SOCIAL JUSTICE AMONG STUDENTS

CHAPTER 7

FLUX OF DIGITAL ACTIVISM TO LEVERAGE PEACE AND HUMAN RIGHTS

Anil Shukla and Kshama Pandey

ABSTRACT

Plato and contemporary thinkers including American philosopher Martha Nussbaum have emphasized the need for political consciousness among the youth. Cultivating Humanity: A Classical Defence of Reform in Liberal Education *by Nussbaum expressed that*

It would be catastrophic to become a nation of technically competent people who have lost the ability to think critically, to examine themselves, and to respect the humanity and diversity of others.

Ideologically, it has been proven that advancement in technology can shift social ethos if we use it intelligently and then technology can lead to activism.

Digital activism can be defined as the use of electronic communication devices, for example, social media, Twitter, Facebook, YouTube, e-mail, e-blogging, micro-blogging and podcast for different forms of activism. It enables citizens to express ideology and spread information to a large audience regarding human rights. In this context, researchers have explored the level of digital activism among pupil teachers and found very little awareness regarding the same. Findings also reveal that the level of digital activism does not have any significant effect on attitude toward human rights and peace. Although findings reveal that attitude toward peace and human rights is positively correlated with each other. Therefore, on the basis of the findings, an intervention program for

International Perspectives in Social Justice Programs at the Institutional and Community Levels
Innovations in Higher Education Teaching and Learning, Volume 37, 91–108
ISSN: 2055-3641/doi:10.1108/S2055-364120210000037007

digital activism has been suggested at the end of this chapter that can foster
digital activism among them.

Keywords: Peace; human rights; attitude toward peace; attitude toward
human rights; digital activism tools; online petitions; social networks;
blogs; micro-blogging; proxy servers; encryption

INTRODUCTION

A wide availability of information and communication technologies and accessibility of online digital tools makes it possible for human rights defenders and peace
activists to protect human rights and sustain peace across the globe. In 2016, the
United Nations Human Rights Council accepted a resolution which endorsed that
"the same rights that people have offline must also be protected online." It promotes
the access of all countries as "promotion, protection, and enjoyment of human
rights on the internet" which do not allow any country that internationally interrupt
internet connection of its citizen (Human Rights Council, 2016, A/HRC/32/L.20).
This freedom of online accessibility facilitates and promotes freedom of expression
and online dialogue among learners also. They can communicate their voice in various innovative ways in which they can turn information into action. Students use
digital devices to have their voices heard and to synchronize actions that challenge
their relationship with governments.

To achieve success in the twenty-first century depends on having a purpose,
a sense of self-efficacy, a growth mindset and the right tools or access to those
tools. The responsibility of the school should assist learners to identify the right
tools, learn them how to use and take initiatives that support better knowledge
of local circumstances that can be used to prevent human rights (Dickinson,
2018). Learners can select online tools from virtual platform and participate in
realistic and reasonable movements. On such canvasses, learners become digital
activists and they leverage networked technologies – YouTube, Twitter, Facebook,
blogs, SMS text messaging – for social and political change campaigns (Rabali.
ca, 2001). Digital activism exists where digital tools (the internet, mobile phones,
social media, etc.) are used toward bringing about social and/or political change.

The activists who fight to protect human rights have more consideration to
sustain peace, and they use social media as an outlet to make their voices loud.
Instagram, Twitter, Facebook and YouTube are all proving more and more popular when it comes to activism across the world, providing a space where people
come together, exchange ideas, learn from one another, organize and have their
say. According to RESET (2018) from 2004 onward, social media is supporting
digital activism where entire campaigns are online having wide reach. But is this
availability enough?

Many argue that digital tools alone do not perform better for sustaining
human rights. In 2016, Eileen Donahoe (2016), Director of Global Affairs, stated
in her article that China has an advance vision of cyber repression. The Chinese

government protects human rights with the combination of digital devices for mass surveillance, censorship and social monitoring to provide a rich and comprehensive means of social and political control. Regarding this, the following questions are to be addressed in this chapter.

1. What opportunities and problems exist for use of digital activism in peace building?
2. How the new media might contribute or be capable of contributing to the digital activism?
3. How might this digital activism be conceptualized – as a new movement, or through the lenses of some existing or other reflections?
4. In what ways the messages shared on social media be considered democratic, and what are the ways in which they could be helpful in accessing human rights?
5. Does digital activism develop positive attitude toward human rights and peace?

In this chapter, we also examine and highlight the enormous potential of these fairly digital activism and attitude toward peace and human rights that they present to humankind as platforms for democratic and participatory communication and governance – especially in grassroots educational and social movements activism. In order to analyze the relationships between digital activism and attitude toward peace, researchers will make an effort to study the social activism and attitude toward peace and human rights of preservice teachers. To accomplish the objectives of study, researcher will make a layout of questions related to digital activism and attitude toward peace and human rights.

WHAT IS PEACE?

According to NCF (2005),

Peace education encompasses respect for human rights, tolerance, cooperation, social responsibility, social justice, and equality and cultural diversity, in addition to a firm commitment to democracy and non-violent conflict resolution. (p. 61)

Reardon (2012) insists that "peace is the absence of violence in all its forms – physical, social, psychological, and structural" (p. 16). But Copi and Cohen (1994) disagree with this negative concept of peace and argue that this connotation has failed to provide a positive picture of peace. Therefore, it can be concluded that negative concept of the peace is the non-appearance of any type of direct violence, that is, physical, verbal and psychological between individuals, groups and governments.

However, Galtung (1967) describes the word "peace" as an "umbrella concept." To him, it is a state of mind felt as a consequence of the actualization of certain stated human desires. That is, it is a feeling of internal serenity as a result of external stability. But at a first glance, Galtung (1967, p. 12) describes it as an "umbrella concept" and defines peace as a state of mind felt as a consequence of the actualization of certain stated human desires.

Galtung (1967) also explains peace as affecting the concept of law and order. Peace maintains social harmony and does not ignore violence; rather it establishes regulations and outlines punishments to produce and sustain peace. Therefore, on the basis of the above definitions, it can be concluded that peace is a phenomenon that includes harmony, goodwill, friendliness, truth, beauty and love.

ATTITUDE TOWARD PEACE

Attitude toward peace can be defined as to manage interpersonal relationships and eradicate conflicts in order to control, contain and reduce actual and potential violence. It sustains social equality and justice, equality and equity, ecological balance; protects from riots and terrorists; and provides basic human rights. It also involves the elimination of the root causes of war, violence and injustice and the conscious effort to build a society that reflects these commitments. Positive peace assumes an interconnectedness of all living beings. Attitude toward peace promotes the value of peace and nurture the belief that peace is possible and achievable with certain norms, that is, equality, diversity, empathy, nonviolence and social responsibility. Attitude toward peace requires to promote the belief that peace is not illusion and can be achieved. Attitude toward peace can be nurtured by containing the following values:

- *Equality*: Peace can be promoted by fostering the core value of equality and can be achieved by respecting and appreciating the sense of human rights.
- *Diversity*: Diversity incorporates the belief in antidiscrimination, the active challenging of stereotypes, the desire to understand and respect those different from self-tolerance, the recognition of each person's dignity.
- *Empathy*: Empathy is a sensitive attitude; it makes a person to listen to others and not overpower them.
- *Nonviolence*: It is a skill to resolve conflicts and maintain harmony and develop tolerance.
- *Social responsibility*: It develops interpersonal relationship with the sense of human duty for improving the peace and ensuring the dignity of all human beings.

HUMAN RIGHTS

Human rights are fundamental and innate to all human beings, beyond any discrimination and disparity. These rights are inherent to all human beings irrespective of their nationality, sex, ethnicity, color, caste, creed, race, religion, language or any other position. These rights are all interrelated, interdependent and indivisible.

Human rights ensure the right to life and liberty, freedom from slavery and torture, freedom of opinion and expression, the right to work and education and many more. Everyone is entitled to these rights, without discrimination (United Nations, 1948).

Human rights are inalienable, indivisible and interdependent. It means that these rights cannot be lost or cease. These rights cannot be condemned because the right has least viability. These rights are interdependent, for example, your ability to participate in your government is directly affected by your right to express yourself, to get an education and even to obtain the necessities of life (Human Rights Resource Centre, http:www.hrusa.org).

DIGITAL ACTIVISM

Digital activism energizes the action that attempts to reach beyond conventional politics, usually being additional vigorous, zealous, innovative and dedicated. Action includes e-mail complaints, government grievance portal, blogs, social media, etc. The world of social media and blogs has unlocked numerous doors for making injustices known, and students can share information across their accounts to maximize their reach. Social media can be used to advance nearly any cause.

Digital Activism Tools

The tools used by digital activists are vast and changing constantly as technology evolves. The following digital tools have been considered as digital activism tools in this study.

- *Online petitions*
  By this service, people can use website to connect with others across the world regarding their issues.
- *Social networks*
  A huge number of users are involved with this tool for various interests. They can also use it to promote human rights.
- *Blogs*
  Blog is a form of citizen journalism for the masses; it provides an effective means to express about any topic and is used in numerous online campaigns.
- *Micro-blogging*
  Micro-blogging sites such as Twitter, Joomla, Medium, Blogger and WordPress are used to help spread awareness of an issue or activist event.
- *Mobile phones*
  Mobile phones having various applications such as communication applications, web-based applications, multiple apps, hybrid applications, fun applications, security applications, etc., provide activism in single hand.
- *Proxy servers*
  As a means of circumventing government intervention when it comes to online protesting, many people deploy proxy servers, which act as intermediaries between a user and a site, thus essentially circumventing national restrictions on any site.
- *Encrypting e-mails*
  In this encrypting process of e-mail, it is possible to protect the information in the e-mail and maintain privacy by end-to-end encryption. There are mainly

three methods for e-mail encryption namely (i) Pretty Good Privacy is a hybrid approach; (ii) digitally signing MIME-based e-mail data and its public key encryption; and (iii) transport layer security (TLS) for security between client/ server apps.

- *Protecting data*
  This specific feature does not allow unauthorized access by other users. This is about maintaining your data access, the secrecy and integrity of data.

THEORETICAL FRAMEWORK OF THE STUDY

Nowadays digital action has become more prominent in civic engagements; digital technology and resources are significant and relevant instruments for social movements. But several times, learners find inequalities in social participation and acquiring basic human rights which generate conflicts among scholars. Stiglitz (2003) revealed

> The actual number of people living in poverty has actually increased by almost 100 million. This has occurred at the same time that total world income increased by an average of 2.5% percent annually.

Similarly, World Health Organization stated:

> Poverty wields its destructive influence at every stage of human life, from the moment of conception to the grave. It conspires with the deadliest and painful diseases to bring a wretched existence to all those who suffer from it. (Farmer, 2003, p. 50)

An understanding of economic, social and cultural rights also demands recourse to the right to development (Piovesan, 2004). Due to paucity of resources and literacy in India, majority of the academics do not involve actively in social movements. Bennett & Segerberg, 2013; Bimber, Stohl, & Flanagin, 2012; earl & Kimport, 2011 have revealed in their studies that online intensity of digital activism can lower participation costs and render collective action (Olson, 1965). These, resource mobilization theories are less supported to newer theories of mobilization in the digital era (Mccarthy & Zald, 1977). Resource mobilization theory addresses individuals as wise activists (Spier, 2017). The suggestion is that reduced costs remove participation barriers to enable more people to do more organizing with fewer resources. But we have not yet known if everyone has been able to harness these lowered costs of participation, nor if and how any variation in these costs shapes online participation in social and political movements. This study has been formulated based on the previous studies to examine how these theories of online activism extend to movement groups from different social classes. This literature tends to focus on extraordinary moments of online political organizing (e.g., Vasi & Suh, 2016), relying heavily on events such as anti-globalization protests, the Arab Spring and Occupy Wall Street. The emphasis on these exceptional cases initially made sense as social media activism began to emerge, as they had highly visible levels of online activity. But this focus leaves researchers with more information on emergent movements of the digitally plugged-in and less data on existing organizations from different social classes. Socioeconomic inequality is the most significant and basic demographic factor driving digital inequality, age not withstanding (Martin, 2007; Schradie, 2012; Zhang, 2014). Research reveals that most digitally successful movements have created a selection bias and carelessly confuse on differences with internet access and use. But some studies suggested that digital activism literature can be promoted by facilitating attractive studies and scholarships (McAdam & Boudet, 2012). Stornaiuolo and Thomas (2017) suggested that educational researchers understand digital activism by themselves about how to disrupt educational inequalities. These research trends expressed that most of the studies on digital activism were not designed to understand students' activism. Analysis of researches shows that online activism has started, but it is in the basic level, and few studies have been found on how digital activism ensures human rights and continues peace for humanity. Therefore, this study has made an attempt to explore the perceived knowledge regarding digital activism. What is the relationship between digital activism and human rights? Does digital activism ensure human rights and peace across society?

OBJECTIVES OF THE STUDY

Following objectives have been formulated for the study:

1. To explore the digital activism among preservice teachers.
2. To compare the attitude toward peace of preservice teachers having high and low digital activism.
3. To compare the attitude toward human rights of preservice teachers having high and low digital activism.
4. To find out the relationship between attitude toward peace and attitude toward human rights.

HYPOTHESES OF THE STUDY

In this study, the following hypotheses have been formulated to achieve the objectives:

1. There is no significant difference in attitude toward peace of preservice teachers having high and low digital activism.
2. There is no significant difference in attitude toward human rights of preservice teachers having high and low digital activism.
3. There is no significant relationship between digital activism and attitude toward human rights.

METHODOLOGY

The study was conducted on a sample of 200 preservice teachers recruited from four teacher training institutions affiliated to M.J.P. Rohilkhand University,

Bareilly. The sample comprised of 70 and 130 male and female preservice teachers, respectively. Mixed method was used for data analysis. Self-developed tools (Digital Activism Questionnaire cum interview schedule, scales of attitude toward peace and human rights) were applied to collect data.

Digital Activism Questionnaire is based on various literature and studies related to online activism or digital activism. This questionnaire includes 30 items. A structured interview has been conducted to explore the understanding of digital activism. Eight open-ended items have been incorporated in the same questionnaire to conduct the interview. Item analysis and content validity (I-CVI) is calculated. Content validity of this tool is based on expert rating and calculated item level content validity index. It shows that 84% of the total items are judged as content valid.

Peace attitude scale is developed by the researcher, and it is based on Peace Attitudes Li' Scale, PALiS (Eryilmaz, 2008), to investigate individuals' attitudes toward peace. It is a Likert-type scale with 25 items. Higher scores indicate a higher level of peace attitudes, while lower scores indicate a negative attitude toward peace. Its split-half reliability is 0.70.

The researcher has developed human rights attitude scale. For this purpose, the researcher has discussed and analyzed items of Attitude Toward Human Rights Inventory, ATHRI GUIDE (2006), developed by Darcia Narvaez, Steve Thoma, and Irene Getz. Thereafter, Inventory items have been adopted in Indian context. Digital activism has been defined in social and cultural context of India. The final draft of this scale has been prepared by selecting the items having t-values greater than or equal to 1.75 at 0.05 level of significance.

The preservice teacher who scored higher than 35 (above third quartile) were included in high digital activism group, whereas preservice teachers who scored less than 16 (below first quartile) were included in low digital activism group.

Mixed method was used for data analysis. Quantitative data were analyzed with the help of percent analysis, t-test and coefficient correlation technique. Semantic analysis has been adopted to analyze open responses obtained by the structured interview.

RESULTS AND DISCUSSIONS

The data have been analyzed and interpreted by keeping in view the formulated objectives (Table 1):

Observation from Table 2 shows that the value of t-ratio is 1.22 which is not significant at 0.05 level. So, the null hypothesis that there is no significance difference in attitude toward peace of preservice teachers having high and low digital activism is accepted. It means that both groups have similar attitude toward peace. It shows that activism has itself adequate democratic beliefs, and digitalization does not make it more operational. In India, majority of learners possess digital device, but education is still in the traditional mode so that they have fear to be active in democratic life and civil engagement. It can be supposed that peace can be publicized without digital instruments if only activism can lead positive attitude toward peace.

Table. 1. Exploration of Awareness Toward Digital Activism Tools Among Preservice Teachers.

S. No.	Digital Activism Tools	Awareness Toward Digital Activism Tools (%)	Result and Discussion
1.	Online petitions	35	Only 35% preservice teachers have knowledge of online petition. But they have never used this for the protection of their human rights. It shows that web tools are not in use for legal protection. Traditional modes of justice are still in use by common people. It shows that scholars are not aware of online mediums. They suppose that digital mode may not be more easier in comparison to conventional mode.
2.	Social networks	95	95% Preservice teachers have their own account in various social networking sites. They are using these sites for fun and social interaction. Sometimes they are involved in social campaign but never use these medium in protection of human rights or spreading in peace. It shows that they are not aware of its strengths and peculiar features which can promote peace and become part of social activism.
3.	Blogs	65	65% Preservice teachers are aware of blogs. Out of them, only 15% preservice teachers read others' blogs but no preservice teacher found who has created their own blog. Preservice teacher does not know how to write blogs although ICT is the integrated part of curriculum. It reflects that ICT skills should be integrated into the pedagogy of practice teaching and make them more competent by providing opportunity of practice. Practice of ICT skills should be made part of internship so that they become proficient in practical behavior.
4.	Micro-blogging	35	Only 35% preservice teachers are aware of Twitter, and out of them only 15% preservice teachers engage in such types of micro-blogging. Micro-blogging can become a major tool of activism. So, it seems relevant that micro-blogging should be integrated as part of curriculum.
5.	Mobile phones as activism tool	15	100% Preservice teachers are mobile users, but negligible number of preservice teachers (15%) are applying their devices as an activism tool. Mobile phone is a handy device for learning and spreading knowledge. It must be the responsibility of teacher educators that they ensure that their preservice teachers use their device for teaching and learning also. They focus learning strength of mobile device and make them competent to use this device to maintain social harmony and sustain peace across globe. They also use their mobile phone for disseminating local issues such as activism and can find appropriate solution.
6.	Proxy servers	15	Only 15% preservice teachers are aware of proxy servers. They have often heard proxy server as an activism tool. They are not aware that it can be used as a tool to disseminate peace and maintain harmony. Little knowledge regarding proxy server shows that scholars perceive that simple and conventional mode can be easy for activism.

Table. 1. (*Continued*)

S. No.	Digital Activism Tools	Awareness Toward Digital Activism Tools (%)	Result and Discussion
7.	Encryption e-mail	58	Encryption is the facility for online security. In this study, the researcher found that 58% preservice teachers are aware of this peculiar feature of e-mail. But very few scholars know that how they secure their e-mail in a high-risk situation. So, it is very important to make them aware of security features of e-mail.
8.	Protecting data	75	Unauthorized access could lead to the theft of data, the loss of user's access or to unauthorized changes to your own data. This study reveals that 75% preservice teachers are skilled to protect their data. They expressed some following methods which can be used for data protection: Use antivirus, regular data backup, computer password, start–restart computer, activate screen saver and protect web-browsing history.

Table. 2. Mean, SD and *t*-Ratio Showing the Difference in Attitude Toward Peace of Preservice Teachers Having High and Low Digital Activism.

S. No.	Level of Digital Activism	N	Mean	SD	t-Ratio
1.	High	25	42.36	6.61	1.22
2.	Low	29	40.24	5.70	

Observation from Table 3 shows that the value of *t*-ratio is 0.069 which is not significant at 0.05 level. So, the null hypothesis that there is no significance difference in attitude toward human rights of preservice teachers having high and low digital activism is accepted. It means that both groups have similar attitude toward human rights.

If an individual is mistreated by society and faced social injustice, then it can produce a sense of activism. In the case of preservice teachers' activism, this may relate to student maltreatment by the school administration. Issues extend from racism and sexism to access to health care or education, and students often join with larger activism groups to amplify their collective voice. Therefore, it is not necessary to have digital devices to spread activism. Now it is clear that both levels of digital activism have equal attitude toward human rights. The reason may be that the unavailability of resources does not make them active to fight against human rights. Although researches suggest that readily available online resources

Table. 3. Mean, SD and *t*-Ratio Showing the Difference in Attitude Toward Human Rights of Preservice Teachers Having High and Low Digital Activism.

S. No.	Level of Digital Activism	N	Mean	SD	t-Ratio
1.	High	25	47.72	8.53	0.069
2.	Low	29	47.55	9.36	

can generate new tactics that can make possible large democratic participation in political contention among preservice teachers. So, it can be concluded that stratification in the use of such resources implies that the incorporation of new technologies will be uneven (Schradie, 2018).

Observation from Table 4 reflects that the values of coefficient of correlation are 0.123 and 0.094 for attitude toward peace and attitude toward human rights, respectively. Both of them are not significant at 0.05 level. So, the null hypothesis that there is no significant difference between attitude toward peace and attitude toward human rights has been accepted.

Table. 4. Coefficient of Correlation Between Attitude Toward Peace and Attitude Toward Human Right.

S. No.	Dependent Variable	Value of Correlation
1.	Attitude toward peace	0.123
2.	Attitude toward human rights	0.094

The person who possesses digital activism needs a support network because standing up for human rights can be physically and emotionally develop the sense toward human duties. It can prevent common burnout. Therefore, it seems relevant to know our limitations and surround ourselves with people who can understand feelings. Fighting for human rights can develop the sense of peace and humanity. So, peace can sustain the dignity of human being and protect human rights.

DESIGNING INTERVENTION PROGRAM TO DEVELOP DIGITAL ACTIVISM

On the basis of finding, it can be concluded that there is an essential need to design an intervention program related to digital activism for preservice teachers. An intervention program should be an organized, purposeful effort to create change, and it should be guided by thoughtful planning. Before executing a successful intervention program, it is relevant to learn all possible aspects about as mentioned below:

- The current reality.
- Target audience.
- What possible issues both positively and negatively?
- What transformation can elevate the situation?
- What resources, strategies and tools are available to implement an intervention program that will address the issue?

So, keeping all points, the researcher has planned to develop and execute an intervention program as follows:

Fig. 1 exhibits the execution framework of the digital activism intervention program. In the first phase, it seems imperative to make them competent in

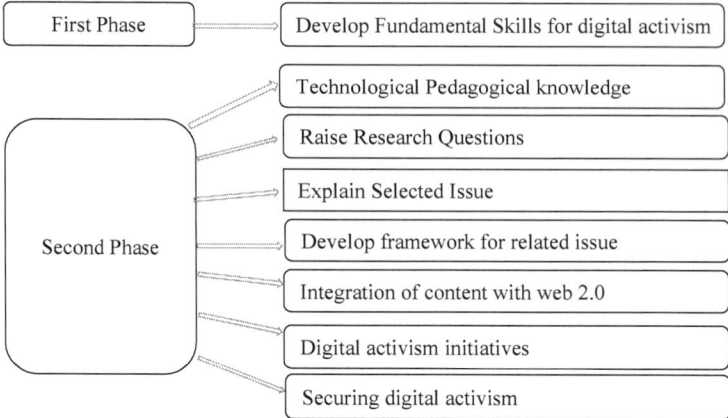

Fig. 1.   Planning Framework of Intervention Program of Digital Activism.

technical skills. Activism can disseminate in various forms. Each type of social issue can be part of digital activism requiring its own set of skills. First of all, it is imperative to understand what are the fundamental skills and how it can be executed to elevate digital activism among preservice teachers.

a) First phase:

Fundamental skills for digital activism

An understanding of why and how digital tools would be appropriated by users in their activism skills is called only activism can lead positive attitude toward peace. Digital activism skills also incorporated critical and reflective analysis skills and develop argument skills that belong among the essential twenty-first-century cognitive skills. The following skills can be included to foster digital activism among preservice teachers:

I. *Fundamental Skills*

Interpersonal	Analytical	Background Knowledge
• Develop academic writing skills and research aptitude that make them able to translate scientific and sociological studies into compelling narratives for policy-makers and the general public	• Develop critical and reflective analysis skills and develop argument skills that belong among the essential twenty-first-century cognitive skills. We face complex issues that require careful, balanced reasoning to resolve	• Develop digital skills including website design and information management
• Second-language skills and knowledge of global cultures and customs.	• Business management skills, including project and personnel management skills	• Statistical research analysis ability
• Physical stamina and a willingness to travel and work unconventional hours	• Fundraising and budgeting and knowledge of legal requirements	• E-blog writing, online survey ability

Source: American Chemical Society (2009).

b) Second phase:

i. *Technological pedagogical knowledge*

Technological pedagogical content knowledge (TPACK) is an emerging concept that integrates technology with pedagogy and content knowledge. To nurture digital activism among preservice teachers, the following objectives can be addressed in the digital activism intervention program:

- Define the mode of online activism with their pears.
- Elucidate the strengths and weakness of internet as a tool of digital activism.
- Consider the prospects of social media as the medium of digital activism.
- Define the negative aspects of social media as the medium of human rights violation.
- Identify the issues from society to disseminate across the society.

II. *Research Questions*:

To accomplish the objectives of the digital activism intervention program, there is a need to create a design challenge to empathize with the related issue. These questions can assist them to define the design challenge.

- How can digital tools be applied to achieve social transformation?
- What may be the strengths and weaknesses of the internet as a medium for activism?

c) Explain what is digital activism?

In this intervention program of digital activism, design challenge approach has been applied. Hence, after defining the issue or concept of digital activism, preservice teachers reach the phase of prototype. Now they are skilled to explore innovative solutions. In this phase, it is the responsibility of a teacher to explain the basic concept of digital activism And then identify a problem related to human rights with social relevance. Digital activism can be started through collective action integrated with digital devices. Collective actions may involve democratic values which leads to conflict resolution. To resolve conflicts, it is essential to foster conflict resolution skills based on design thinking. This innovative approach can develop attitude toward human rights and attitude toward peace. Digital activism is explained in Fig. 2.

d) Framework of digital activism:

To develop the framework of digital activism among preservice teachers, it is a basic requirement to narrate the seriousness of issues related to human rights. It would be better if the issue relates to local society or teaching institute. Then need to discuss with class or preservice teachers about their strategy to protect rights of concerned persons. Instructor can ask them what initiatives or measures can be taken to resolve the conflicts of victim. Scientific literacy can elucidate the major aspects of particular rights. Finally deliver a lesson based on design thinking to promote the knowledge about the issue related to human rights. Digital activism framework can be understood from Fig. 3.

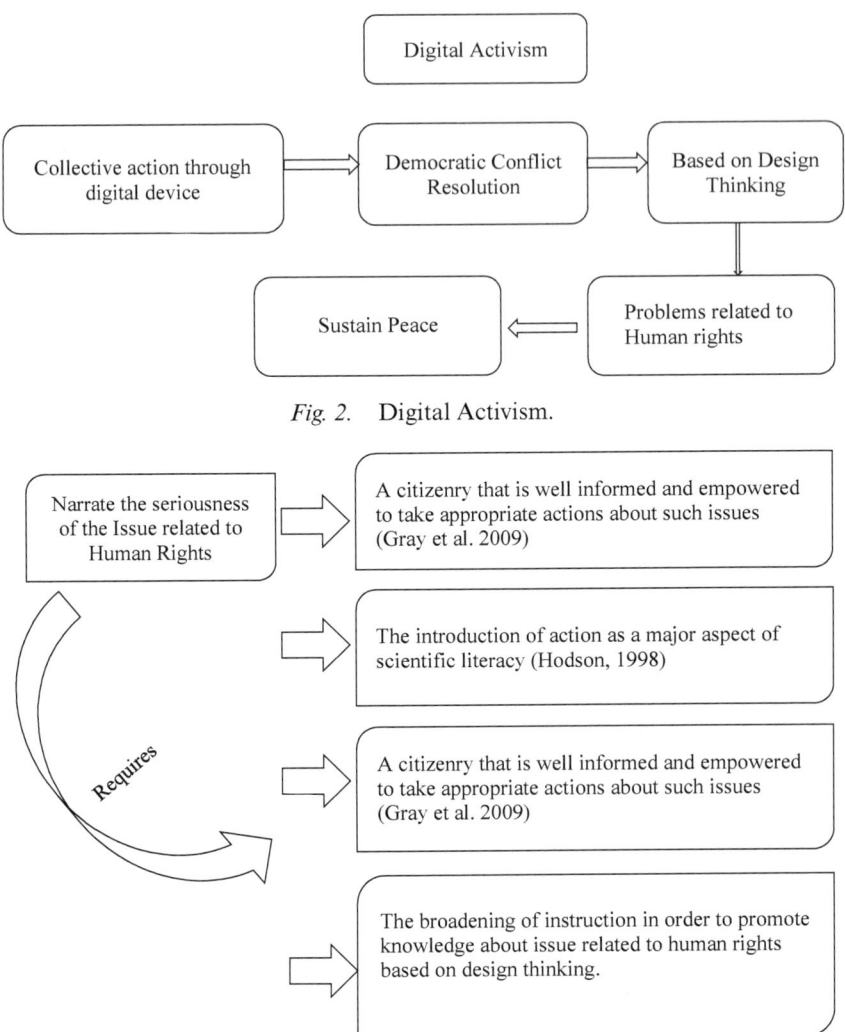

Fig. 2.   Digital Activism.

Fig. 3.   Framework of Digital Activism.

e) Procedure of digital activism:

Digital activism is a social phenomenon which leads to continue peace and protect human rights. Preservice teacher can start with a relevant issue related to human rights. They can start with online petition, e-blogging, social networking, mobile apps and micro-blogging. They can spread related knowledge and attitude through media and internet. These devices make them possible to participate in related campaign and exhibition and propose innovative solutions to resolve conflicts that protect human rights. This solution can develop attitude toward human duties and sustain peace across the globe. This application can nurture conflict resolution skills and develop a sense of living together. Fig. 4 exhibits the procedure of digital activism.

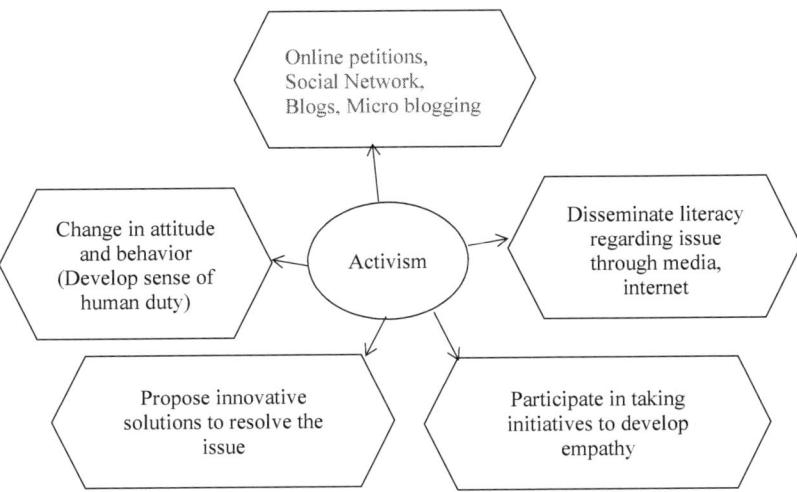

Fig. 4. Procedure of Digital Activism.

f) Integration of content with Web 2.0:

In this step of the intervention program, there is a basic requirement to develop learning objectives for the identified issue related with human rights. This issue should have social relevance and can be practical in nature. Learning outcomes should be applicable in learning environment and capable to transform human attitude in a positive manner. There are various approaches that exist for teaching and learning, but it should be relevant while choosing best approach for teaching social issues. Therefore, it seems relevant to select design thinking approach to spread awareness regarding issue through Web 2.0 tools. Design thinking approach involves empathy, prototype and then produce innovative solution. This integration process of digital activism can be seen in Fig. 5.

g) Digital activism initiatives:

There are various ways to take initiatives for the protection of human rights and protection of global peace, for example:

- Blogs about life survival.
- E-blogs about child labor.
- Micro-blogging about public session and manifest on the decreasing quality of basic human needs.
- Radio talks about shelter.
- Blogs and posters about environmental degradation.
- Vodcast and YouTube related to untouchability.
- Survey and public session about health.
- Legal women rights awareness campaign.

h) Securing digital activism:

In digital activism, it is very much important to make preservice teachers aware of online security. Online security can develop a feeling about communication, and data will be safe from other users.

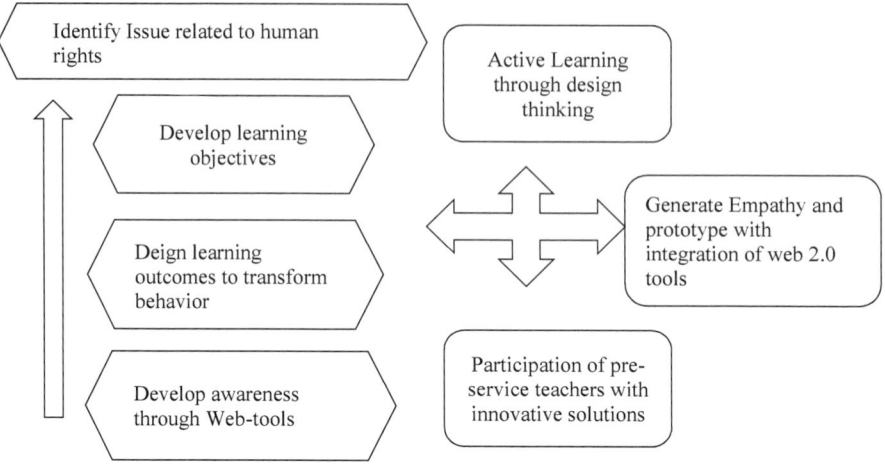

Fig. 5.   Integration of Content With Web 2.0.

There are two main areas to consider when a user set up his or her online security:

- *Protecting identity*
  It is very important that learners have adequate knowledge about protecting identity. They have has a sense that no one can access identity without permission. This includes making sure that no one can use e-mail account, social networking spaces or credit card information and making anonymous online.
- *Protecting your data*
  This feature keeps data safe from others and all other information about the user and group. It also makes secure access of online files. This protects computer files from unauthorized users, keeps computer virus-free and takes backup files and data.

CONCLUSION

One of the benefits of student activism is how it helps a student to look at life globally and not locally. One of the bright spots about social media is how important information is passed with ease among users. It should not be permissible to post flyers on blogs or mobile poles. It may be suggested that they should post on their own page, their friend's page or use a popular hashtag. Today's student activists feel empowered by this. Drama activities and exhibitions about SSI can raise questions, elicit personal reflection and stimulate conversations between students and visitors, transforming both of them into learners and political activists (Stegmann, Weinberg, & Fischer, 2007). These research findings can be implemented to develop digital activism among preservice teachers.

Web 2.0 tools provide students with powerful means to express their voices and visions, fostering interactive and decentralized forms of communication/intervention and a participatory model of democracy. (Nicholson, Levinson, & Parry, 2008)

These activities may develop the feeling that they are not alone fighting this issue and can get attention within seconds of a post. This sense of community emotion drives a more passionate feeling of human rights and produces an attitude toward peace. These movements of change should be viewed as a vehicle of doing good and should be encouraged by the older generations.

From the findings of this study, it can be suggested that attitude toward peace is positively associated with human rights. However, scores of digital activism are not significant among preservice teachers, so it is imperative to enhance the following skills among preservice teachers:

1. Skills related to Web 2.0 should be introduced as a core subject in the curriculum of teacher education as a practical part.
2. Human rights activities and peace activities should be made part of the teacher education program in order to inculcate peace values in the learner.
3. Appropriate pedagogical training such as technological pedagogical knowledge should be made part of pedagogy.
4. Design thinking approach should be adopted to learn digital activism by teacher education institutions.

REFERENCES

Bennett, W. L., & Segerberg, A. (2013). *The logic of connective action: Digital media and the personalization of contentious politics*. Cambridge: Cambridge University Press.

Bimber, B., Flanagin, A., & Stohl, C. (2012). *Collective action in organizations: Interaction and engagement in an era of technological change*. Cambridge: Cambridge University Press.

Copi, I., & Cohen, C. (1994). *Introduction to logic* (9th ed.). New York, NY: Macmillan.

Dickinson, D. (Ed.). (2018). *Transforming the education: Empowering the students of today to create the world of tomorrow*. Australia: Microsoft National Library of Australia.

Donahoe, E. (2016). Digital disruption of human rights. *Just Security*. Retrieved from https://www.hrw.org/news/2016/03/25/digital-disruption-human-rights

Earl, J., & Kimport, K. (2011). Table of Contents. In *Digitally Enabled Social Change: Activism in the Internet Age* (pp. V–Vi). Cambridge, Massachusetts; London, England: The MIT Press. doi: 10.2307/j.ctt5hhcb9.2

Eryilmaz, A. (2008). Investigating the peace attitudes with respect to self-esteem and gender. *Balikesir University Journal of Social Sciences Institute, 12*.

Farmer, P. (2003) *Pathologies of power*. Berkeley, CA: University of California Press.

Galtung, J. (1967). *Theories of peace: A synthetic approach to peace thinking*. Oslo: International Peace Research Institute.

Gray, D., Colucci-Gray, L., & Camino, E. (Eds.). (2009). *Science, society and sustainability: Education and empowerment for an uncertain world*. London: Routledge Research.

Hodson, D. (1998). *Teaching and learning science: Towards a personalized approach*. Buckingham: Open University Press.

Human Rights Council. (2016, June 16). The promotion, protection and enjoyment of human rights on the internet. Retrieved from https://www.article19.org/data/files/Internet_Statement_Adopted.pdf

Martin, B. (2007). Activism, social and political. In G. L. Anderson & K. G. Herr (Eds.), *Encyclopedia of activism and social justice* (pp. 19–27). Thousand Oaks, CA: Sage.

McAdam, D., & Boudet, H. (2012). *Putting Social Movements in Their Place: Explaining Opposition to Energy Projects in the United States, 2000-2005*. New York: Cambridge University Press.

McCarthy, J., & Zald, M. (1977). Resource Mobilization and Social Movements: A Partial Theory. *American Journal of Sociology, 82*(6), 1212–1241. Retrieved from http://www.jstor.org/stable/277793

Narvaez, D., Thoma, S., Getz, I. (2006). Athri Guide, Center for Ethical Education University of Notre Dame. Retrieved from https://www3.nd.edu/~dnarvaez/documents/ATHRIguide061_000.pdf

National Council for Research and Training. (2005). National curriculum framework. Retrieved from http://www.ncert.nic.in/rightside/links/pdf/framework/english/nf2005.pdf

National Curriculum Framework. (2005). Retrieved from https://ncert.nic.in/nc-framework.php?ln=

Nicholson, H., Levinson, R., & Parry, S. (Eds.). (2008). *Creative encounters: New conversations in science, education and the arts*. London: The Wellcome Trust.

Olson, M. (1971) [1965]. *The Logic of Collective Action: Public Goods and the Theory of Groups* (Revised ed.). Cambridge, MA: Harvard University Press.

Piovesan, F. (2004). Social, economic and cultural rights and civil and political rights. *Translation: Regina de Barros Carvalho and Jonathan Morris. São Paulo, 1*, 21–48.

Rabali.ca. (2001). Digital activism. Retrieved from https://rabble.ca/toolkit/rabblepedia/digital-activism

Reardon, B. (2012). Conception of "Peace" and its Implications for a Philosophy of Peace Education. *Peace Studies Journal, 5*(3).

RESET. (2018). Digital and online activism. Retrieved from https://en.reset.org/knowledge/digital-and-online-activism

Schradie, J. (2012). The trend of class, race, and ethnicity in social media inequality. *Information, Communication & Society, 15*(4), 555–571.

Schradie, J. (2018). The digital activism gap: How class and costs shape online collective action. *Social Problems, 65*(1), 51–74. https://doi.org/10.1093/socpro/spx042

Social Impact/Activism. (2009). American chemical Society. Retrieved from https://www.acs.org/content/acs/en/careers/college-to-career/chemistry-careers/social-impact.html

Spier, S. (2017). Tehran, Tunis, Tahrir: Social media and the formation of collective action collective. *Action 2.0*. Retrieved from www.sciencedirect.com/science/article/pii/B9780081005675000037

Stegmann, K., Weinberg, A., & Fischer, F. (2007). Facilitating argumentative knowledge construction with computer-supported collaboration scripts. *Computer-Supported Collaborative Learning, 2*, 421–447.

Stiglitz, J. E. (2003). *Globalization and its discontents*. New York, NY: W. W. Norton & Company.

Stornaiuolo, A., & Thomas, E. E. (2017). Disrupting educational inequalities through youth digital activism. *Review of Research in Education, 41*, 337–357.

Vasi & Suh (2016). Online Activities, Spatial Proximity, and the Diffusion of the Occupy Wall Street Movement in the United States. *Mobilization: An International Quarterly, 21*(2), 139–154.

Weaver, J. B. (2011). Issues in the association of women with peace activism, *Aberystwyth University, E-International Relations*. Retrieved from https://www.e-ir.info/2011/04/17/issues-in-the-association-of-women-with-peace-activism/

Zhang, L. (2014). Linking information through function. *JASIST, 65*(11).

CHAPTER 8

PROMOTING INTERNATIONAL HUMAN RIGHTS VALUES THROUGH REFLECTIVE PRACTICE IN CLINICAL LEGAL EDUCATION: A PERSPECTIVE FROM ENGLAND AND WALES

Irene Antonopoulos and Omar Madhloom

ABSTRACT

The global Clinical Legal Education (CLE) movement transcends borders as law teachers worldwide try to inculcate law students and future legal practitioners with social justice values. One method of achieving this is through developing reflective practitioners. Kolb, finding common ground in the work of Lewin, Dewey, and Piaget, formulated the four stages in the experiential development of concrete experience, reflective observation, abstract conceptualization, and active experiment. Although Kolb's model is used in legal education literature, students may not be provided with the relevant conceptual tools required to engage in reflective practice. This often results in students providing subjective analysis of their work, which fails to fully contribute to their educational experience. One of the reasons for omitting analytical tools is that reflective practice suffers from a lack of conceptual clarity. According to Kinsella, the "concept remains elusive, is open to multiple interpretations, and is applied in a myriad of ways in educational and practice environments".

International Perspectives in Social Justice Programs at the Institutional and Community Levels
Innovations in Higher Education Teaching and Learning, Volume 37, 109–127
Copyright © 2021 by Emerald Publishing Limited
All rights of reproduction in any form reserved
ISSN: 2055-3641/doi:10.1108/S2055-364120210000037008

A further issue hindering reflective practice relates to Donald Schön's critique of the positivist approach adopted by law schools.

This chapter will apply a human rights framework to CLE to develop reflective practitioners. The two main reasons for this are, first, human rights as formulated by the Universal Declaration on Human Rights are universal, inter-related, and indivisible and, second, reflection based on these universal human rights values will benefit cross-jurisdictional societies in assisting vulnerable clients affected by emerging implied and direct human rights challenges.

Keywords: England and Wales; experiential learning; human rights; law students; legal education; legal practitioners; policy-makers; reflection; Universal Declaration of Human Rights

INTRODUCTION

In this chapter, we argue that legal education, in England and Wales, which is almost exclusively a national undertaking, is ill-equipped to train students to become global practitioners. Apart from the study of International Law and European Law, legal education focuses primarily on its jurisdiction-specific law and legal institutions. Law is predominantly taught in a manner which excludes normative[1] concepts such as duty, justice, and virtue. This is mainly due to the case method,[2] which is the dominant approach used in law schools. Christopher Columbus Langdell is credited with introducing the case method in 1870 (Duxbury, 1991, p. 81; Kimball, 2006, p. 192), which replaced the existing approach for the study of law from a book-and-lecture to a system founded on the study of reported appellate opinions using inductive reasoning. However, he did not discover this method (Hall, 1955, p. 99). Keener wrote that:

> The teaching of law by the study of cases is but the application to the study of law of a method that has been almost universally accepted in other departments of education. (Keener, 1894, p. 473)

Thus, a judge reaching a decision in a case where the law was in dispute is under no requirement, according to the case method, to consider what the effects of a rule were, or whether the rule was moral or not. This form of judicial reasoning is demonstrated by the following quote from Lord Justice Ward in the case of *Re A (Children)* [2000] EWCA Civ 254: "This court is a court of law, not of morals, and our task has been to find, and our duty is then to apply the relevant principles of law to the situation before us". This quote highlights that there is no necessary connection between law and morality.

Similarly, in relation to the application of the case method to legal education, the following Criminal Law problem-based question illustrates the absence of normative values in legal education:

> Amanda is late for her Criminal Law lecture. As she is rushing out of her flat, she realises that she cannot find her Criminal Law textbook. She notices that her flat mate's Criminal Law

textbook on the floor and remembers that her flat mate was away visiting their parents. Amanda decides that her flat mate would not mind if Amanda took their textbook. Discuss Amanda's criminal liability, if any.

This type of scenario is found in substantive law modules such as Contract Law, Tort, and Land Law. The above problem-based question requires the application of case law (previous judicial decisions) and statute (in this scenario section 1 of the Theft Act 1968). The case method requires students to apply previous judicial decisions and reasoning (*ratio decidendi*) to the problem-based question. This scenario shows that the case method fails to provide students with the opportunity to engage in concepts of justice and morality. This model of teaching law constitutes a "corporatised or positivist approach" (Walsh, 2008, p. 123).

There is a risk that students, whose legal education is based on the case method, will resort to applying this positivist approach when dealing with similar facts as the above scenario. The absence of notions of justice (e.g., Rawls' justice as fairness) prevents students and legal practitioners from engaging in values to arrive at substantively just outcomes. The term "values" is used to refer to principles, ideals, standards, which act as points of reference in decision-making or the evaluation of beliefs or actions and are closely connected to personal identity (Halstead, 1996, p. 5). Empirical data show that this positivist approach only addresses the needs of a minority of students. Some students enter law school with the desire to effect social change (Schwartz, 1980, p. 437). However, some students might not wish to pursue legal careers. Inculcating such students with notions of social justice can provide them with the necessary intellectual nourishment that they need to find satisfaction in their studies (Thornton, 1991, p. 19).

In relation to the suitability of the jurisdiction-specific case method which is devoid of morality and notions of social justice, it is necessary to provide an overview of the impact of globalization on the legal profession and communities generally. The United Nations (UN) has, for more than 15 years now, recognized that "[g]lobalization has increased contacts between people and their values, ideas and ways of life in unprecedented ways" (UNDP, 2004). Globalization is also affecting the practice of the law (Alemanno & Khader, 2018, p. 14). A brief survey of Big Law[3] reveals that corporate law firms such as Baker McKenzie, Clifford Chance, DLA Piper, and Kirkland & Ellis have offices on most continents. Alemanno and Khader highlight the international dimension of legal practice:

> The transnational judicial dimension of legal practice is today epitomized by the EU, a legal order characterized by a plurality of sources, judicial authorities, and the introduction of new modes of governance that have profoundly shaped the nature and practice of the law. This constellation is further complexified by the numerous agreements concluded by the EU with third countries as well as international organizations (such as the World Trade Organization [WTO]) that entail the operation of dispute settlement mechanisms, or by the existence of legal sources, also operationalized by dedicated judicial bodies, such as the ECHR. (Alemanno & Khader, 2018, p. 16)

Thus, global lawyers are expected to understand the jurisdictional competencies of international courts such as the European Court of Human Rights (ECHR) and the Court of Justice of the EU (CJEU). The implications of globalization of legal services lead us to conclude that law schools can no longer afford to simply teach the law relevant to their own jurisdiction. Any reform to legal education ought to address the increasing global nature of the profession. As a result of these global changes, law schools should "rethink what type of new knowledge and what type of graduates our future societies need" (Gregersen-Hermans, 2012, p. 24).

In addition to globalization of the legal profession, recently there has been an emergence of legal issues which transcend national jurisdictions, such as the COVID-19 pandemic outbreak as well as climate change and the recent migrant crisis (Fulconbridge & Muzio, 2009, pp. 1335-1360). The National Intelligence Council envisages that by 2025:

> [N]ation-states will no longer be the only - and often not the most important - actors on the world stage and the "international system" will have morphed to accommodate the new reality. But the transformation will be incomplete and uneven. Although states will not disappear from the international scene, the relative power of various nonstate actors - including businesses, tribes, religious organizations, and even criminal networks - will grow as these groups influence decisions on a widening range of social, economic, and political issues. (National Intelligence Council, 2009).

It is, therefore, no longer acceptable to teach law in a manner devoid of the complexities of legal practice. In response to changes in the legal profession and the wider world, this chapter will argue that the dominant case method used in law schools, which privileges theory over practice and domestic law over international law, is no longer a viable method for preparing students for a global market. The dominant legal pedagogic method is an inferior mode of academic pursuit (Hutchinson, 1999, p. 302).

Teaching students to identify and address emerging global problems is best understood by viewing globalization to mean world community. In other words, every person and every region are affected by the same threats, and their responses affect us all (Bloch, 2008, p. 113). We argue for the restructuring of the law school curriculum to train students for roles as "policy makers" in society (Lasswell & McDougal, 1943), by inculcating them with universal values. For the purposes of this chapter, the source of these normative values is the Universal Declaration of Human Rights (UDHR).

In addition to exploring the limitations of the case method, this chapter discusses the implications of the proposed new qualification route for aspiring solicitors. We identify the universal values as embodied in UDHR as a normative framework for teaching law students to become global policy-makers. The final section embeds these values, through reflective practice, within a pedagogical movement which transcends national jurisdictions, namely Clinical Legal Education (CLE).

By applying a normative approach to CLE (Madhloom, 2019), students are provided with the opportunity to confront the complex realities of the "law in action" (Pound, 1910). CLE, similar to substantive modules, cannot expose students to all laws. However, CLE may contribute to the denationalization of the law curriculum by teaching students to reflect on what law ought to be through the lens of universal values.

CLE IN ENGLAND AND WALES

The LawWorks Clinics Network recorded 229 active clinics across England and Wales (LawWorks, 2018).[4] A total of 39,937 clients were given legal advice at a clinic, a 14% increase from the previous year (2016). University law clinics account for 41% of the network, and collectively, they dealt with over 19,000 enquiries. The importance of law school clinics in relation to facilitating access to justice is demonstrated by the fact that they account for 51% of all clients receiving general information, signposting, or referral (LawWorks, 2018, p. 15). Chart 1 sets out the breakdown of volunteers that supported clinics between April 2017 and March 2018.

Chart 1 shows that the largest category of volunteers is students, with 4,632[5] participating in clinics (LawWorks, 2018). In the UK, over 70% of law schools now provide clinical or pro bono experience to their students. CLE is clearly now mainstream (Duncan, 2016, p. 390). The popularity of university law clinics among student volunteers could be due to the fact that they provide an opportunity to apply theory to practice and enhance student employability through client interaction, the acquisition of soft skills, and case management (McKeown, 2017). Another significant factor is the general need for pro bono legal support, which may have prompted universities to engage in corporate social responsibility through law clinics (Marson, Wilson, & Van Hoorebeek, 2005). The Sentencing and Punishment of Offenders Act 2012 (LASPO) introduced funding cuts to legal aid and narrowed the scope and financial eligibility criteria. This resulted in fewer people gaining access to legal advice and representation in areas such

VOLUNTEER BREAKDOWN

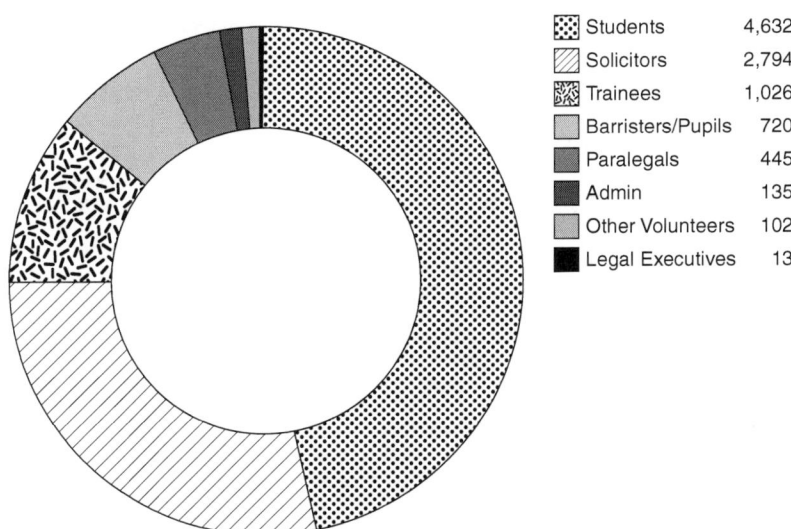

Students	4,632
Solicitors	2,794
Trainees	1,026
Barristers/Pupils	720
Paralegals	445
Admin	135
Other Volunteers	102
Legal Executives	13

Fig. 1. Breakdown of volunteters hat supported clinics between April 2017 and March 2018 (LawWorks, 2018, p.20).

as family, employment, and welfare benefits law. The number of clients provided with early legal advice, including social welfare law cases covering areas such as debt, benefits, employment, and housing, fell from 573,737 in 2012/2013 to 140,091 in 2016/2017 (Law Centres Network, 2018, p. 4). The most significant impact of this legislation has been in the area of access to early legal advice, especially in social welfare law, tribunal procedures and family law (LawWorks, 2019). Access to justice, according to LawWorks, "is eroding" (Ntephe, 2017). The Equality and Human Rights Commission (EHRC), in their recent work on the impact of legal aid reforms, have referred to the "over-representation of people with certain protected characteristics in areas of law excluded by LASPO" (EHRC, 2018). As a result of an increase in the number of people who are unable to afford professional legal representation, more individuals are relying on pro bono legal assistance. It is, therefore, imperative that clinic students acquire reflective tools to act in the best interest of their clients and to critique the law and political institutions.

CLE is a form of experiential learning. Law schools have long recognized the value of experiential learning techniques such as simulations, moots courts, and mock trials. Experiential learning has been a feature of legal education since medieval times. In England and Wales, formal legal education existed in response to the emergence of the legal profession in the twelfth century. Although the Universities of Cambridge and Oxford offered legal instruction, their curriculum was based on the Roman and canon law and omitted any instruction in common law (Brand, 1992, pp. 143-146). It would appear that this model of education was not utilized to provide the legal education necessary for the emerging profession (Rose, 1998, p. 31). Instead, legal education adopted an experiential approach which involved on-the-job learning and by observing experienced lawyers and judges (Rose, 1998, p. 32). Writing in the fifteenth century, Sir John Fortescue refers to this model of experiential learning as "public stadium",[6] which he considered to be intellectually and geographically more well-suited to its educational task than the university (Fortescue, 1997, p. 67). This public stadium appears to be an early form of CLE. However, a version of the case method is the dominant form of legal education in the UK, and until recently CLE rarely featured in law schools. There are two possible reasons for the prominence of the case method. First, judicial decisions/cases are the law, and therefore, lawyers must be able to extract the law from them (Slawson, 2000, pp. 344-346). While this still holds true in the sense that even statutes require judicial interpretation and, thus, become overlaid with judges interpreting them, it is inadequate as the only teaching method. It fails to provide students with an insight into public policies which law seeks to serve. Moreover, the case method does not provide students with the necessary skills to determine which evidence[7] is required to support their client's case, how to act in their client's best interests, or how to resolve ethical dilemmas. Second, according to Langdell, "law is considered as a science", and all the available materials are contained in books dealing with judicial opinions (Langdell, 1871). This positivist approach privileges source knowledge over practice. Legal positivism is the belief that it is both tenable and valuable to offer a purely conceptual theory of law, whereby the analysis of law is kept strictly separate from its evaluation (Bix, 2000, p. 1615). The English jurist John Austin formulated legal positivism in the following manner:

> The existence of law is one thing; its merit or demerit is another. Whether it be or be not is one enquiry; whether it be or be not conformable to an assumed standard, is a different enquiry. A law, which actually exists, is a law, though we happen to dislike it, or though it vary from the text, by which we regulate our approbation and disapprobation. (Austin, 1995, p. 157)

Legal positivists argue that the validity of the law is derived from its source, not its merit (Gardner, 2001, p. 199). It is not difficult to see how such a doctrine can become the dominant approach in law schools, which are rarely concerned with practice and are removed from the individuals affected by legal/political institutions and the operation of the law (Evans et al., 2017, p. 163).

This positivist approach is present in the Solicitors Regulation Authority's (SRA) new route to qualification.[8] In October 2016, the SRA announced a new route for aspiring solicitors: the Solicitors Qualifying Examination (SQE) (SRA, 2016). This overhaul was in response to the Legal Education and Training Review's (LETR) report, which concluded that the current[9] qualification "provides, for the most part, a good standard of education and training" (LETR, 2013, p. ix), but identified a need for clarity in relation to what is expected of a solicitor at the point of admission and an outline of the level ability expected (LETR, 2013).

The SQE will consist of two stages. Stage 1 (Functioning Legal Knowledge) will be assessed through multiple choice questions. This stage will not require candidates to "call case names or cite statutory authority except where specified", and they "will not be assessed on the development of the law" (SRA, 2017). This seems an unusual decision given that England and Wales operate a common law system which combines not only the passing of legislation but also the creation of precedent through case law. Stage 2 (Practical Legal Skills) will assess skills such as client interviewing and practical legal research (SRA, 2020a). All candidates will need to complete at least two-year full-time (or equivalent) qualifying work experience (SRA, 2020b). The significance of the SQE is that a law degree and the "conversion" Postgraduate Diploma in Law (GDL) will no longer mandate a prerequisite to qualifying as a solicitor. Moreover, the requirement to successfully complete the vocational stage (the Legal Practice Course)[10] has been replaced by the SQE.

We identify three pedagogic limitations associated with the SQE. First, the SQE is underpinned by a doctrinal[11] methodology and is focused on the law as "is" rather than what the law "ought" to be (Hume, 1973).[12] This might result in future solicitors lacking analytical and legal reasoning skills leading to a decrease in the value of England and Wales' legal education/qualification, as far as international employers are concerned (Madhloom, 2019). The SQE does not involve the analysis of judicial decisions, gaining an understanding of the development of law and principles, nor is there a requirement to address fundamental questions such as "as should one obey unjust or immoral laws?"

Second, future solicitors' moral and ethical reasoning will be limited to the SRA's Codes of Conduct. The Codes are client centric and as such omit analysis of concepts such as lawyer paternalism, client autonomy, judicial activism, and legal issues outside England and Wales. The third reason, which draws on the first two concerns, relates to the fact that the SQE is not designed to develop reflective practitioners. The absence of legal theory, normative values, and case analysis suggests that future solicitors risk confining themselves to simply solving legal issues without analyzing the implications of the relevant law and policies.

SOURCING UNIVERSAL VALUES

The skills and knowledge to address global problems are dependent on the attitudes and values that underpin a student's future practice. Being a member of a global community of legal practitioners requires a common desire to respond to global issues and concerns. It has been shown that legal education in England and Wales is lacking in a value-based approach due to its positivist approach. This form of legal education ignores the fact that international documents, such as those of the UN and the European Union, which regulate the training and conduct of lawyers, stress the importance of a value-based approach to professional activities (Office of the High Commissioner for Human Rights, 1990, Article 12; Council of Bars and Law Societies of Europe, 2007).

Recognizing these universal values for the global reflective practitioner requires identifying the source of these universal values. In its Preamble, the UDHR states that:

> Recognition of the inherent dignity and of the equal and inalienable rights of all members of the human family is the foundation of freedom, justice and peace in the world. (UN General Assembly, 1948)

This appears to echo the work of Lasswell and McDougal, who in 1943 argued that the fundamental value of democracy is "the realization of human dignity in a commonwealth of mutual deference" (Lasswell & McDougal, 1943, p. 217). In relation to legal education "the proper function" of law schools is to train students for "policy-making" (Lasswell & McDougal, 1943, p. 206). A pedagogic framework focused on training students to become policy-makers not only ensures that legal education caters those who do not wish to enter the legal profession but also provides the foundations for inculcating students with normative values. According to Schwieler and Ekecrantz:

> [N]ormative values are about how things "ought to be". What is just and fair? How should students behave? What is good and bad? What is important? Emotions are associated with teaching, such as feelings of joy, frustration, indifference or satisfaction. (Schwieler & Ekecrantz, 2011, p. 59)

Largely uncontroversial in its provisions, the UDHR creates an accessible introductory framework for students to apply to their studies when reflecting on their own attitudes and practice, thereby introducing normative concepts into the positivist approach associated with the case method. Utilizing the UDHR as a guide for good practice and as a tool for instilling human rights within education is to be found in its preamble:

> Whereas recognition of the inherent dignity and of the equal and inalienable rights of all members of the human family is the foundation of freedom, justice and peace in the world, ... The General Assembly proclaims this Universal Declaration of Human Rights as a common standard of achievement of all peoples and all nations, to the end that every individual and every

organ of society, keeping this Declaration constantly in mind, shall strive by teaching and education to promote respect for these rights and freedoms ... (UN General Assembly, 1948, Article 1)

However, the UDHR is not a legally binding document. It omits legalistic language and instead creates a set of moral rights and duties. Despite the lack of legal sanctions for non-compliance with its provisions, the UDHR makes the protection of rights, free from discrimination on any grounds, a priority for all nation-states (Nickel, 1987). The UDHR illustrates that these rights are recognized irrespective of their implementation or non-implementation in national legal systems, but they still remain a normative priority over national laws (Nickel, 1987, p. 3). The UDHR implies that state and non-state actors have duties to protect human rights by establishing "minimal standards of decent social and government practice" (Nickel, 1987, p. 4).

Cho believes that exposing students to the values contained in the UDHR promotes a sense of global citizenship assisting the protection of human rights as they enter their professional lives as practitioners and policy-makers (Cho, 2019). The emergence of Human Rights Education (HRE) signaled the focus on the "educational strategies" to achieve human rights protection (Bajaj, 2011, p. 482). The United Nations Declaration on HRE and Training explains:

Human rights education and training is essential for the promotion of universal respect for and observance of all human rights and fundamental freedoms for all, in accordance with the principles of the universality, indivisibility and interdependence of human rights. (UN Human Rights Council, 2011)

Recognizing that legal education can rely on one set of values implies an assumption over the universality of its application. Questions over the value of human rights law in a world of inequalities (Moyn, 2018), the effectiveness of human rights treaties (Posner, 2014), as well as the perceived universality of human rights (Langford, 2018, pp. 72-73), have been some of the concerns raised by human rights critics. For example, Andreopoulos and Claude explain, there is a perceived attempt by HRE to make education "value neutral" (Andreopoulos & Claude, 1997). The underlying principle of HRE, which is that of ensuring a culture of human rights, can be misconstrued as an attempt to align personal values with universal human rights values (Ahmed, 2018). However, Caney explains that universality can be divided in "universality of scope" and "universality of justification". The former relates to the application of one value - in this case rights - to all people. The latter relates to the justification of this value (Caney, 2006).

CLINICAL LEGAL EDUCATION

To qualify as solicitors on the SQE route, students will be required to complete at least two years qualifying work experience (SRA, 2020b).This period can be spent in one or more of the following:

- on placement during a law degree;
- working in a law clinic;

- at a voluntary or charitable organization such Citizen Advice or a law center;
- working as a paralegal; and
- on a training contract (SRA, 2020b).

For our purposes, we will focus our analysis on university law clinics. These are a form of experiential learning and can take various forms ranging from providing basic assistance and advice to clients to being incorporated entities that carry out similar activities to law firms but on a pro bono basis. Some clinics provide only online support, while others choose to offer face-to-face support. The student-led client facing model is the common type of university law clinic. Students work on their cases (usually in pairs or small groups) under the supervision of legally qualified academics. In this way, law clinics are similar to university teaching hospitals. Law clinics are a component of CLE. Duncan notes that "[i]n recent decades CLE has moved from a predominantly US phenomenon to one that informs legal education throughout the world" (Duncan, 2016, p. 390). Organizations such as the Global Justice Alliance for Justice Education (GAJE) and the European Network of Clinical Legal Education (ENCLE) have established an international framework devoted to CLE and social justice. In addition to the generic law clinics, the past decade has witnessed the emergence of European Union Law and European Convention of Human Rights specialist clinics. Examples include the University of Bristol's Human Rights Law Clinic (University of Bristol, n.d.), Columbia University's Human Rights Clinic (Columbia Law School, n.d.), the EU Rights Clinic in Brussels, and the Women's Law Clinic of the University of Ibadan (Adelakun-Odewale, 2018). Writing in relation to European legal education, Alemanno and Khader state that:

> [L]egal teaching - historically formulistic, doctrinal, hierarchical, and passive (lecture- and textbook-based) - is coming under increasing pressure to reimagine itself as pragmatic, policy-aware, and action oriented (Alemanno & Khader, 2018, p. 4).

However, despite the emergence of a "global clinic movement" (Bloch, 2010), CLE remains a non-essential component of legal education in England and Wales. This could be due to the fact that CLE ranges from a non-assessed module to a module which is integrated into the curriculum and is underpinned by legal ethics, moral philosophy, and jurisprudence.[13] Unlike other established modules such as Criminal Law, Contract Law, or Tort, there is no universally accepted definition of CLE. According to Grimes, CLE is:

> [A] learning environment where students identify, research and apply knowledge in a setting which replicates, at least in part, the world where it is practiced ... It almost inevitably means that the student takes on some aspect of a case and conducts this as it would ... be conducted in the real world. (Grimes, 1996)

Meghdadi and Nasab state that:

> Clinical legal education is a course of study combining a classroom experience with representation by students of clients with real cases or projects, under the supervision of a full-time faculty member whose background includes extensive law practice ... Clinical legal education implies a method of teaching that, in most instances, has a social justice dimension. (Meghdadi & Nasab, 2011, p. 3015)

A more comprehensive definition which outlines the different conceptions CLE can take is provided by ENCLE:

> Clinical legal education is a legal teaching method based on experiential learning, which fosters the growth of knowledge, personal skills and values as well as promoting social justice at the same time. As a broad term, it encompasses varieties of formal, non-formal and informal educational programs and projects, which use practical-oriented, student-centered, problem-based, interactive learning methods, including, but not limited to, the practical work of students on real cases and social issues supervised by academics and professionals. These educational activities aim to develop professional attitudes and foster the growth of the practical skills of students with regard to the modern understanding of the role of the socially oriented professional in promoting the rule of law, providing access to justice and peaceful conflict resolutions, and solving social problems. (ENCLE, 2019)

The above definitions not only emphasize the experiential and social justice dimensions of CLE but also draw attention to the fact that CLE can accommodate a variety of teaching methods and forms, to which we will add universal human rights values as presented in the UDHR. The above definitions share a commitment to professional attitudes, access to justice, and resolving social issues. These definitions do not define the key terms which underpin their definitions. For example, ENCLE does not define "values", "attitudes", and "access to justice". A further limitation of definitions is the absence of reflective practice. The significance of reflection in CLE is that it turns experience into learning (Murray, 2011, p. 227) and promotes continued professional development.

REFLECTION

It is now universally acknowledged that reflection is a valuable learning tool for students and practitioners to learn effectively from experience (Boud, Keogh, & Walker, 1985, p. 19). However, law students continue to be trained as domestic lawyers, using a predominantly positivist approach which overemphasizes "technical rationality". According to Schön:

> Technical rationality holds that practitioners are instrumental problem solvers. Who select technical means best suited to particular purposes. Rigorous professional practitioners solve well-formed instrumental problems by applying theory and technique derived from systematic preferably scientific knowledge. (Schön, 1987, pp. 3-4)

Because technical rationality is an epistemology of practice rooted in the heritage of positivism, it risks reducing normative questions such as "how ought I act?" to a merely instrumental questions about the means best suited to achieve one's ends (Schön, 1983, p. 33). The gap between legal education and legal realities appears particularly striking in England and Wales, and in Europe generally, where legal scholars and their universities continue with their historical reluctance to engage in self-reflection (Alemanno & Khader, 2018, p. 2). Therefore, there is a dearth of "soul-searching and thinking" beyond legal texts and lectures (Alemanno & Khader, 2018, p. 2).

Similar to CLE, there is not one universally agreed upon definition of reflection. According to Dewey, "reflective thinking" involves two sub-processes:

(a) a state of perplexity, hesitation; and (b) an act of search or investigation directed toward bringing to light further facts which serve to corroborate or to nullify the suggested belief. (Dewey, 1910, p. 9)

Thus, CLE involves learning from experience. But how does CLE promote learning from experience? One method is through reflection. Without engaging in reflection, CLE risks being downgraded to work experience (Murray, 2011, p. 227).

What does it mean to engage in reflection? In the context of professions, including law, the capacity to engage in reflective practice is a means of enhancing the quality of the work and prompting learning and development through a continuous reflexive process (McGill & Brockbank, 2004, p. 94). Donald Schön is credited with developing the notion of reflective practice as a means of enhancing a person's critical and reflective abilities (Cossentino, 2002; Kibble, 1998; Kinsella, 2010; McGill & Brockbank, 2004, p. 94; Mickleborough, 2015). Schön (1982, 1987) was interested in how and when professionals use reflection to build professional knowledge and expertise. Those who teach disciplines tend to create and promote largely propositional knowledge "knowing that" and what Ryle has termed "knowing how" (Ryle, 1949, p. 32). Schön was of the view that such propositional knowledge, on its own, is of limited value for the emerging professional (examples includes lawyers, social workers, nurses, and teachers) (Schön, 1987, p. 22). Limiting student learning to the acquisition of professional knowledge risks limiting their ability to develop into reflective practitioners because propositional knowledge does not take into account the realities and complexities of professional practice (McGill & Brockbank, 2004, p. 94).

Emergent professionals, such as solicitors, enter practice and are effective despite not having had formal training on how to reflect. They develop practical experience and professional knowledge, which includes propositional knowledge acquired to enter their chosen profession (McGill & Brockbank, 2004, p. 94). To engage in their practice areas effectively, an additional element is required. Schön (1987) observes that, traditionally, professional legal education has been based on a model in which practitioners are instrumental problem solvers, rather than problem setters, who select the technical methods best suited to particular purposes:

In the varied topography of professional practice, there is a high hard ground overlooking a swamp. On the high ground, manageable problems lend themselves to solution through the application of research-based theory and technique. In the swampy lowland, messy, confusing problems defy technical solution. (p. 3)

Schön (1983) distinguishes the high ground from the messy indeterminate swampy lowland of professional legal practice. He posited a new epistemology of practice which allows practitioners to enhance their practice while they are engaging in it:

If the model of Technical Rationality is incomplete, in that it fails to account for practical competence in "divergent" situations, so much the worse for the model. Let us search instead for an epistemology of practice implicit in the artistic, intuitive processes which some practitioners do bring to situations of uncertainty, instability, uniqueness, and value conflict. (p. 49)

Schön's (1987) epistemology of professional practice distinguishes between two types of reflection: reflection-in-action (p. 29), while the actions are taking place - and reflection-on-action (Schön, 1987, p. 36), reflecting after the event. Retrospective reflection allows practitioners to reflect on *their* reflection-in-action and indirectly shape their future actions (Schön, 1987, p. 31). There is a risk that without a framework, students are unable to engage in reflection-in-action due to their limited experience in dealing with clients. Similarly, in relation to reflection-on-action, students might engage in a purely descriptive and/or subjective analysis of their experience.

HRE AND REFLECTION IN PRACTICE

Kreiling (1981) contends that "clinical education should reach beyond skills training to provide students with a method from future learning from their experiences" (p. 284). Without a methodology which can be transferred to the world of professional practice, student experience and law school resources may be squandered by merely providing exposure to an unreflective world of practice (Kreiling, 1981, p. 284). Practitioners who continue to learn through the course of their careers should be more competent lawyers (Kreiling, 1981, p. 286).

Dewey (1944) argues that experience "is whatever conditions interact with personal needs, desires, purposes, and capacities to create experience which is had" (p. 44). Therefore, the value of reflection can also extend beyond a student's own personal development. Teaching through human rights means that diversity, equality, and dignity remain at the center of teaching and learning. This ensures that the student as a future legal professional will live by human rights (Cargas, 2019, p. 297). Reflection allows students to assess the compatibility of their attitudes and behavior with human rights values. This allows students to set their own roadmap for their future learning and practice. As Cargas (2019) explains, the results of this process are not uniform for all students. This requires a critique of the methods employed and their improvement in order to help students learn to critique their own attitudes and hopefully generate a will to participate in change (p. 297). Aligned with the UN's recommendation that reflective practice should be combined with experiential learning (UNESCO & UN High Commissioner for Human Rights, 2012), CLE provides the vehicle for reflecting on experience. Johnson and Johnson define experiential learning as:

Generating an action theory from your own experiences and then continually modifying it to improve your effectiveness. The purpose of experiential learning is to affect the learner in three ways: (1) the learner's cognitive structures are altered, (2) the learner's attitudes are modified, and (3) the learner's repertoire of behavioural skills is expanded. These three elements are interconnected and change as a whole, not as separate parts. (Johnson & Johnson, 2003, p. 49)

CLE provides a vehicle for reflecting on experiences between the students and their peers, clients, and (global) community. The experiential approach is illustrated by a model of learning known as the learning cycle (Kolb, 1984). Kolb (1984), building on the theories of Dewey, Lewin, and Piaget (Evans et al., 2017, p. 159), defines learning as "the process whereby knowledge is created through transformation of experience" (Kolb, 1984, p. 38). The Kolb cycle of learning is commonly used to illustrate the differences between concrete experience (doing), reflective observation (thinking), abstract conceptualization (extrapolating), and active experimentation (testing). Although the learner can enter the cycle at any point, Kolb appears to link the cycle to concrete experience, and reflection flows from Kolb's learning model (Evans et al., 2017, p. 159). However, Kolb's cycle does not provide guidance on how a learner should engage in reflection, nor which values should underpin a learner's reflective observation.

Commentators have highlighted the benefit of teaching theory in an integrated manner by arguing that a theoretical underpinning allows students to better understand reflection (Wrenn & Wrenn, 2009). Fook (1991) writes:

> In order to understand the idea of critical reflection and the processes involved, it is helpful to explore the main traditions of thinking from which it arises. I have identified four main ones that are involved: reflective practice, reflexivity, postmodernism/deconstruction and critical social theory. These traditions are not mutually exclusive and, of course, share many commonalities. It is helpful to understand some of the basic tenets of each of these traditions in order to build up a more complex understanding of the theoretical underpinnings of critical reflection. (p. 442)

Having discussed the global reach of CLE and the importance of developing practitioners who are able to apply normative values such as those espoused by the UDHR, we will now address how the CLE can incorporate HRE. An understanding of the HRE is particularly important and is defined as:

> [A] movement to promote awareness about the rights accorded by the Universal Declaration of Human Rights and related human rights conventions… intended to be one that skills, knowledge, and motivation to individuals to transform their own lives and realities so that they are more consistent with human rights norms and values. (Tibbits & Fernekes, 2010, pp. 87, 93)

However, human rights is offered as an optional module. While other compulsory modules offer an introduction to human rights, such as Land Law, there is little exposure to the normative aspect of human rights unless the student selects a specialized human rights module. This chapter suggests that the CLE curriculum should include an introduction to the UDHR. This introduction will cover the background of the UDHR, its provisions, and its significance to democracy and Human Rights Law, considering the elements of dignity, equality, and social justice. The introduction should inspire law students in identifying the values on which they can rely when reflecting on their interactions with clients.

Embedding human rights within education has been supported by the UN, which suggested the adopting a human-rights-consistent teaching style in order for students to "learn tolerance and respect for the dignity of others and the means and methods of ensuring that respect in all societies" (UN General Assembly, 2005). In addition, the Universal Declaration on HRE and Training pointed to the UDHR as the source of these human rights values. The UN General Assembly clarified that the aim of HRE is ensuring the respect of dignity in all societies (UN General Assembly, 2005), bringing at the center of HRE, dignity.[14] The Guidelines for National Plans of Action for HRE, suggested that:

> Human rights are promoted through three dimensions of education campaigns:
>
> (a) knowledge: provision of information about human rights and mechanisms for their protection;
>
> (b) values, beliefs and attitudes: promotion of a human rights culture through the development of values, beliefs and attitudes which uphold human rights;
>
> (c) action: encouragement to take action to defend human rights to prevent human rights abuses. (UN General Assembly, 1997, 13(c))

The importance of (a) and (b), notwithstanding, CLE can act as a vehicle for influencing future "policy-makers' "values, beliefs and attitudes" through a combination of experiential learning and reflection (UN Human Rights Council, 2010, 27(b)(iii)), "promoting the development of the individual - in this case, the future policy-maker - as a responsible member of a free, peaceful, pluralist and inclusive society" (UN Human Rights Council, 2011, Article 4).

CONCLUSION

This chapter argued that CLE should be the vehicle for embedding normative values into legal education through reflective practice. These normative values should derive from a universally recognized moral guide, such as the UDHR, which transcends geographical and cultural boundaries. Knowledge of human rights leads to knowledge for human rights: supporting the development of the students' attitudes and values aims at responding to global problems as global policy-makers in government, law firms, non-governmental organizations (NGOs), or international organizations. However, it is not suggested that this normative approach becomes the sole method for developing global policy-makers; rather, these universal values are used as a point of reference for addressing jurisdiction-specific and global issues.

In relation to implementing our proposed normative framework for reflective practice, students advising law clinic clients would not only address the individual client's legal needs using domestic law but also would reflect on their interaction with the client and the role of the State in terms of limiting or removing the right to a public-funded lawyer. Students should treat the client with respect and do so in an unbiased manner, which should be influenced by the principles found in Articles 1 and 2 (dignity and equality, respectively). This provides a framework for students to address any biases they might have toward their clients. Students might conclude that LASPO is contrary to Article 7 (equal protection of the law), Article 8 (a right to a fair remedy), and Article 10 (right to a fair hearing) of the UDHR.

In real-world practice, problems do not simply present themselves to policy-makers. Instead, they must be constructed from the materials of problematic situations which are puzzling, troubling, and uncertain (Schön, 1983, pp. 39-40). By applying our proposed framework of embedding UDHR into CLE, future practitioners are trained to become policy-makers by not only solving legal problems based on domestic law but also identifying global threats to human rights.

NOTES

1. By "normative", we mean what the law ought to be as opposed to what it is.
2. A system of instruction focused upon the analysis of court opinions.
3. An industry term which describes global law firms that employ more than 1,000 lawyers and have offices in different continents.
4. Law Works is the operating name for the Solicitors Pro Bono Group, a charity working across England and Wales.
5. Almost 10,000 individuals volunteered across the Law Works Clinics Network, a 33% increase in the number of volunteers reported in previous year (LawWorks, 2018a).
6. Meaning "a place of study".
7. In England and Wales, Law of Evidence, whether civil or criminal, is not a compulsory module/unit.
8. The regulatory body for solicitors in England and Wales.
9. The current position is that the SRA and the BSB jointly set out the requirements for the qualifying law degree, and the SRA approves and monitors LPC providers.
10. The Legal Practice Course is a postgraduate degree and is the final vocational stage for becoming a solicitor in England and Wales.
11. Doctrinal or "black letter" methodology refers to a way of conducting research which is focused traditional sources of law such as case law and statutes. It is not concerned with an interdisciplinary approach.
12. The difference between "is" and "ought" was highlighted by David Hume in his Treatise on Human Nature: "In every system of morality that I have hitherto met with, I have always remarked that the author proceeds for some time in the ordinary way of reasoning, and establishes the being of a God, or makes observations concerning human affairs; when of a sudden I am surprised to find that instead of the usual copulations of propositions, is, and is not, I meet with no proposition that is not connected with an ought, or an ought not. This change is imperceptible; but is, however, of the last consequence .... A reason should be given for what seems altogether inconceivable, how this new relation can be a deduction from others, which are entirely different from it".
13. At the University of Bristol, the CLE module includes lectures on normative ethics, moral reasoning, and Rawls' theory of justice.
14. Protecting human rights as a means to protecting dignity entails moral considerations (Lukow, 2018). Associating human dignity with the action of ensuring human rights protection entails a question of universality of justification (Caney, 2006). The attempt to define human dignity could potentially find obstacles within the cultural interpretations of dignity, and such an exercise should remain independent from the overall adoption of the principles of the UDHR (Lukow, 2018).

REFERENCES

Adelakun-Odewale, O. S. (2018). Role of clinical legal education in social justice in Nigeria. *Asian Journal of Legal Education, 5*(1), 88–98.

Ahmed, K. (2018). Bridging the 'Values Gap': Human rights education, ideology and the global-local nexus. In M. Zembylas & A. Keet (Eds.), *Critical human rights, citizenship, and democracy education: Entanglements and regenerations.* London: Bloomsbury Academic.

Alemanno, A., & Khader, L. (2018). *Reinventing legal education: How clinical education is reforming the teaching and practice of law in Europe.* Cambridge: Cambridge University Press.

Andreopoulos, G. J., Claude, R. P., & Koenig, S. (1997). *Human rights education for the twenty-first century.* University of Pennsylvania Press.

Austin, J. (1995). *The province of jurisprudence determined.* Cambridge: Cambridge University Press.

Bajaj, M. (2011). Human rights education: Ideology, location and approaches. *Human Rights Quarterly, 33*, 481–508.

Bix, B. (2000). On the dividing line between natural law theory and legal positivism. *Notre Dame Law Review, 75*, 1613–1624.

Bloch, F. S. (2008). Access to justice and the global clinical movement. *Washington University Journal of Law and Policy, 28*, 111–139.

Bloch, F. S. (2010). *The global clinical movement: Educating lawyers for social justice.* New York, NY: Oxford University Press.

Boud, D., Keogh, R., & Walker, D. (1985). *Reflection: Turning experience into learning.* Falmer: Routledge.

Caney, S. (2006). *Justice beyond borders: A global political theory.* Oxford: Oxford University Press.

Cargas, S. (2019). Fortifying the future of human rights education. *Journal of Human Rights, 18*(3), 293–307.

Cho, H.-J. (2019). Rethinking democracy and human rights education on the seventeenth anniversary of the Universal Declaration of Human Rights. *Asia Pacific Education Review, 20*(2), 171–180.

Columbia Law School. (n.d.). Experiential learning. Retrieved from https://www.law.columbia.edu/clinics/human-rights-clinic

Cossentino, J. (2002). Importing artistry: Further lessons from the design studio. *Reflective Practice, 3*(1), 39–52.

Council of Bars and Law Societies of Europe (CCBE). (2007). *CCBE Recommendation on Training Outcomes for European Lawyers.* Europe: CCBE.

Dewey, J. (1910). *How we think.* New York, NY: D. C. Heath & Co.

Dewey, J. (1944). *Democracy and education.* New York, NY: Free Press.

Duncan, N. (2016). Book review: Jeff Giddings, promoting justice through clinical legal education. *The Law Teacher, 50*, 390–393.

Duxbury, N. (1991). The birth of legal realism and the myth of Justice Holmes. *Anglo-American Law Review, 20*, 81–100.

Equality and Human Rights Commission. (2018). *Response of the equality and human rights commission to the post-implementation review of part 2 of the legal aid, sentencing and punishment of offenders act 2012.* London: EHRC.

European Network of Clinical Legal Education (ENCLE). (2019). *Report on ENCLE roundtable on standards for clinical legal education in Europe.* Valencia: ENCLE.

Evans, A., Cody, A., Copeland, A., Giddins, J., Joy, P., Noone, M. A., & Rice, S. (2017). Reflective practice: The essence of clinical legal education. In A. Evans, A. Cody, A. Copeland, J. Giddins, P. Joy, M. A. Noone, & S. Rice (Eds.), *Australian clinical legal education: Designing and operating a best practice clinical program in an Australian law school* (pp. 153–178). Acton: Australian National University Press.

Fook, J. (1991). Reflective practice an clinical reflection. In J. Lishman (Ed.), *Handbook for practice learning in social work and social care* (pp. 440–454). London: Jessica Kingsley Publishers.

Fortescue, J. (1997). Sir John Fortescue: On the laws and governance of England. In S. Lockood (Ed.), *Cambridge texts in the history of political thought* (pp. 66–68). Cambridge: Cambridge University Press.

Fulconbridge, J., & Muzio, D. (2009). Legal education, globalization, and cultures of professional practice. *Goergetown Journal of Legal Ethics, 21*, 1335.

Gardner, J. (2001). Legal positivism: 5½ myths. *American Journal of Jurisprudence, 46*(1), 199–227.

Gregersen-Hermans, J. (2012). To ask or not to ask: That is the question. In J. Beelen & H. De Wit (Eds.), *Internationalisation revisited: New dimensions in the internationalisation of higher education* (pp. 23–36). Amsterdam: Centre for Applied Research on Economics and Management.

Grimes, R. (1996). The theory and practice of clinical legal education. In J. Webb & C. Maugham (Eds.), *Teaching lawyers' skills.* (p. 138) London: Butterworths.

Hall, J. (1955). *Teaching law by case method and lecture.* Articles by Maurier Faculty Paper, pp. 99–106.

Halstead, J. M. (1996). Values and values education in schools. In J. M. Taylor (Ed.), *Values in education and education in values.* London: Farmer Press.

Hume, D. (1973). *Treatise on human nature book III, part I: 'Of Virture and Vice in General'.* Oxford: Oxford University Press.

Hutchinson, A. C. (1999). Beyond black-letterism: Ethics and law and legal education. *Law Teacher*, *33*(3), 301–309.

Johnson, D. W., & Johnson, F. P. (2003). *Joining together: Group theory and group skills.* Boston, MA: Allyn & Bacon.

Keener, W. A. (1894). Inductive method in legal education. *Proceedings of the American Bar Association*, *17*, 473–490.

Kibble, N. (1998). Reflection and supervision in clinical legal education: Do work placements have a role in undergraduate legal education? *International Journal of the Legal Profession*, *5*(1), 83–116.

Kimball, B. A. (2006). The proliferation of case method teaching in american law schools: Mr Langdell's Emblematic "Abomination", 1890–1915. *History of Education Quarterly*, *46*, 192–247.

Kinsella, E. A. (2010). The art of reflective practice in health and social care: Reflections on the legacy of Donald Schön. *Reflective Practice*, *11*(4), 565–575.

Kolb, D. (1984). *Experiential learning.* London: Prentice Hall.

Kreiling, K. R. (1981). Clinical education and lawyer competency: The process of learning to learn from experience through properly structured clinical supervision. *Maryland Law Review*, *40*(2), 284–337.

Langdell, C. C. (1871). *A selection of cases on the law of contracts: Prepared for use as a text-book in Harvard Law School.* Boston, MA: Little, Brown & Co.

Langford, M. (2018). Critiques of human rights. *Annual Review of Law and Social Science*, *14*, 69–89.

Lasswell, H. D., & McDougal, M. S. (1943). Legal education and public policy: Professional training in the public interest. *Yale Law Journal*, *52*(2), 203–295.

Law Centres Network. (2018). *LASPO act 2012 post-implementation review: Submission from the Law Centres Network.* London: Law Centres Network.

LawWorks. (2018). *LawWorks clinics network report: April 2017–March 2018.* LawWorks.

LawWorks. (2019). Retrieved from https://www.lawworks.org.uk/about-us/who-we-are

Legal Education and Training Review (LETR). (2013). *Setting standards: The future of legal services education and training regulation in England and Wales.* LETR.

Łuków, P. (2018). A difficult legacy: human dignity as the founding value of human rights. *Human Rights Review*, *19*(3), 313-329.

Madhloom, O. (2019). A normative approach to developing refelctive legal practitioners: Kant and clinical legal education. *The Law Teacher*, *53*(4), 416–430.

Marson, J., Wilson, A., & Van Hoorebeek, M. (2005). The necessity of clinical legal education in university law schools: A UK perspective. *International Journal of Clinical Legal Education*, *7*, 29–43.

McGill, I., & Brockbank, A. (2004). *The action learning handbook: Powerful techniques for education, professional development and training.* Abingdon: Routledge.

McKeown, P. (2017). Pro bono: What's in it for law students? The students' perspective. *International Journal of Clinical Legal Education*, *24*(2), 43–80.

Meghdadi, M. M., & Nasab, A. E. (2011). The role of legal clinics in human rights education: Mofid University legal clinic experience. *Procedia – Social and Behavioral Science*, *15*, 3014–3017.

Mickleborough, T. (2015). Intuition in medical practice: A reflection on Donald Schön's reflective practitioner. *Medical Teacher*, *37*(10), 889–891.

Moyn, S. (2018). *Not enough: Human rights in an unequal world.* Cambridge: The Belknap Press of Harvard University Press.

Murray, V. (2011). Reflection. In K. Kerrigan & V. Murray (Eds.), *A student guide to clinical legal education and pro bono* (pp. 226–249). Basingstoke: Palgrave Macmillan.

National Intelligence Council. (2009). *Global trends 2025: A transformed world.* Washington, DC: DIANE Publishing.

Nickel, J. W. (1987). *Making sense of human rights: Philosophical reflections of the universal declaration of human rights.* London: University of California Press.

Ntephe, A. (2017). Pro bono in practice: 'The LawWorks Secondary Specialisation Programme'. Retrieved from https://www.lawworks.org.uk/about-us/news/pro-bono-practice-lawworks-secondary-specialisation-programme

Office of the High Commissioner for Human Rights (OHCHR). (1990). *Basic principles on the role of lawyers.* Geneva: OHCHR.

Posner, E. A. (2014). *The twilight of human rights law.* New York, NY: Oxford University Press.

Pound, R. (1910). Law in books and law in action. *American Law Review, 44*(1), 12–36.

Rose, J. (1998). The legal profession in Medieval England: A history of regulation. *Syracuse Law Review, 48*(1), 1–137.

Ryle, G. (1949). *The concept of mind.* London: Hutchinson.

Schön, D. A. (1983). *The reflective practitioner: How professionals think in action.* New York, NY: Basic Books.

Schön, D. A. (1987). *Educating the reflective practitioner: Toward a new design for teaching and learning in the professions.* New York, NY: Jossey-Bass.

Schwartz, A. J. (1980). Law, lawyers and law school: Perspectives from the first-year class. *Journal of Legal Education, 30,* 437.

Schwieler, E., & Ekecrantz, S. (2011). Normative values in teachers' conceptions of teaching and learning in higher education: A belief system approach. *International Journal for Academic Development, 16,* 59–70.

Slawson, D. W. (2000). Changing how we teach: A critique of the case method. *Southern California Law Review, 74,* 343–346.

Solicitors Regulation Authority (SRA). (2016). *A new route to qualification: The solicitors qualifying examination.* London: SRA.

Solicitors Regulation Authority (SRA). (2017). Assessment specification for SQE stage 1 pilot. Retrieved from https://www.sra.org.uk/sra/policy/sqe/pilot/sqe-assessment-specification

Solicitors Regulation Authority (SRA). (2020a). Solicitors Qualifying Examination (SQE). Retrieved from https://www.sra.org.uk/students/sqe/

Solicitors Regulation Authority (SRA). (2020b). SQE Update – February 2020. Retrieved from https://www.sra.org.uk/sra/news/sqe-update/february-2020/

Thornton, M. (1991). Portia lost in the groves of academe wondering what to do about legal education. *Law in Context, 9,* 9.

Tibbits, F., & Fernekes, W. R. (2010). Human rights education. In S. Totten & J. Pedersen (Eds.), *Teaching and studying social issues: Major programs and approaches.* Charlotte, NC: Information Age Publishing.

UN General Assembly. (1948). *Universal declaration of human rights.* Paris: UN General Assembly.

UN General Assembly. (1997, October 20). *Report of the Secretary-General on the United Nations Decade for Human Rights Education (1995–2004) and public information activities in the field of human rights. A/52/469/Add.1.* Paris: UN General Assembly.

UN General Assembly. (2005, July 14). *World programme for human rights education: Resolution adopted by the General Assembly. A/RES/59/113 B.* Paris: UN General Assembly.

UN Human Rights Council. (2010, July 27). *Draft plan of action for the second phase (2010–2014) of the World programme for human rights education – Note by the United Nations High Commissioner for Human Rights. A/HRC/15/28.* Geneva: UN Human Rights Council.

UN Human Rights Council. (2011, April 8). *United Nations Declaration on Human Rights Education and Training: Resolution adopted by the Human Rights Council. A/HRC/RES/16/1.* Geneva: UN Human Rights Council.

UNDP. (2004). *Human development report 2004: Cultural liberty in today's diverse world.* New York, NY: UNDP.

UNESCO & UN High Commissioner for Human Rights. (2012). *World programme for human rights education, second phase: Plan of action.* Geneva: UNESCO.

University of Bristol. (n.d.). Human rights law clinic. Retrieved from http://www.bristol.ac.uk/law/careers-and-employability/human-rights-law-clinic/

Walsh, T. (2008). Putting justice back into legal education. *Legal Education Review, 17,* 119–142.

Wrenn, J., & Wrenn, B. (2009). Enhancing learning by integrating theory in practice. *International Journal of Teaching and Learning in Higher Education, 21*(2), 258–265.

CHAPTER 9

BRIDGING THE GAP: IMPLEMENTING EQUITY-MINDED ACADEMIC AND MENTORING SUPPORT SERVICES FOR FOSTER YOUTH WITHIN UNIVERSITY WRITING PROGRAMS

Paul Beehler and Rory Moore

ABSTRACT

The authors use their university and its writing program as a case study to interrogate established wraparound support systems for foster youth and the role that additional, volunteer faculty – led support services can play in retention and graduation rates. This chapter first provides research on college-going foster youth in the United States. Then, it considers the foster youth population and established support programs at the University of California, Riverside. Next, this chapter reviews the benefits of faculty – student mentoring and tutoring, specifically in composition studies, and how those benefits can contribute to a successful college-going experience. The chapter then shifts to offering a model for those interested in establishing a similar program. Using business, communication, composition, education, and psychosocial theory to ground the discussion, the authors provide a detailed account of the proposal, implementation, and ongoing programmatic administration processes, including the rationale undergirding decision-making. Ultimately, they show how equitable supplemental academic support led by composition faculty can

International Perspectives in Social Justice Programs at the Institutional and Community Levels
Innovations in Higher Education Teaching and Learning, Volume 37, 129–149
Copyright © 2021 by Emerald Publishing Limited
ISSN: 2055-3641/doi:10.1108/S2055-364120210000037009

bridge the gap between existing foster youth services and outstanding needs, an innovative approach that relies on the natural mentoring relationships which organically evolve from faculty–student interaction.

Keywords: Resource equity; social justice; equity programming; foster youth; supplemental support programs; academic support programs; at-risk student populations; writing programs

A BRIEF INTRODUCTION

After two years as a Higher Education Opportunity Program (HEOP) administrator and adjunct associate professor at Long Island University in Brooklyn, New York, in 2017, Rory Moore returned to the University of California, Riverside (UCR) as a lecturer in the University Writing Program (UWP). She brought back with her a revised and expanded understanding of diversity, and by working almost exclusively with economically and educationally disadvantaged students legally recognized as requiring wraparound support for college success, her pedagogical and relational approaches shifted. Alongside the expectations that she has always had for students – that they commit themselves to the work at hand and produce results that align with university-level standards – she also expanded her own role as instructor. To help students achieve their academic goals and make progress in their skill acquisition, Moore needed to guide students in ways that required her to become more than just their instructor. By posting online and speaking regularly with students about various campus programs, she became a resource. Offering replacements of low-stake assignment scores should her students attend university-hosted grammar workshops and tutorials, Moore identified effective ways to help students improve essential skills needed for success in academia. Such a sharpening of skill sets also assisted in students' professional pursuits. Relying on disclosing her own vulnerability by sharing some academic and personal struggles, she formed authentic, reciprocal connections that welcomed students who, in turn, shared their vulnerabilities with her. This vulnerability allowed her insight into their thinking processes and (sometimes) limiting mindsets, resulting in refined and thoughtful responses to student needs, academic, or otherwise. Gently addressing behavior or disclosures she interpreted as negatively impacting students' potential for academic success, in her class if not also at the university, Moore became an integral part of their whole-student support system, a role she had valued in HEOP, especially when a student was also a current or former foster youth. In sum, Moore became an informal mentor to any student of hers who sought that relationship type from her.

Early in her return to UCR, and with this expanded vision of what she thought she ought to be for students, Moore identified a problem that needed a solution. While in office hours reviewing a current assignment, a student in a class Moore was teaching disclosed their foster youth status and revealed some of the specific challenges the foster youth population grappled with both on campus and off.

After the student's unsuccessful attempt to pass the course (a result of juggling school with overnight-shift Amazon warehouse hours and a second, on-campus job), Moore began to research which types of support at UCR were available for some of America's – and the university's – most at-risk populations. Concluding that additional action was needed, Moore turned to Paul Beehler, this chapter's co-author, to develop a supplemental academic support program within the UWP to address a critical gap in foster youth student support at UCR: compositional consultation and mentoring by specially trained, volunteer faculty. Together, and with the support of UCR's Office of Foster Youth Support Services (OFYSS), in September 2018, they launched what would become the all-volunteer Writing and Foster Youth Alliance (WAFYA), the subject of this chapter.

CHAPTER OVERVIEW

It is no surprise for those working in higher education in the United States and elsewhere that students benefit from mentoring relationships. The word *mentor* has been difficult to parse because of the looseness of its signification (Allen & Eby, 2011). However, in their cross-discipline, meticulous review of the literature on mentoring, Tammy Allen and Lillian Eby (2011), psychology professors at the University of South Florida and the University of Georgia, respectively, have identified common factors present in mentorship: establishing a "unique relationship between individuals" (Allen & Eby, 2011, p. 33); entering into "a learning partnership" (Allen & Eby, 2011, p. 33); undertaking a "process, defined by the types of support agreed upon by the mentor and the protege [student]" (Allen & Eby, 2011, p. 33); marking the "relationship as reciprocal, yet asymmetrical" (Allen & Eby, 2011, p. 33), with the protege achieving the majority result; and recognizing the "dynamic" nature of mentoring, which changes over time, and with outcomes improving the longer the relationship exists (Allen & Eby, 2011, p. 33). When students connect with faculty, either through a formal mentor-protege process or through an informal, self-selected undertaking, studies show that academic gains (grade point average (GPA), persistence, rate of credit completion) and retention rates generally are greater than those achieved by non-mentored student groups (Campbell & Campbell, 1997; Crisp & Cruz, 2009). Foster youth represent a small, but high-risk, community that profits from mentoring relationships in higher education. This understanding served as the guiding principle for the founding of WAFYA within the UWP at UCR, a comprehensive R1 research university and one of the 10 campuses of the renowned University of California (UC) system.

WAFYA's social justice- and equity-minded mission seamlessly aligns itself with other public and private foster youth support programs across the US education system, including at UCR. Equity-minded, WAFYA provides professional composition assistance and mentorship to all foster youth on campus, current and former, in order to improve retention and increase their chances of degree completion.

BACKGROUND

External and systemic factors face college-attending foster youth in the United States: lack of familial support; placement in lower-performing K-12 schools; high levels of school turnover; higher rates of trauma and abuse, resulting in mental health issues and cognitive and other disabilities; and lack of "soft skills" knowledge and advocacy training (Geiger & Beltran, 2017; Geiger, Piel, Day, & Schelbe, 2018; Wolanin, 2005). These circumstances directly contribute to the plight of foster youth and their categorization as a higher-risk population than first-generation or low-income students outside of foster care (Gross, 2019). Foster care students are less likely to graduate, too (Day, Dworsky, & Feng, 2013; Day, Dworsky, Fogarty, & Damashek, 2011). Approximately 440,000 foster youth in care each year (Children's Bureau, 2018), and around 65,000 age 16 or older enter the college-going years (Children's Bureau, 2018). Few end up doing so, though, especially when compared with the general population. Despite 70% of foster youth reporting a desire to attend postsecondary schools, only 10% matriculate (Geiger & Beltran, 2017); 3–5% of all foster youth persist to graduate with a bachelor's degree (Geiger & Beltran, 2017). Comparatively, 81% of first-generation, low-income students expected to matriculate at a postsecondary school and did so, at a rate of 24% (Redford, 2017); 90% of continuing-generation students (those with at least one parent with a bachelor's degree or higher) anticipated entering college and achieved this goal at a rate of 42% (Redford, 2017). Twenty-three percent of first-generation students completed a bachelor's degree or higher – 55% of continuing-generation students did (Redford, 2017). The 18-20- and 50-52-point gaps between foster youth and first-generation, low-income, and continuing-generation students' bachelor's degree graduation rates, respectively, are astounding. Intentional, focused attention on this special student population is necessary from the perspective of equity to address the disparity between groups in college matriculation and graduation. From a position of social justice, foster youth deserve the opportunity to earn a college degree, a degree which, in the United States, correlates with increased potential for upward social mobility (Greenstone, Looney, Patashnik, & Yu, 2013; National Center for Education Statistics (NCES), 2019).

Affirming their heightened risks and support needs, in 2008, the US Congress made certain that foster youth had access to federally funded TRIO programs by writing their eligibility for programming into the House of Representatives (HR) bill 4137, the Higher Education Opportunity Act, which was a reauthorization of an earlier law, the Higher Education Act. TRIO (named for three programs that make up the designation) provides pre-college, college, and adult-entry support (advising, counseling, tutoring, mentoring, financial literacy, grants and scholarships, and more) to first-generation, low-income, and disabled individuals (G. Miller, 2008). Thirty-one states, too, promote foster youth-specific resources by offering state tuition waivers and/or state-funded support programs (Michigan, n.d.). Campus-based foster youth support programs at four-year colleges and universities exist at approximately 84 sites across the United States (Michigan, n.d.).

UCR hosts the federally funded TRIO Student Support Services (SSS) program, also known as TRIO Scholars. At the date of publication, TRIO Scholars does not count any foster youth among its approximately 140 students it serves annually (N. Borgonia, personal communication, November 18, 2019); in the current grant cycle (academic years 2015–2016 through 2019–2020), two foster youth have been program participants; one has graduated and the other is still pursuing their degree (N. Borgonia, personal communication, November 18, 2019). Academic advising, financial aid navigation, peer mentoring/tutoring, and excursions that promote learning as well as community are some of the benefits for TRIO Scholars (N. Borgonia, personal communication, October 14, 2019). While UCR does not have a state-funded Educational Opportunity Program (EOP) (Educational Opportunity Program (EOP)|UC Admissions, n.d.), foster youth who meet specific criteria do benefit from federal Pell, state Chafee, and campus grants to offset the costs of attending.

UCR also has a dedicated space for OFYSS, the primary supplemental support center for the school's foster youth. OFYSS matches students to resources and offers a facilitation of the process in-house, too. Workshops and community-building events are available to all of the campus's approximately 150 foster youth (T. Yates, personal communication, May 28, 2019), academic and skills development seminars, with regular guest speakers from the campus's career and academic resource centers, among others. For the approximately 80 foster youth in care after age 13, OFYSS also pays for textbooks and maintains an exclusive food and toiletries pantry for emergency needs (T. Yates, personal communication, May 28, 2019). Also housed in OFYSS is the privately funded Guardian Scholars program, which provides intensive wraparound support and merit-based scholarship funds to 30 of the most at-risk campus foster youth, typically those who have aged out of foster care and have no familial base of support (T. Yates, personal communication, May 28, 2019). In addition to OFYSS services, students in Guardian Scholars can receive year-round housing; access to a storage locker off campus stocked with furniture and other domestic supplies (K. L. Whitman, personal communication, September 3, 2019); waivers to shop at participating community-based second-hand stores for clothing and other goods; and whole-person care (K. L. Whitman, personal communication, September 3, 2019). The program also hosts Thanksgiving, winter holiday, graduation, and back-to-school events each year (T. Yates, personal communication, May 28, 2019).

In many ways, campus support for foster youth at UCR is robust and certainly contributes to students overcoming some of the barriers foster youth face once matriculated. Across the United States, data confirm that foster youth entering college at a four-year institution have higher completion rates than those that begin at two-year colleges (Okpych & Courtney, 2018). Okpych and Courtney (2018) explain that when a student identifies with the mission and population of a university campus, and when an institution dedicates resources to academic and support services as well as instruction, graduation rates correspondingly rise. UCR's mission encompasses an explicit desire to educate and graduate a diverse student body through a commitment to diversity, equity, and inclusion (About the University of California Riverside, n.d.; Diversity, Equity & Inclusion, n.d.). Multiple measures indicate its success in doing so (Ranks and Facts|University of California, Riverside, n.d.). Consistent with these metrics, graduation rates for UCR's foster youth are higher than the national average of 3–4% (Geiger & Beltran, 2017). In the group for which data are available, UCR's Guardian Scholars, their five-year 75% degree completion average (T. Yates, personal communication, May 28, 2019) is slightly higher than the campus's already-impressive 73% five-year rate (33 out of 44 Guardian Scholars (T. Yates, personal communication, May 28, 2019) versus 13,578 out of 18,506 non-Guardian Scholars (Institutional Research, n.d.)). The overall national graduation rate at public universities for all students in a five-year period is 49% (The Integrated Postsecondary Education Data System, n.d.).

As important as private, public, and institutional support is, so, too, is the high level of resilience that foster youth bring to higher education (Hines, Merdinger, & Wyatt, 2005), exhibiting in their pursuit of a degree what psychologists describe as a capacity to adapt positively to threats to their "system" (Masten & Barnes, 2018), be it a risk to their ability to function, survive, or develop in the future. Rather than interpreting the extraordinary hardships foster youth experience as a challenge to degree completion, educators and administrators instead can look to the high levels of resilience that foster youth have developed as a powerful means to navigate new environments like college and, consequently, increase the likelihood of successfully navigating those environments. This subset of the student population has the ability to adapt and continue to develop their psychological fortitude while coping with extensive periods of stress and hardship (Masten & Barnes, 2018), a skill uncommon in the general foster youth population (Hines et al., 2005), but clearly evident in the college-going foster youth that earn bachelor's degrees, including here on the UCR campus.

EQUITABLE OPPORTUNITY: WAFYA

With the strong track record of foster youth retention and graduation at UCR, establishing an academic support and mentoring program for foster youth within a writing program office may seem like an unnecessary addition to the cadre of already-available on-campus programming. No doubt, foster students can do well at UCR, especially if they qualify for one of the 30 comprehensive support slots within Guardian Scholars. However, what the numbers fail to illuminate are how many foster youth are not accounted for and/or supported, nor, when accounted for and/or supported, how prepared they are for competitive grant, scholarship, graduate school, and employment opportunities.

Since 2008, the wraparound support program Guardian Scholars, inclusive of one full-time program director, a part-time student coordinator (20 hours weekly, sometimes split between two students), a volunteer executive director, and volunteer advisory committee, has buttressed 33 foster youth as they progressed to their bachelor's degree at UCR. Guardian Scholars continues to produce meaningful results, but its efforts are not scalable. Excluding staff and administrative expenses, the cost of year-round campus housing, food, scholarships, seminars, events, and miscellaneous expenses account for an average per capita expenditure of $5,000, largely funded by private donors (T. Yates, personal communication, November 14, 2019). Moreover, each Guardian Scholar still must take out $5,000–10,000 in annual loans (T. Yates, personal communication, November 14, 2019). OFYSS offers support for the approximately 120 remaining foster youth on campus, but use of that support by the larger foster youth community remains low, in part due to OFYSS's lack of visibility on campus: it is not listed on the campus's clubs and organization website, *HighlanderLink* (Labs, 2019), and rather than being physically located alongside the majority of student special services and programs in Costo Hall and the Highlander Student Building (HUB), both central campus buildings, OFYSS is situated a half mile away from the center of campus, adjacent to graduate student apartments in Bannockburn Village ("Map of UC Riverside," Unknown, n.d.). To date, OFYSS simply is not a well-known nor publicized program, nor is its office easily accessible or physically visible.

Located in the HUB and with a nationally recognized moniker, TRIO Scholars has higher visibility than Guardian Scholars. Their cohort size is exponentially larger, too, with 140 academically disadvantaged low-income, first-generation, and disabled students participating; currently, none is identified as foster youth (N. Borgonia, personal communication, November 18, 2019). According to its current director, owing to its size and scope, TRIO Scholars is unable to capture all foster youth on campus who are in need (N. Borgonia, personal communication, October 14, 2019), nor does the office actively recruit from the matriculating foster youth population, though they plan to consider adding foster youth-specific recruiting strategies in the future (N. Borgonia, personal communication, October 14, 2019). Between these two programs, 30 out of 150 foster youth have been consistently identified and supported on campus, leaving 120 without such support. It can be assumed that some use the university's Academic Resource Center, but these data are not tracked. Unaccounted foster youth may not benefit from support in these and other programs because of a lack of desire on the part of the student, but more likely their absence can be explained by a lack of programmatic resources, visibility, and, in the case of TRIO Scholars, training and outreach. Significantly, no supplemental or wraparound support programs, including those offered to the general student population through UCR's Academic Resource Center, offer faculty-led, expert academic assistance in composition and related areas.

Impressive supports and infrastructure are in place for UCR's foster youth population for those who both know about and are eligible/selected to benefit from them, but a service gap looms large: the campus's overlooked foster youth (those not in a program) and, more generally, the composition needs of all foster youth-identifying students, including those participating in campus-affiliated support services programming. College composition, as one scholar puts it, is an act that "initiat[es] [students] into the academic discourse community" (Bizzell, 1982, p. 206). Composition literacy enables students' success in their chosen academic disciplines. Eminent theorists have long understood – and shared – how important language and writing are to discovery and conceptual facility, as well as how important an understanding of rhetorical situation is for both writers who produce work and readers who experience it (Bakhtin, 2010; Vygotsky, 1978). The components that constitute composition – critical reading, thinking, and writing, as well as researching and speaking – also shape students into active community members, locally, nationally, and globally. These skills, in others words, form the bedrock of students' competence in higher education, and the skill sets are indispensable for broad-based academic success and civic engagement. Post-degree employment, too, hinges on compositional aptitude. The *World Economic Forum*, in anticipating the workforce needs in 2020, identified 10 skills employers are looking for in new hires, as the world continues to automate; while nearly all 10 are potential learning outcomes of composition literacy, the top three skills are quite clearly achieved in the study of composition: complex problem-solving, critical thinking, and creativity (The 10 Skills You Need to Thrive in the Fourth Industrial Revolution, n.d.). Without composition acuity and precision, success in the collegiate, civic, and professional arenas can be frustratingly elusive.

Writing programs might best address their campus's foster youth population's composition deficits. At UCR, and with the exception of transfer students, the UWP provides some writing instruction to every student on campus. All students who matriculate as freshmen are required to fulfill the UWP's English 1A, B, C sequence of composition courses (2019-20 UCR General Catalog, n.d.), which range from beginning to applied intermediate composition. Those matriculating who have not yet satisfied the UC-wide analytical writing base standard, the Entry-Level Writing Requirement (n.d.), must also take one or more basic English speaking, reading, and writing classes (2019-20 UCR General Catalog, n.d.). The course learning outcomes are steeped in composition and rhetoric, as well as leading theoretical approaches to the analysis and interpretation of texts, and include meeting standards in critical reading, thinking, and writing, in addition to rhetorical and research literacies (2019-20 UCR General Catalog, n.d.). Moreover, UCR's composition courses are unofficially classified as "gatekeepers," classes which a student must pass in order to remain at the university and advance to degree completion. The writing program's scope coupled with the transferable knowledge and composition skills taught, which are applicable to all campus majors, makes the UWP the largest, most student-engaged program at UCR.

Because of higher incidents of academic and soft skills deficits in the foster youth student population (Geiger & Beltran, 2017; Geiger et al., 2018; Wolanin, 2005), foster youth-identifying students at UCR who fit this paradigm are due, in the authors' view, access to additional composition and mentoring support for any class they take at UCR, whether it be one designated as a UWP course or not. Following the advice of scholars focused on the college-going experiences of foster youth (Dworsky & Perez, 2009; Emerson, Duffield, Salazar, & Unrau, 2012; Geiger et al., 2018; J. Miller, Benner, Kheibari, & Washington, 2017; Okumu, 2014), this service-driven mission forms the foundation of the UWP's WAFYA program. Students with experience in the foster system have "limited avenues to access of knowledge," yet they also recognize how mentoring relationships can help them to acquire that knowledge and "remove barriers to their educational success ... disentangl[ing] them from a myriad of initially perplexing institutional systems" that can inhibit it (Wallace, Abel, & Ropers-Huilman, 2000, pp. 94–95). Mentoring relationships are made possible when instructors can develop interpersonal relationships with students (Buell, 2004) and are most successful when a mentor and student view the mentor's role as one that involves teaching, guiding, and modeling behaviors, which make more likely the student's goal attainment (Buell, 2004). When done well, mentoring is recognized as one of the most effective ways for students to increase their self-esteem and fulfill their potential (Lasley, 1996).

WAFYA provides many options for students to select from in their search for academic and mentoring support. Ever-evolving, current programming entails one-on-one faculty consultations, which aid in assignment-focused sessions and building a mentoring relationship. Seminars offer key insights into general composition and rhetoric, such as the writing process and general knowledge of rhetorical situations. Drop-in writing labs for just-in-time tutoring are scheduled during critical weeks in the academic session, including midterm and finals weeks. Offering access to familiar and highly trained instructors, these sessions ease the pressure surrounding high-stakes work and provide feedback for any writing-related assignment at any stage in the process. Knowing that foster youth also can benefit from non-academic compositional needs, WAFYA encourages students to ask for help from faculty with expertise in scholarship, grant, graduate school, and employment applications. Specific seminars are offered for these extra-academic areas of need, and faculty are available to consult with and mentor students on an individual basis as well.

Mentoring can occur in person, online (ZOOM, FaceTime, Skype), over e-mail, and via phone, based on the mentors' and students' preferences. In its advocacy efforts, WAFYA relies on its relationship with the Office of Undergraduate Education (UE) and Jennfier Brown, Vice Provost and Dean of Undergraduate Education (VPDUE), to highlight UCR's foster youth-specific support services, including OFYSS and Guardian Scholars, in addition to WAFYA. WAFYA also lobbies for more foster youth representation and inclusion in programs devoted to at-risk and underrepresented students but not designated just for foster youth. Most recently, WAFYA communicated to TRIO Scholars the need for modified outreach approaches for foster youth eligible for their services (R. Moore, personal communication, October 19, 2019).

Programs measure success by the achievement of desired outcomes. Though nascent, WAFYA has met one significant goal: Guardian Scholars has credited WAFYA as being the catalyst for its program participants' collective highest-ever average quarterly GPA, a 2.9 for the spring quarter, 2019 (K.L. Whitman, personal communication, September 3, 2019). In his memoir, *Between the World and Me*, the writer Ta-Nahisi Coates describes how he thinks of the American Dream as one that is not accessible to all demographics; rather, it is a dream limited to those in power, predominantly white people. It is a dream only made possible through the oppression of those in America without a voice: people of color, especially blacks, and other marginalized groups (Coates, 2015). The divide between those who have and have not in the United States became starkly apparent in the 2018 college admissions scandal (*The New York Times*, 2019), which exposed flagrant institutionalized inequity and made plain gaining entry into college, for many the vehicle necessary to achieve what they hope will be the American Dream, is a rigged game. Arguably, the American social system may lack distributive justice, as well as resource equity. Philosophically, WAFYA positions itself on the side of justice, of resource equity. By providing additional academic support and mentoring to the foster youth community at UCR, WAFYA is attempting to level the playing field. In meeting foster youth where they are educationally and without judgment, WAFYA conveys to them that they are seen and valued, deserving access to highly qualified expertise. Ultimately, WAFYA wants to bridge the gap between existing campus support programs and overlooked supplemental academic support needs particularly suited to being met by the competence and compassion of a trained and dedicated writing program faculty. WAFYA's success is its students' success. A work-in-progress, the program nevertheless has been thoughtfully, consistently, and recursively implemented.

A NEW PROGRAM STEEPED IN THE GOALS OF SOCIAL JUSTICE

The genesis of a project like WAFYA can be, for all parties involved, an intensely creative, frenetic, and even chaotic time. The following analysis of the process resulting in WAFYA is designed to focus the service-oriented impulses of interested instructors and administrators alike while simultaneously removing possible missteps. Because of the powerful social dynamics at play with the foster youth community, all communication involving WAFYA is an integral and sensitive component that involved potentially complicated interactions from the outset of the WAFYA project. Anyone interested in establishing an organization like WAFYA should reflect deeply on how communication is designed to operate in the realm of foster services and the complex dynamics that can emerge (Braithwaite & Baxter, 2006). Administrators of all ilk involved in the OFYSS and Guardian Scholars communities serving foster youth are well aware of the range and depth of complications WAFYA students face. As such, a certain defensive and protective approach can be detected in even the most innocuous communications. WAFYA communication that occurs across varying communities involve what Kelly M. Quintanilla and Shawn T. Hall identify as a formal communication network and, more importantly, an informal communication network (Quintanilla & Wahl, 2017). The kind of project WAFYA embodies is one that routinely relies on bridging communication outside of the defined formal network and directly privileges the "white space" or "part of the organizational chart that is not prescribed" (Quintanilla & Wahl, 2017, p. 123) because foster youth programs on campus transcend traditional disciplinary demarcations. The kind of communication that takes place is in many ways more fluid than structured and professional communication.

As such, anyone interested in founding such a program must take great pains, even from the inception of the program, to safeguard against miscommunication and, especially, the concept of "malcommunication" – communication that inadvertently fosters either active or passive hostility through an informal, though occasionally formal, communication process. Standard communication can involve challenging negotiations, but any communication around the foster youth community is often charged and easily given to malcommunication because of the audience involved and the highly emotional nature of the subject.

Many people working or advising foster youth support services programs do so precisely because they themselves were foster youth, had or have a connection to the foster youth community, or faced traumas that align with foster youth experiences; this population may not self-disclose. Thinking about this dynamic and operating under the assumption that all communication about foster youth, or WAFYA in this case, involves personal associations with the foster youth population can help all involved to avoid or at least mitigate malcommunication, whether or not communication occurs in an online medium.

Early in the process of reflecting on what service the UCR UWP could provide to campus foster youth, Moore was quick to introduce the concept of WAFYA to an associate director of the UWP and co-founder of WAFYA, Beehler. This initial communication was valuable because the official process of constituting an organization could begin with the administrative support of the UWP. Academics interested in establishing these kinds of programs would benefit from such intense discussions because vision and structure are the invariable results of these dialogues. While some communication at the earliest point in the project took place electronically out of convenience, such discussions were delicate and easily given to miscommunication or even malcommunication because "e-mail messages are devoid of nonverbal communication and inflection. The hope is that the person at the other end understood what you were really trying to say" (Powers & Dutt-Doner, 1998, p. 1177). Still, Beehler and Moore were able to begin the creative process through dyadic interactions (Quintanilla & Wahl, 2017) over e-mail because of their similar backgrounds: two academics with backgrounds in British literature and an interest in serving the broader university by engaging foster youth. Even with this shared background, though, the discussions around WAFYA necessarily had to develop through one-on-one in-person communication. Through this open and ongoing dyadic dialogue, Beehler and Moore developed a formal proposal that was subsequently presented to the UWP's director, John Briggs. That formal proposal served as the articulated vision for WAFYA. Meetings, as has been discussed in recent research (Boemer, Schaffner, & Gebert, 2012), are an essential vehicle – perhaps most especially to WAFYA – to establish a culture of trust among personnel from different parts of UCR. In this way, these regular meetings cultivated a number of the powerful benefits Jing Cai and Adam Szeidl (2016) identify in "Interfirm Relationships and Business Performance." Specifically, Cai and Szeidl "found significant, robust, large, and persistent effects ... on innovation and management" as well as "learning and partnering" (Cai & Szeidl, 2016, p. 33). In other words, meetings occurring between people from different fields generated a culture of productivity and innovation, one that helped propel the WAFYA project forward. The formal proposal, a document academics should plan to craft early in the founding process for a multitude of reasons, consists of several sections and sub-sections: Proposal

Overview, Background Information, Proposal, Initiative Description, Outreach, Budget, Desired Outcome, Research, and Works Cited.

ORIGIN AND UNDERLYING PHILOSOPHY OF WAFYA

The creation of a formal proposal served several functions. First and foremost, the proposal articulated a deliberate vision. The co-founders had an opportunity, through the generation of a formal proposal, to discuss at length the purpose and philosophy behind the program, so the formal approach enabled a guiding foundation for WAFYA to be formulated and enshrined for future consultation and recursive consideration. The need to establish a deep understanding of the project between the co-founders was predicated on John Rawls' *A Theory of Justice* (1971) in that "Men are to decide in advance how they are to regulate their claims against one another and what is to be the foundation charter of their society" (Rawls, 1999). The exercise of considering all aspects of the program and determining how to chart the most effective course provided a blueprint that was useful throughout the genesis of WAFYA. Even an element as basic as a name required considerable thought because the name had to reflect the intersection between the foster youth population and the writing program. As Beehler and Moore thought in advance about how the program would operate, a series of names evolved. Part of this evolution was instigated by a growing awareness of the diversity among the foster youth population and the range of services the UWP faculty could provide given the right training and resources.

Names and labels as they apply to foster youth programs are charged subjects and often given to debate. Guardian Scholars Writing Alliance (GSWA) was the first name conceived and was warmly received by Guardian Scholars' directors and members of its advisory board because it highlighted an alliance between the groups. A couple of concerns, however, emerged as the name circulated, and these complications helped illuminate the function of the organization and the populations it serves. Using the name "Guardian Scholars," while easily recognized among the most vulnerable of the foster youth population, also inadvertently signaled that the full foster youth population might not be invited to enjoy the benefits of the service. Working under GSWA, while directly appealing to an established organization that serves the most vulnerable of the campus's foster youth, still signaled exclusivity among the foster youth population at large – an unintended act of miscommunication and even malcommunication.

The name likewise did not emphasize the important role the UWP played because the word "writing" was sublimated to "Guardian Scholars." An emphasis on the word "writing" was necessary to indicate the principal function of the group and to indicate where this organization was housed – in the UWP. Because of the many different organizations that typically have some interaction with foster youth at UCR, confusion over such points could result in confusion about the services offered, even the purpose of the program.

From this initial name evolved another, one that was much more cumbersome: Foster Youth Support Services and University Writing Program Writing

Alliance (FYSSWA). FYSSWA fully and directly communicated the main entities involved. Of note, though, the repetition of "writing" was a somewhat misguided, perhaps even clumsy, attempt to call attention to the important role of writing in the organization. Needless to say, the desire to be precise in naming the entities, while well-intentioned, spawned an impractical acronym. In the chapter "Words Get Their Meanings from Other Words," Dylan B. Dryer considers Ferdinand de Saussure's argument that "In language itself, there are only differences" (Adler-Kassner, Wardle, & Land, 2015, p. 118). Dryer correctly recognizes in Saussure that,

> because there is no necessary connection between any sounds or clusters of symbols and their referents (otherwise different languages would not exist), the meanings of words are relational – they acquire their meanings from other words. (Adler-Kassner et al., 2015, pp. 23-24)

The meanings derived from the hyper-accurate FYSSWA utilized the context of words to precisely capture the alliance between writing and the entire foster youth community, but at the expense of linguistic accessibility. Just as Kevin Roozen identifies how writing is bound to the "deeply social and rhetorical dimensions" of social systems (Adler-Kassner et al., 2015, pp. 17–19), the use of labels expresses that rhetorical function in the university, so identifying accurate nomenclature remained a high priority because of the need to communicate the purpose and position of this new organization at UCR. Because writing was again subordinated to the foster youth component in this new incarnation, discussions about the name of the organization continued. Eventually, these conversations resulted in the current iteration of WAFYA (Writing and Foster Youth Alliance). This name places, appropriately, the concept of writing at the fore and maintains the seminal idea of alliance. Further, the name was intentionally less specific to become more inclusive. All foster youth, and not just the Guardian Scholars, are the concern of WAFYA. In addition, all manner of writing and not just the UWP is the principal function of the organization. The name WAFYA now provides enough generality to extend the flexibility needed to communicate both function and audience while privileging the primary occupation of the organization – writing.

ANATOMY OF "THE PROPOSAL"

Each part of the proposal provides an explanation and justification of the program. Succinct in nature, the "Proposal Overview" introduces the direct and clear recommendation

> that a group of experienced and trained lecturer-volunteers extend their office hours to accommodate all students to ensure that, if wanted, foster youth have an accessible expert able to offer assistance. (Beehler & Moore, 2018, p. 1)

This sentence illustrates the value that a formal proposal plays in establishing such a program as well as Rawls' concept of justice. Generating visibility within the university is another important priority. In an attempt to recruit and inform instructors about WAFYA during its inaugural year, one of the panels at the annual orientation for the UWP at UCR was dedicated to internal innovative practices. WAFYA featured prominently on this panel, and interest in the program resulted in discussions about the purpose and structure of the services being offered through the UWP.

At one point, a teaching assistant (TA) asked whether he could participate in WAFYA, expressing enthusiasm about the possibility of serving as a mentor. The moment was one that reflected a general misunderstanding of duties and expectations, as explored in several articles – "Superior-subordinate communication: The state of the art" (Jablin, 1979), "Communication and participative decision-making: An exploratory study" (Harrison, 1985), and "Context matters: Combined influence of participation and intellectual stimulation on the promotion focus – employee creativity relationship" (Zhou, Hirst, & Shipton, 2011). While an intriguing possibility, opening the program to TAs would have compounded some of the delicate challenges that even seasoned instructors grapple with. Career faculty often can draw from a wealth of experience and maturity that is essential in establishing mentoring relationships. The more established lecturers also often have greater insights into how to engage with students in a tutoring environment, a particular concern when working with students enrolled in other instructors' courses. Maintaining the integrity of the tutoring program is of paramount importance when establishing such an organization because such a concern speaks directly to the credibility of the program within the university.

Fortunately, and in keeping with Rawls' principles, Beehler and Moore carefully considered the parameters of participation well before any general discussion of WAFYA took place. That the "Proposal Overview" unambiguously described the WAFYA cohort as "experienced and trained lecturer-volunteers" (Beehler & Moore, 2018, p. 2) helped definitively answer the request without provoking a defensive reaction from the TA or diminishing the TA's enthusiasm. Further, the Proposal Overview required advanced thought about the issue. That means the discussion about precluding TAs was an informed one, and an explanation as to why "experienced and trained lecturer-volunteers" (Beehler & Moore, 2018, p. 2) rather than less experienced TAs helped illuminate the specific role that expertise plays with at-risk populations like foster youth. The language from the "Proposal Overview" also helped initiate a discussion about the ambassadorial role the lecturer-volunteers assume on the broader campus as they fulfill their function as mentors. These benefits from a formal "Proposal Overview" were instrumental in avoiding either miscommunication or malcommunication.

Like other sub-sections of the proposal, "Background Information" serves the dual purpose of informing the administration of the current level of support on campus for students identifying as foster youth and justifying the need for WAFYA, especially at an R1 university, as detailing the catalogue of services underscores the importance of WAFYA and its position at UCR. "Background Information" also introduces Guardian Scholars Founder and Executive Director Tuppett Yates, from the Department of Psychology, and Program Director Kenyon Lee Whitman, PhD candidate in UCR's Graduate School of Education. Both are foster studies scholars and longtime advocates for foster youth; securing their support of WAFYA was integral to establishing credibility with and access to UCR's foster youth community, especially given the complementary program missions, and to marking clear distinctions between WAFYA and Guardian Scholars for the administration.

Similar to the "Proposal Overview," the section, "Proposal," provides an estimate of how many lecturer-volunteers might be required to serve the 30 students in the Guardian Scholars program. The initial estimate of lecturer-volunteers was set at 5–10, but in practice far more lecturer-volunteers were ultimately trained – 22 in total – as the response to the call for volunteers was surprisingly robust. A comprehensive list of current mentors and the full parameters of the program can be found at uwp.ucr.edu/wafya. Identifying the number of actual students in Guardian Scholars also helped audiences outside of WAFYA gain a perspective of the potential benefits of the program. The proposal, though, could have been strengthened had it acknowledged the full contingent of foster youth on campus, some 150 students, because WAFYA is a program that serves all foster youth.

"Initiative Description" offers a detailed explanation of the training required to certify instructors. This section identified the expectations for the writing faculty and clarified the relationship shared with Guardian Scholars:

> Lecturers will not necessarily be teaching the same texts or assigning the same assignments; still, the experienced pool for instructors likely will be able to offer valuable insight and instruction regardless of the specific assignment. (Beehler & Moore, 2018, p. 2)

Capturing this aspect of the mission helps establish bright lines or boundaries. While this language was not directly cited during the training or even during actual sessions, the language was instrumental in providing a definitive set of parameters and expectations for the program.

When working with faculty, the recognition of boundaries is vital because a sensitivity to ownership of the classroom furthers the service-oriented mission of WAFYA. The interaction between tutoring services and official classrooms is not always complicated or rife with tension, but that interaction can still be fraught with challenges. Sometimes, instructors can be protective of their classroom and the work that occurs in that space. Without doubt, this impulse is a healthy one and should be respected. When another academic influence is introduced in the form of a tutor, questions about authority can, potentially, result in awkwardness or, worse, defensiveness. Other factors, like labor conditions and stability, can intensify such reactions. Proceeding with an awareness of the social and professional dynamics can prevent problematic situations altogether, and one of the best avenues to establish that awareness is through language in the "Initiative Description." Reasoning like this informed the decision to use the unequivocal sentence "This program has no expectation or intention to align classes in any way" (Beehler & Moore, 2018, p. 2), which helps to formally maintain an understanding of the autonomous position of courses and the service-oriented position of WAFYA faculty.

Peppered throughout the proposal are references to "experienced" instructors, and such is the case in "Initiative Description." This reinforcement is important to the health of the program because the strongest of UWP instructors have the greatest likelihood of successfully navigating mentor-based relationships with foster youth. Recognizing and applauding the strengths of the instructors is important as the culture for WAFYA has developed, and the instructors have responded to public and professional signs of appreciation. Letters detailing WAFYA mentors' contributions to the program are written yearly and placed in their employment record. The letters are a vehicle to recognize professional service through a formal personnel file and process. Second to this function, though, the letters increase the visibility of WAFYA because the personnel files are circulated widely throughout campus circles. Understanding the role such a letter plays in the program is articulated in the "Proposal Initiative" with a line that, again, recognizes the essential and specialized function of the writing faculty: "In return for their participation in the training and program, all lecturers will receive a certificate of completion indicating their specialized skill set" (Beehler & Moore, 2018, p. 2). For this professional recognition, the opportunities for continued professional development, and the opportunity to serve an at-risk population, lecturer support for WAFYA remains high. Of the 25 lecturers who volunteered in the inaugural year of WAFYA, 22 returned. Of the three lecturers who did not return two left UCR to pursue other professional opportunities and one lecturer retired.

Also included in "Proposal Initiative" is a delineation of the five-part orientation program for UWP faculty interested in volunteering as WAFYA mentors. This material not only provides a schedule but also explanations of the panels and activities that constitute the orientation. The mentoring partnerships between students and faculty are a core part of WAFYA and featured prominently in the orientation programming. Partnerships between organizations also play an important role, though. The orientation began with a half-hour panel titled "Guardian Scholars Presentation." The panel set the tone for the alliance that was in the process of being forged between the campus's foster youth community and the UWP. The Guardian Scholars' executive and program directors, along with Guardian Scholars students, introduced themselves and detailed their program's mission after the UWP's director welcomed the prospective volunteers and invited panelists. Careful orchestration of the leadership of both entities was a delicate matter because all members needed to recognize that the shared goal of providing supplemental academic support services to the particularly vulnerable population of foster students required a synchronized effort. In a way, such an introduction provides a kind of performative, organizational chart. Having those in leadership explain their roles and how WAFYA works in the greater university structure was helpful for all involved because the discussion provided clarity about the complementary programmatic missions and the ways WAFYA volunteers could provide unique, essential services. Additionally, the panel was a nexus for familiarizing different programs with each other and beginning the process of cultivating important and powerful alliances across the campus, alliances that might not otherwise flourish. The remainder of the orientation was dedicated to best practices in behavioral interaction (half hour), discussion of campus resources devoted to foster youth (half hour), and a consideration of how to provide feedback to the foster youth community (half hour). The final hour of the orientation was reserved for instruction in specialized tutoring skills as they apply to foster youth.

The proposal then shifts, in "Outreach," to approaches for connecting foster youth to WAFYA. Personal, face-to-face interactions to build trust and community was and is prioritized. To date, the most effective means of establishing WAFYA mentor–student interactions has transpired through thoughtful dialogue with administrators who work directly with foster youth. Attending OFYSS and Guardian Scholars events like orientations and monthly luncheons remain essential to establishing positive WAFYA mentor–student relationships, as do personal invitations to participate in WAFYA services once foster youth self-identify, which can and does happen in UWP writing classes. Less personal, faculty announce WAFYA events in UWP classes, whether or not the course instructors are WAFYA volunteers. More traditionally, and by utilizing networks open to academic units, UE assists WAFYA in communicating with undergraduates directly through mass e-mail; this form of communication, while impersonal, provides yet another layer of visibility for WAFYA.

Next in the proposal is the "Budget" section. The initial budget was negligible; however, as the program continues to grow, a larger budget is anticipated and will need to be established to provide funding for WAFYA events and continued training. Securing grants and soliciting funds from entities within the university (like the VPDUE) will become primary components for establishing a budget that can sustain the organization. Equally important, though, will be the ability to secure grants outside the university because such awards can raise the profile of the program and insure against reductions in university support during difficult fiscal periods.

The penultimate section, "Desired Outcome," is brief but essential. The goals for the program are several: professionalizing UWP lecturers, increasing the visibility of the UWP, elevating foster youth composition skills, reducing time to completion of UCR's composition course requirements for foster youth, and increasing UCR's retention and graduation rates.

Finally, because UCR is an R1 research university, the section, "Research," concludes the proposal by identifying possible research interests: tracking student achievement of learning outcomes, participation in the program, progression through the composition sequence, and metrics involving confidence in interaction with faculty. WAFYA's focus on research has led to an application with UCR's Institutional Review Board (IRB), as well as a preliminary search for grant monies.

Communication remains a seminal element to the success of a program like WAFYA, and that communication occurs at myriad levels: students, colleagues, administrators, and external agents. While the communication initially begins with the founders of the program, the development of a formal proposal will aid in ensuring the longevity of the program. Administrators and academics interested in establishing this kind of program should take every measure to mitigate and eliminate both miscommunication and malcommunication. Negotiating the dynamics of the university is a complicated process, but crafting a foundational document like the one outlined here will preserve a vision of the program that is indispensable.

CONCLUSION

Now in its third year, WAFYA continues to expand its services by working closely with the different stakeholders. Maintaining a strong connection to OFYSS and Guardian Scholars, as well as building a relationship with TRIO Scholars, remains a primary focal point, as does working more extensively with UE to raise WAFYA's profile. WAFYA and programs like WAFYA have the potential to increase retention and graduation rates among the most vulnerable of college-going students; elevating inter-program and administrative networks is essential to this goal.

WAFYA has enjoyed an auspicious beginning, but continued research on its efficacy and a continued expansion of its services will be the challenges before it. Sustained collection of foster youth data such as GPA and retention rates coupled with analysis should continue as WAFYA grows because the research will help determine how effective WAFYA is in the broader university community. WAFYA's outreach and engagement also is a research focus: the program's ability to assist foster youth relies on communication principles to establish strong mentoring relationships and advance administration of the program, writing faculty involvement, and campus visibility. Future research will investigate the actual effectiveness of WAFYA writing instruction. Such an endeavor, though, will almost certainly be complicated because the research directly involves human subjects and a particularly vulnerable student population. Interrogating and refining best practices of WAFYA, however, could result in enhanced results for future foster youth at UCR. The approach toward such research will necessarily involve a careful consideration of malcommunication and a close working relationship with IRB to safeguard against any ethical concerns applicable to the campus's foster youth population. In pursuing these and other research questions that inform policy, theory, and practice, WAFYA can contribute to a growing body of knowledge offering insight into foster youth support services in higher education.

Ultimately, WAFYA is a program that can be replicated on other campuses, with the potential of generating similar positive results, and continued research on WAFYA's effectiveness could likely serve as a model for other institutions of higher education to follow. The implementation of comparable programs would be a powerful expression of social justice that affects the lives of a vulnerable student population, one that richly benefits from professional, academic support. The foster youth research cited in this chapter is definitive: this resilient student population is poised for strong gains in higher education and beyond if program leadership and mentoring provided by composition faculty can be harnessed and steadfastly sustained in concert with traditional support models.

DECLARATION OF INTEREST

Paul Beehler is the co-founder/co-director of WAFYA and collaborates regularly with the Office of Foster Youth Support Services and Guardian Scholars at the University of California, Riverside. Rory Moore is the co-founder/co-director of WAFYA and collaborates regularly with the Office of Foster Youth Support Services and Guardian Scholars at the University of California, Riverside. Paul Beehler declares no financial interest in WAFYA. Rory Moore declares no financial interest in WAFYA.

ACKNOWLEDGMENTS

The authors wish to thank the Office of Foster Youth Support Services and Guardian Scholars and their executive director, Tuppett Yates, and director, Kenyon Lee Whitman, as well as TRIO Scholars and its director, Norman Borgonia, for their willingness to share their respective programs' unpublished data and professional insights.

REFERENCES

2019-20 UCR General Catalog. (n.d.). Retrieved from https://registrar.ucr.edu/registering/catalog. Accessed on November 24, 2019.

About the University of California Riverside. (n.d.). Retrieved from https://www.ucr.edu/about. Accessed on October 26, 2019.

Adler-Kassner, L., Wardle, E., & Land, R. (2015). *Naming what we know: Threshold concepts of writing studies*. Logan, UT: Utah State University Press, an imprint of University Press of Colorado.

Allen, T. D., & Eby, L. T. (2011). The Blackwell handbook of mentoring: A multiple perspectives approach. Retrieved from https://play.google.com/store/books/details?id=jJdRSJBhhEsC

Bakhtin, M. M. (2010). The dialogic imagination: Four essays. Retrieved from https://play.google.com/store/books/details?id=cblaBAAAQBAJ

Beehler, P., & Moore, R. (2018). Proposal for an Extended Student Support Initiative for UCR's Current and Former Foster Youth.

Bizzell, P. (1982). College composition: Initiation into the academic discourse community. *Curriculum Inquiry*, *12*(2), 191–207. https://doi.org/10.2307/1179517.

Boemer, S., Schaffner, M., & Gebert, D. (2012). The complementarity of team meetings and cross-functional communication: Emperical evidence from new services development teams. *Journal of Leadership & Organizational Studies*, *19*(2), 1–11.

Braithwaite, D. O., & Baxter, L. A. (Eds.). (2006). *Engaging theories in family communication: Multiple perspectives*. Thousand Oaks, CA: SAGE Publications. doi:10.4135/9781452204420

Buell, C. (2004). Models of mentoring in communication. *Communication Education*, *53*(1). https://doi.org/10.1080/0363452032000135779

Cai, J., & Szeidl, A. (2016). *Interfirm relationships and business performance*. NBER Working Paper Series. Cambridge, MA: National Bureau of Economic Research.

Campbell, T. A., & Campbell, D. E. (1997). Faculty/student mentor program: Effects on academic performance and retention. *Research in Higher Education*, *38*(6), 727–742. https://doi.org/10.1023/A:1024911904627

Children's Bureau. (2018). *The AFCARS report: Preliminary FY 2017 estimates as of August 10, 2018.* No. 25. Children's Bureau, US Department of Health and Human Services, Washington, DC.

Coates, T.-N. (2015). *Between the world and me*. New York, NY: Penguin Random House.

Crisp, G., & Cruz, I. (2009). Mentoring college students: A critical review of the literature between 1990 and 2007. *Research in Higher Education*, *50*(6), 525–545. https://doi.org/10.1007/s11162-009-9130-2

Day, A., Dworsky, A., & Feng, W. (2013). An analysis of foster care placement history and post-secondary graduation rates. *Research in Higher Education Journal*, *19*, 1–17. Retrieved from https://eric.ed.gov/?id=EJ1064665

Day, A., Dworsky, A., Fogarty, K., & Damashek, A. (2011). An examination of post-secondary retention and graduation among foster care youth enrolled in a four-year university. *CYSR Children and Youth Services Review, 33*(11), 2335–2341. Retrieved from https://ucr.worldcat. org/title/an-examination-of-post-secondary-retention-and-graduation-among-foster-care-youth-enrolled-in-a-four-year-university/oclc/590248317l&referer=brief_results

Diversity, Equity & Inclusion. (n.d.). Retrieved from https://deanofstudents.ucr.edu/diversity. Accessed on October 27, 2019.

Dworsky, A., & Perez, A. (2009). *Helping former foster youth graduate from college: Campus support programs in California and Washington State*. Chicago, IL: Chapin Hall at the University of Chicago.

Educational Opportunity Program (EOP)|UC Admissions. (n.d.). Retrieved from https://admission. universityofcalifornia.edu/campuses-majors/campus-programs-and-support-services/educational-opportunity-program-eop.html. Accessed on October 26, 2019.

Emerson, J., Duffield, B., Salazar, A., & Unrau, Y. (2012). The path to success: Creating campus support systems for foster and homeless students. *Leadership Exchange, 10*(2), 8–13.

Entry-Level Writing Requirement. (n.d.). Retrieved from https://uwp.ucr.edu/elwr. Accessed on November 24, 2019.

Geiger, J. M., & Beltran, S. J. (2017). Experiences and outcomes of foster care alumni in postsecondary education: A review of the literature. *Children and Youth Services Review, 79*, 186–197. https:// doi.org/10.1016/j.childyouth.2017.06.023

Geiger, J. M., Piel, M. H., Day, A., & Schelbe, L. (2018). A descriptive analysis of programs serving foster care alumni in higher education: Challenges and opportunities. *Children and Youth Services Review, 85*, 287–294. https://doi.org/10.1016/j.childyouth.2018.01.001

Greenstone, M., Looney, A., Patashnik, J., & Yu, M. (2013). Thirteen economic facts about social mobility and the role of education. Retrieved from https://core.ac.uk/download/pdf/71362449. pdf

Gross, J. P. (2019). *Former foster youth in postsecondary education: Reaching higher*. Palgrave Pivot, Cham. https://doi.org/10.1007/978-3-319-99459-8

Harrison, T. (1985). Communication and participative decision-making: An exploratory study. *Personnel Psychology, 38*, 93–116.

Hines, A. M., Merdinger, J., & Wyatt, P. (2005). Former foster youth attending college: Resilience and the transition to young adulthood. *The American Journal of Orthopsychiatry, 75*(3), 381–394. https://doi.org/10.1037/0002-9432.75.3.381

Institutional Research. (n.d.). UCR campus statistics. Retrieved from https://ir.ucr.edu/stats.html. Accessed on June 16, 2019.

Jablin, F. M. (1979). Superior-subordinate communication: The state of the art. *Psychological Bulletin, 86*, 1201–1222.

Labs, C. (2019). HighlanderLink. Retrieved from https://highlanderlink.ucr.edu/. Accessed on October 27, 2019.

Lasley, T. J. (1996). On mentoring: What makes so few so special? *Journal of Teacher Education, 47*(4), 307–309. https://journals.sagepub.com/doi/pdf/10.1177/0022487196474009

Masten, A. S., & Barnes, A. J. (2018). Resilience in children: Developmental perspectives. *Children, 5*(7), 98. https://doi.org/10.3390/children5070098

Michigan, F. S. (n.d.). National map|fostering success Michigan. Retrieved from http://fostering-successmichigan.com/campus-support?utm_source=National+Postsecondary+Support+ Map+Launch&utm_campaign=National+Postsecondary+Support+Map+Launch&utm_ medium=email. Accessed on July 13, 2019.

Miller, G. (2008). *Higher Education Opportunity Act*. Public Law No. 4137.

Miller, J., Benner, K., Kheibari, A., & Washington, E. (2017). Conceptualizing on-campus support programs for collegiate foster youth and alumni: A plan for action. *Children and Youth Services Review, 83*, 57–67. https://doi.org/10.1016/j.childyouth.2017.10.028

National Center for Education Statistics (NCES). (n.d.). The Integrated Postsecondary Education Data System [Data set]. Institute of Education Sciences, U.S. Department of Education. Retrieved from https://nces.ed.gov/ipeds/use-the-data. Accessed on November 24, 2019.

Okpych, N. J., & Courtney, M. E. (2018). Barriers to degree completion for college students with foster care histories: Results from a 10-year longitudinal study. *Journal of College Student Retention: Research, Theory & Practice, 16*(1), 127–151. https://doi.org/10.1177/1521025118791776

Okumu, J. O. (2014). Meaning-making dynamics of emancipated foster care youth transitioning into higher education: A constructivist-grounded theory. *Journal of the First-Year Experience & Students in Transition, 26*(2), 9–28. Retrieved from https://ucr.worldcat.org/oclc/19535828698 582&referer=brief_results

Powers, S. M., & Dutt-Doner, K. (1998). Replacing the tin can: Creating an effective electronic communication environment. *Technology and Teacher Education Annual*, 1176–1180.

Quintanilla, K. M., & Wahl, S. T. (2017). *Business and professional communication: Keys for workplace excellence*. London: Sage.

Ranks and Facts|University of California, Riverside. (n.d.). Retrieved from https://www.ucr.edu/about/ranks-and-facts. Accessed on October 26, 2019.

Rawls, J. (1999). A theory of justice revised edition. Cambridge, MA: The Belknap Press of Harvard University Press.

Rawls, J. (1971). In (Ed.). Justice as Fairness. In *A Theory of Justice* (pp. 3–46). Cambridge, MA: Harvard University Press

Redford, J. K. M. H. (2017). *Stats in brief: First-generation and continuing-generation college students: A comparison of high school and postsecondary experiences* (No. NCES 2018–009). Retrieved from https://nces.ed.gov/pubs2018/2018009.pdf

The 10 Skills You Need to Thrive in the Fourth Industrial Revolution. (n.d.). Retrieved from https://www.weforum.org/agenda/2016/01/the-10-skills-you-need-to-thrive-in-the-fourth-industrial-revolution/. Accessed on November 25, 2019.

The Integrated Postsecondary Education Data System. (n.d.). Retrieved from https://nces.ed.gov/ipeds/use-the-data. Accessed on November 24, 2019.

The New York Times. (2019, March 14). College admissions scandal: Your questions answered. *The New York Times*. Retrieved from https://www.nytimes.com/2019/03/14/us/college-admissions-scandal-questions.html

Unknown. (n.d.). Map of UC Riverside. Retrieved from https://campusmap.ucr.edu/map.pdf

Vygotsky, L. S. (1978). *Mind in society: The development of higher mental processes* (E. Rice, Ed. & Trans.). Cambridge, MA: Harvard University Press. (Original work published 1930, 1933).

Wallace, D., Abel, R., & Huilman, B. (2000). Clearing a path for success: Deconstructing borders through undergraduate mentoring. *The Review of Higher Education, 24*(1), 87–102. https://doi.org/10.1353/rhe.2000.0026

Wolanin, T. R. (2005). Higher education opportunities for foster youth: A primer for policymakers. Retrieved from http://www.ihep.org/sites/default/files/uploads/docs/pubs/opportunitiesfosteryouth.pdf

Zhou, Q., Hirst, G., & Shipton, H. (2011). Context matters: Combined influence of participation and intellectual stimulation on the promotion focus-employee creativity relationship. *Journal of Organizational Behavior. 33*(7), 894–909. doi:10.1002/job.779

CHAPTER 10

PROMOTING GENDER EQUALITY IN COLLEGES OF EDUCATION IN GHANA USING A GENDER-RESPONSIVE SCORECARD*

Wisdom Kwaku Agbevanu, Hope Pius Nudzor, Sharon Tao and Francis Ansah

ABSTRACT

This chapter presents the findings of a Gender and Leadership study on promoting gender responsiveness and equality in Ghanaian Colleges of Education (CoEs) conducted in 2017. Specifically, this chapter explores CoEs actors' perspectives on and experiences with using predetermined gender-responsive scorecard (GRS) as a strategy for promoting gender equality within the CoEs. Multiple-case study involving 10 CoEs selected purposively was used to explore the GRS implementation. Data collection and analysis methods included semi-structured interviews and "processual" analysis. The findings revealed a general contradiction among respondents regarding which gender actions/strategies had been implemented in the case study CoEs. Nonetheless, amid reported implementation challenges, there was general acknowledgment of the importance of the GRS in running gender-responsive CoEs in Ghana. The study concludes that the effective use and implementation of the GRS

*This chapter is based on a Gender and Leadership study commissioned by the National Council for Tertiary Education, the National Teaching Council, and the College of Education Principals' Conference and jointly implemented by the Transforming Teacher Education and Learning Program in Ghana. Aspects of the findings from the study are being published in peer-reviewed journals. We have no conflict of interest to disclose.

International Perspectives in Social Justice Programs at the Institutional and Community Levels
Innovations in Higher Education Teaching and Learning, Volume 37, 151–175
ISSN: 2055-3641/doi:10.1108/S2055-364120210000037010

strategies appear imperative in promoting female success in CoEs, not only in Ghana but also in contexts where gender gap is an issue in teacher education.

Keywords: Gender-responsive scorecard; gender equality; teacher education; colleges of education; college actors; multiple-case study

INTRODUCTION

Gender equality and women empowerment remain a central issue in the Sustainable Development Goals and continue to receive significant attention across the world. According to UNESCO (2015), mainstreaming gender equality in system-wide teacher education institutions is crucial for two main reasons. First, owing to the gender disparity between men and women across the world, gender equality has become a priority on the international development agenda. Second, teachers are central to the education system for the key roles they play in the transmission of values and knowledge, and their role in the development of human potential and skills in young people. A gender-responsive scorecard (GRS)[1] has the potential to play a significant role in measuring, monitoring, mainstreaming gender equality, women empowerment, and gender-specific programming (UNESCO, 2019) in teacher education institutions. As the literature suggests, GRS can help the management of teacher education institutions to better reflect on the gender sensitivity and responsiveness of their institutions and to more effectively make all necessary changes so that gender equality prevails in their institutions (UNESCO Bangkok, 2009).

Over the past decade in Ghana, Initial Teacher Education (ITE) has witnessed major policy reform changes exclusively with the view to ensuring that teacher training in the country is guided by national goals of education, policies and national objectives on reforms, international commitments, and distinctive features of the teaching specializations. Among these remarkable reform changes was, first, the change of status of initial teacher training institutions from postsecondary teacher training institutions to CoEs in 2008 (Newman, 2013). In 2012, the full operationalization of Act 847, which elevated all CoEs across the country to tertiary status to enable them to offer tertiary programs in teacher education came into effect (Ansah, Nudzor, & Awuku, 2018). Finally, in 2018, the curriculum of CoEs was reformed from a focus on awarding a three-year Diploma in Education qualification to a four-year Bachelor of Education degree-awarding status. This latest curriculum reform covers both pre-tertiary education and CoEs levels and includes institutional reform of CoEs and their affiliation to universities, improvement in leadership and management, and pedagogy at the CoEs (Ministry of Education (MoE), 2017).

As part of strengthening the CoEs, the Government of Ghana, with funding from the UK's Department for International Development (DFID), also introduced a program known as Transforming Teacher Education and Learning (T-TEL), with the implementation period starting from 2014 to 2018, and later extended to 2021. Essentially, the T-TEL program aims to support preservice teacher professional development and management to strengthen preservice teacher education institutions to produce professionally effective and efficient teachers for the country's pre-tertiary education, which hitherto was not clearly emphasized. The main goal of these new T-TEL's reform initiatives is to transform ITE institutions to prepare highly qualified, motivated new teachers who can inspire their pupils to achieve improved outcomes in basic education, and to improve the life chances of Ghana's children and young people (MoE, 2017; T-TEL, 2017).

A core assumption within T-TEL's "theory of change" is that College Leadership and Management is critical to the transformation of gendered relations in CoE, which received little or no attention. In this line of reasoning, therefore, one of the key research areas of the research component of T-TEL is on examining gendered structures, cultures, and practices within Ghanaian CoEs. T-TEL's preliminary research activities in this regard indicate a growing body of research investigating different issues about gender within Ghanaian tertiary institutions, which focuses primarily on universities. For example, Prah (2002) explores the lives of female academics and administrators at the University of Cape Coast; Tsikata (2007) looks at gender, institutional cultures, and the career trajectories of faculty at the University of Ghana; Manuh, Gariba, and Budu (2007) discuss sexual harassment and sexual transactions for grades within Ghana's public and private universities; Apaak (2015) investigates sexual harassment from the perspective of Ghanaian female university athletes; and Morley, Leach, and Lugg (2009) focus on how gender and socioeconomic status constrains and facilitates student and staff participation within Ghanaian universities. On the whole, this body of literature highlights the interest and concerns surrounding female participation and representation in higher education, as well as the growing alarm regarding sexual harassment issues.

As interesting as the literature is, the specific insights recounted demonstrate the dearth of gendered research relative to the context of CoEs in Ghana. In other words, as Ghana's CoEs were upgraded to tertiary status, and ITE policy reform changes are beginning to unfold, the gendered structures, cultures, and practices of CoEs which could create the environment to promote gender equity are not been investigated to the extent of those in Ghanaian universities (Nudzor, Tao, Ansah, & Agbevanu, 2019). A recent publication for UNESCO, *Teacher Education Policies from a Gender Perspective: The Case of Ghana, Nigeria and Senegal* (Mulugeta, 2012), is worth isolating for commendation as one of the few research studies conducted on the topic in recent times in the entire sub-Saharan African region. Mulugeta's study explores gendered practices and structures relative to female students and staff participation in the activities of CoEs in the aforementioned three countries. Although important, there are, however, a few limitations that perhaps affect the validity and reliability of this study. In the case of Ghana, the main respondents for the study consisted of only the MoE officials and only one principal from a CoE who did not constitute a representative sample. This methodological pitfall conveys a key message about the Ghanaian educational context worth highlighting. In particular, this weakness in Mulugeta's research demonstrates the need for a more robust investigation into the different issues about gender within Ghana's CoEs, not only to address the gap in the research but more importantly, to produce knowledge and evidence that contributes to the development of gender policy and practice for the CoEs.

It is against this backdrop that the Gender and Leadership study on which this chapter reports was undertaken. The Gender and Leadership study was commissioned by the National Council for Tertiary Education (NCTE), the National Teaching Council (NTC), and the College of Education Principals' Conference (PRINCOF) and jointly implemented by T-TEL Program. The study, which was conducted from May to June 2017 at 10 case study CoEs, explored the perceptions and experiences of key CoEs actors to provide an in-depth understanding of gender and leadership issues within the colleges.

The current chapter details one area of the Gender and Leadership study: it explores the perspectives and experiences of CoEs actors (i.e., college principals, vice principals, quality assurance (QA) officers, gender champions, tutors, and students) on the use of GRS strategies for promoting gender equality in the CoEs in Ghana. This chapter addresses the following research questions:

1. How do CoEs actors interpret the concept of the GRS?
2. What GRS strategies do CoEs actors consider helpful in mainstreaming gender equality/equity in their CoEs?
3. What challenges do CoEs actors face in implementing the GRS strategies to promote and maintain gender sensitivity and equality in the CoEs?

Our overriding assumption and rationale underpinning the Gender and Leadership study on which this chapter draws is that investigating the salient gender issues within preservice teacher education in Ghana is akin to interrogating how these issues can be addressed (through programs like T-TEL) to strengthen future cadres of Beginning Teachers. In this line of reasoning, and more importantly, to enable readers to understand the context within which the Gender and Leadership study on which this chapter reports were conducted, next section, the details the "GRS" that was used as a toolkit to self-assess the CoEs based on which the follow-up research activities were undertaken.

THE GRS

A "GRS" is a standardized assessment of gender mainstreaming practices, which is designed to foster adherence to minimum standards for gender equality processes across institutions (Commonwealth of Learning, 2017; Esser, 2017) and serve as an accountability framework for assessing the effectiveness of gender mainstreaming. The GRS has been described as an institutional tool for gender mainstreaming, which comprises ongoing audits of organizations' policies and/or strategies to promote gender equality (Bloom, Owen, & Covington, 2003). As a management and planning tool, gender audits examine the quality and effectiveness of gender-related practices and systems of organizations, as well as allows institutions to take a comprehensive look at the status of its gender mainstreaming practices to see what is working, what is not working, and what gaps need filling (Commonwealth of Learning, 2017; Esser, 2017; European Institute for Gender Equality, 2018; Learn4dev Gender Expert Group, n.d.; UNESCO, 2019).

Besides, a GRS measures the extent to which gender equality is effectively institutionalized in the policies, programs, organizational structures and proceedings (including decision-making processes), and in the corresponding budgets. Thus, as the literature points out, GRSs as self-assessment tools are designed to assist staff and members of institutions to self-assess their gender sensitivity and equality (United Nations Development Programme, 2014; United Nations Economic Commission of Africa, 2016).

The European Institute for Gender Equality (2018) outlines several reasons for the use of GRSs in institutions. First, the scorecard, among others, seeks to assist institutions in identifying areas in which they are meeting or not meeting minimum standards and then stimulate a constructive dialogue within the institution about the status of gender mainstreaming and how practices can be improved. Besides, GRSs are meant to identify where technical assistance can support the achievement of minimum standards, as well as share best practices in supporting national priorities for gender mainstreaming. Furthermore, as an institutional self-assessment tool, the gender scorecard seeks to ascertain whether gender equality goals (women's empowerment and equality of women and men) have been attained. Finally, the gender scorecard seeks to assess processes and strategies put in place to mainstream gender in institutions.

In the context of CoEs in Ghana, and as part of its routine targeted capacity development support for CoEs, the Leadership and Management component of the T-TEL's program prepared a special training manual, *The Leadership Programme Resources for College Leaders*, which was used to provide periodic and consistent training to CoEs leaders. *The Leadership Programme Resources for College Leaders* was organized into six units[2] with a focus on issues of professional development and QA.

In the Leadership and Management training workshop conducted on Unit 2 (Systems Leadership) in 2016, CoEs leaders were introduced to ideas on how they could improve and/or strengthen their institutions through, for example, developing policies and procedures for effective college systems. Part of this unit was on the subject of inclusion and was therefore dedicated to gender-responsive college management, which provided an introduction on how to create an environment that promotes gender equity, particularly through removing all forms of discrimination against females and those considered to be most marginalized and/or disadvantaged. This introduction discussed 13 competencies that, together, constitute a holistic approach to ensuring a gender-responsive CoE. These competencies also included specific strategies that contribute to the achievement of each competency. Such an approach was aimed at demonstrating that gender responsiveness goes *beyond* "gender sensitivity" (which is the ability to *recognize* gender issues) or "gender awareness" (which is the ability to *identify* problems arising from gender inequality, even if they are not obvious). In our view, "gender responsiveness" is an "embracing concept" that refers to *taking comprehensive action* to correct gender bias/discrimination to ensure equitable outcomes.

Box 1 shows a list of the 13 competencies discussed and examples of some of the accompanying or corresponding strategies for ensuring gender-responsive institutions.

Box 1. Gender-Responsive Competencies and Strategies..

1. *All members of the CoE have received gender training* (including tutors, leaders, nonteaching staff, and students).
2. *Classroom practice is gender-responsive* (pedagogy that enhances opportunities for all students to participate, take leadership roles, feel confident, etc.).
3. *Tutors challenge traditional gender roles during lessons* (examples and activities allow females and males feel confident to challenge traditional gender roles such as boys cooking, girls being doctors, boys running errands, etc.).
4. *CoE practices and protocols are gender-responsive* (equally assigned leadership roles and chores, a gender club is organized, corporal punishment is banned, etc.).
5. *CoE infrastructure is gender-responsive* (especially accommodation, toilets, changing rooms, etc.).
6. *All female students/staff have equal access to CoE resources* (resources such as TLMs, extra-curricular clubs, ICT, etc.).
7. *CoE teaching practice is gender-responsive* (strategies that ensure that mentees are safe, comfortable, and equitable, especially for female mentees).
8. *CoE staff procedures are gender-responsive* (which includes treatment of staff, nurturing of females, the appointment of a gender champion).
9. *The CoE has a sexual harassment policy that is fully implemented* (which includes all reporting procedures and a dissemination strategy).
10. *CoE policies are developed and/or amended to be gender-responsive* (all policies are gender-responsive, such as code of conduct, QA policy, health and safety, etc.).
11. *CoE data are collected and analyzed in a gender-responsive way* (data are collected and analyzed for female enrollment, achievement, female tutors, senior management, etc.).
12. *CoE planning is gender-responsive* (there are targets and strategies to improve female enrolment, achievement, tutor recruitment, senior management, etc.).
13. *CoE budgeting is gender-responsive* (budgets are allocated for gender training, infrastructure, recruitment, implementation of strategies, etc.) (T-TEL, 2014, 2017, n.d.).

Note. These competencies and strategies were presented in a scorecard format so that CoEs could conduct self-assessments and measure the degree of implementation of gender-responsive strategies within their colleges.

METHOD

The Gender and Leadership study employed a qualitative multiple-case study design to examine the views of key actors in CoEs in Ghana. The multiple-case study design allows the researchers to explore the phenomena under review through the use of a replication strategy (Merriam, 1997; Stake, 2006; Yin, 2003; Zach, 2006). According to Zach, there are no hard-and-fast rules about how many cases are required to satisfy the requirements of a replication strategy in the multiple-case study design. However, Yin suggested that six to 10 cases, if the results turn out as predicted, are sufficient to provide compelling support for the initial set of propositions. For Yin, the approach does not rely on the type of representative sampling logic used in survey research, thus, the typical criteria regarding sample size are immaterial. Yin and Zach agreed that in a multiple-case study approach, the sample size should be determined by the number of cases required to reach saturation, data collection until no significant new findings are revealed.

Given Yin's (2003) and Zach's (2006) suggestions on sample size and for this study, 10 case study CoEs were sampled from five geographical zones in Ghana, namely Northern/Upper East & West, Ashanti/Brong Ahafo, Volta, Central and Western, and Eastern/Greater Accra. The characteristics/criteria used for the selection included the geographical location of the CoE and demographic characteristics of the respondents. While the CoEs selected did not constitute a representative sample, they provided for robust case study comparisons (Yin, 2003) about the selection criteria. Table A1 shows the lists these characteristics for the first 38 CoEs[3] to receive T-TEL leadership training. The CoEs in grey color were the case studies proposed and approved by NCTE, NTC, and PRINCOF.

First, geography was considered to provide geographical representation across the country, and thus, two CoEs per zone were selected to ensure at least some within-zone range. This range focused on rural (rural <150,000 population) and urban locations to see how and to what extent such locales might affect the recruitment and attrition of female staff (see Table A1). As to gender, both

Table. 1. Selected Case Study CoEs.

Zone	Name of CoE	Student Profile M = Mixed SF = Female SM = Male	Locale (Rural vs. Urban)	Gender of Principal (M/F)	Population
Zone 1	1 Gbewaa College of Education	M	Rural	M	1,124
	2 NJA College of Education	M	Urban	F	769
Zone 2	1 Berekum College of Education	M	Rural	M	1,247
	2 St. Louis College of Education	SF	Urban	F	1,017
Zone 3	1 Dambai College of Education	M	Rural	M	702
	2 St. Teresa's College of Education	SF	Urban	F	630
Zone 4	1 Holy Child College of Education	SF	Urban	F	734
	2 Wiawso College of Education	M	Rural	M	1,077
Zone 5	1 Abetifi Presbyterian CoE	M	Rural	M	1,009
	2 Presbyterian Women's CoE	SF	Urban	F	665

Table. A1.   Table of Selected Case Study CoEs.

		Student Profile			
Zone	Name of CoE	M = Mixed SF = Female SM = Male	Locale (Rural vs. Urban)	Gender of Principal (M/F)	Population
Zone 1 Northern/Upper East and West	3 Bagabaga College of Education	M	Urban	M	970
	4 Bimbilla EP College of Education	M	Rural	M	1,088
	5 Gbewaa College of Education	M	Rural	M	1,124
	6 NJA College of Education	M	Urban	F	769
	7 St John Bosco College	M	Rural	M	1,155
	8 Tamale College of Education	M	Urban	M	1,185
	9 Tumu College of Education	M	Rural	M	715
Zone 2 Ashanti/Brong Ahafo	3 Akrokerri College of Education	M	Rural	M	1,201
	4 Atebubu College of Education	M	Rural	M	1,140
	5 Agogo Presbyterian College of Education	SF	Rural	F	732
	6 Berekum College of Education	M	Rural	M	1,247
	7 ampong Technical College of Education	SM	Urban	M	1,194
	8 Ofinso College of Education	M	Rural	M	1,103
	9 St. Joseph College of Education	M	Urban	M	869
	10 St. Louis College of Education	SF	Urban	F	1,017
	11 St. Monica's College of Education	SF	Urban	F	1,078
	12 Wesley College of Education	M	Urban	M	1,026
Zone 3	3 Akatsi College of Education	M	Rural	M	1,126
Volta	4 Dambai College of Education	M	Rural	M	702
	5 Evangelical Presbyterian College of Education	M	Rural	M	599
	6 Jasikan College of Education	M	Urban	M	1,046
	7 Peki College of Education	M	Rural	M	631
	8 St. Francis' College of Education	M	Urban	M	1,013
	9 St. Teresa's College of Education	SF	Urban	F	630

Table. A1. (*Continued*)

Zone	Name of CoE	M = Mixed SF = Female SM = Male	Locale (Rural vs. Urban)	Gender of Principal (M/F)	Population
		Student Profile			
Zone 4 Central and Western	3 Enchi College of Education	M	Rural	F	841
	4 Foso College of Education	M	Rural	M	1,008
	5 Holy Child College of Education	SF	Urban	F	734
	6 Komenda College of Education	M	Rural	M	970
	7 Ola College of Education	SF	Urban	F	1,057
	8 Wiawso College of Education	M	Rural	M	1,077
Zone 5 Eastern/Greater Accra	3 Abetifi Presbyterian CoE	M	Rural	M	1,009
	4 Ada College of Education	M	Urban	M	838
	5 Accra College of Education	M	Urban	F	911
	6 Kibi Presbyterian College of Education	M	Rural	M	776
	7 Mount Mary College of Education	M	Rural	M	1,244
	8 Presbyterian College of Education	M	Urban	M	1,439
	9 Presbyterian Women's CoE	SF	Urban	F	665
	10 SDA College of Education	M	Urban	F	1,076

principals and students were considered, first, to see if the gender of principals affects their views and attitudes toward gender; based on this research question, five male and five female principals were selected for the study. Second, to see how and to what extent student demographics or gender profiles (particularly all-female CoEs) affect the prioritization of gender responsiveness, five mixed and five female single-sex CoEs were selected for the study.

Although the selection criteria aimed to provide a general representation of colleges about geography and demographics, patterns emerged within these selected colleges. For example, out of the 10 case study CoEs, the five rural CoEs all had mixed-sex student populations and male principals. All of the five remaining urban CoEs were headed by female principals, and four of these colleges had single-sex female student populations. These patterns provide a glimpse into the patterns that emerged concerning the recruitment of female leaders and staff, which is discussed at greater length in the comprehensive project report submitted to NCTE, NTC, and PRINCOF. Table 1 outlines the selected case study CoEs.

As indicated earlier in this chapter, the Gender and Leadership study aimed to generate a fine-grained understanding of key college actors' perceptions and experiences. Thus, purposive sampling strategy (Leedy, 1995; Robson, 2002; Saunders, 2011) was used to select the respondents comprising college leaders (such as principals, vice principals, QA officers, and gender champions[4]), female tutors, and female student teachers.[5] These college leaders were selected for the study because of their roles and responsibilities in managing the colleges' visions and their implementation, particularly as they pertained to issues of gender and inclusion. The college leaders, except gender champions, had also participated in T-TEL's Leadership and Management workshops, which meant that they also had some gender training, particularly through the introduction of a Gender Scorecard in 2016.[6] While all the CoEs were mandated by NCTE in 2016 to have a designated gender focal person, many did not have such a person until the concept of a "Gender Champion" was introduced at the later part of Leadership and Management workshops in March 2017. Although many of these champions had just been appointed to their posts, they were also included in the research based on the significance of their role and knowledge of gender scorecards. The two groups of female tutors and students were included because they were salient in triangulating (Cohen, Manion, & Morrison, 2007; Creswell, 2014; Jick, 1979; Robson, 2002) the degree to which gender-responsive strategies had been implemented within the college.

To elicit an in-depth understanding of these respondents' views and experiences, semi-structured interviews (Fontana & Frey, 2000; Thomas, 1995; Wengraf, 2001) were used to probe the research questions outlined. Additionally, the respondents were taken through an abbreviated version of the GRS to gauge how and to what extent strategies from it had been implemented (see Appendix for the interview guide and scorecard) in mainstreaming gender equality. Because our study aimed broadly to explore the perceptions and experiences of key CoE actors to provide an in-depth understanding of gender and leadership issues within the colleges, we employed a "processual analytical approach" (Pettigrew, 1997) in analyzing data obtained. This kind of analysis is underpinned by the assumption that social reality is not at all in a steady state but rather is a dynamic process, perpetually in the process of becoming an accepted norm (Pettigrew, 1997, cited in Nudzor, Dare, Oduro, Bosu, & Addy, 2015, p. 443). Our aim, therefore, was to highlight the current realities of gender and leadership issues in the CoEs in Ghana while recognizing and acknowledging that these realities were not static but changing constantly.

Consequently, although the research project report on which this chapter is based is transparent about the 10 case study CoEs that participated in the Gender and Leadership research, the findings will refer to the colleges by their characteristics only (e.g., rural/mixed-sex CoE or urban/single-sex CoE) to preserve their anonymity (Berg, 2004; Denzin & Lincoln, 2000; Neuman, 2004). For the same reason, where reference is made to individual college leaders in respect of their views, only their official positions and/or designation will be used. It should also be noted that, while quantitative tallies of responses for the gender scorecard were used for analyses and discussion in the full report, the responses were not analyzed in a robust statistical manner. Rather, these tallies have been used for triangulation of answers and to provide a general picture of whether actors from the same college aligned or contradicted one another. The rationale being that consensus, for us, is an indication that a thorough knowledge and implementation of a strategy from management to classroom actors; contradiction indicates inconsistencies in knowledge and/or implementation.

FINDINGS AND DISCUSSION

The aim of this chapter and our research, seeking a fine-grained understanding of perceptions and experiences of key college actors regarding the interpretations of a GRS to promote gender equality and equity in CoEs, is best conveyed by reporting issues emerging from our data analysis using a "narrative approach" (Bates, Greif, Levi, Rosenthal, & Weingast, 1998; Pettigrew, 1985; Pettigrew, Ferlie, & McKee, 1992). Narratives help analyze phenomena contained within a small number of case studies in which social and organizational processes and outcomes are "transparently observable" (Pettigrew, 1990). In such an approach, the analysis consists of a summary of several processes, which are presented in the form of short histories of change events in a chronological order, as well as an indication of the observable outcomes of the processes (Nudzor et al., 2015). For succinctness, we organize the emerging issues in the form of findings around the three key research questions we posed based on CoEs actors' views regarding a GRS, most helpful gender-responsive strategies, and challenges facing the implementation of gender scorecard strategies.

Interpretations of the GRS

The first research question sought to explore the interpretations of respondents about the GRS in Ghanaian CoEs. Our analyses of data suggest that respondents were introduced to the scorecard and asked about the degree to which each of the strategies had been implemented in their CoEs. Overall, there was a general contradiction among respondents regarding which gender actions/strategies had been achieved; this was most vividly seen between college leader answers and tutor/student answers. Such a contradiction is likely due to a theory versus reality divide, whereby college leaders may have been aware of gender policies or strategies that have been discussed (often via leadership training), but tutors and students have not been privy to these discussions and have yet to see anything implemented on the ground.

Despite the inconsistencies regarding the implementation of strategies, a majority of respondents from across the colleges felt that the scorecard and the comprehensive strategies within it, were helpful, not only because the strategies cut across all areas of the college but also because they gave people ideas and actions they had not previously thought of for executing policies supporting gender parity. For example, at one rural/mixed-sex CoE, female respondents indicated their desire to lead the implementation of some of the scorecard strategies because they felt so strongly about them. In her excitement, one female student said: "I can imagine how exciting this campus would be if we had more female tutors. I am looking forward to seeing many more female mentors in the college [*sic.*]."

At another rural/mixed-sex CoE, some leaders highlighted the necessity of these strategies. In particular, the male principals pointed out that implementation of the scorecard would help improve the gender responsiveness of the college. Another respondent, a Head of Department, emphatically stated: "I think they [scorecard strategies] are all important." At another rural/mixed-sex CoE, respondents were generally impressed about the comprehensiveness of the strategies and felt that if all the strategies outlined in the scorecard were implemented and achieved, the college would become truly responsive to gender issues. For example, a female tutor commented: "To me, all these things I do agree with them [*sic.*] provided they will be implemented or structures will be put in place from above." Perhaps, it is important to note here that the leadership buy-in is essential for this tutor because it has not been, or not been fully felt. Another respondent from this college stated:

> I don't think there is any strategy on the list that is left out. They are all very good and for me, I think that if we can implement them, then we will be on the journey towards becoming a gender-responsive college. (QA officer)

Similarly, respondents from the urban/single-sex female CoEs also seemed to value the scorecard, even though some of the strategies were less applicable because of their all-female populations (such as strategies to increase female student recruitment and leadership posts). That said, just because a CoE has female students does not mean that it is automatically gender-responsive. For example, infrastructure such as toilets may not have hygiene bins for sanitary napkins, gender parity among tutors and leaders may not be met, and sexual harassment can still be enacted by male tutors toward female staff and students. Many female respondents did seem to understand this, as demonstrated by their responses when asked whether the scorecard strategies applied to them: "I think they are all important" (female principal); "... they can all be worked at to help build a very good college" (gender champion); "... they are all appropriate" (vice principal); and "I think I agree with them all" (female student). That said, although the male QA officer at this female CoE agreed with the scorecard in principle, he did say that "I think that having a gender focal person is not too necessary." This may be due to a lack of understanding of what a gender champion or gender focal person should do.

Overall, it was clear that after the interviews, respondents at all the case study CoEs seem to have been sensitized to the strategies on the GRS because their understanding of gender responsiveness appeared broader during the latter part of the interviews and they began to think, conceptualize, and interpret gender issues in ways that demonstrated a more comprehensive understanding than the initial stages of the interviews. This shows that even though a brief sensitization via interviews, respondents had come to understand that gender responsiveness was not just about recognizing problems arising from inequality but was also about taking action to correct gender bias to ensure equitable outcomes, which supports the views of Commonwealth of Learning (2017) and European Institute for Gender Equality (2018) that gender "responsive" scorecards be a globally standardized assessment of gender mainstreaming practices, designed to foster adherence to minimum standards for gender equality processes across institutions. Generally, the respondents' interpretations of the GRS as suggested by their views highlight the fact that the scorecard is not only an important tool for mainstreaming gender issues in the leadership and management activities of the CoEs but also an accountability framework for helping to develop policies and strategies to promote gender equality (Esser, 2017).

Helpful GRS Strategies

The second research question sought to identify GRS strategies that were considered most helpful in self-assessing gender equality in the CoEs. In general, there was not one resounding strategy or set of strategies that were deemed to be most salient in achieving a gender-responsive college, which speaks to the holistic nature of gender responsiveness, as well as to respondents valuing strategies that may reflect their world views or position in the college. For example, at one urban/mixed-sex college, the female principal highlighted supporting females assertiveness and exposing gender abuses. The gender champion was in favor of encouraging females to take leadership positions and provide gender-sensitive facilities (e.g., accommodation, toilets, changing rooms, etc.) in the college. And while the female tutors preferred to give increased attention to sexual harassment, the female students favored giving leadership positions to females and providing scholarships to female students and tutors. However, both female tutors and students agreed on each other's priorities.

Interestingly, at a rural/mixed-sex CoE, many of the male respondents thought achieving equal numbers of males and females through effective data collection and analysis was most important. The male college principal stated: "Through effective data management, we hope to achieve parity in the number of male and female tutors and students within the near future." On the other hand, female tutors thought opportunities for professional development and leadership positions were most valuable. For instance, one female tutor said, "We must use affirmative action and hire a female principal for the college soon." At another rural/mixed-sex CoE, leaders thought that bridging the gap between tutors (female and male) and students and providing accommodation facilities and hygiene bins for female students, including those who are pregnant, were the most important strategies. Other strategies emphasized by respondents include "students' admission and providing infrastructure to all," "offering scholarships to female students is gender-responsive," and "allocating budgets for gender training of college staff and students."

In some colleges, there was convergence regarding which strategies were deemed most important. For example, in one urban/single-sex female CoE, a female tutor and student focused on the strategy to improve the performance of females in science and mathematics, while two respondents saw the appointment of a gender champion as most imperative. At another urban/single-sex female CoE, many of the respondents thought that all the strategies that aimed to reverse traditional gender roles were most valuable. For instance, the gender champion said:

> I pray all stakeholders in the college become supporting [*sic.*] gender champions and help us reverse most the traditional gender roles (e.g., sweeping, cleaning, running errands etc.) in the classroom, the halls, the dining hall, among others.

At another urban/single-sex female college, respondents identified strategies for gender-responsive budgeting, provision of appropriate accommodation/infrastructure, recruitment/appointment of qualified staff, and encouraging females to management positions.

Although our results show that most of the GRS strategies are important, it is not clear how the results support or contradict existing findings because of the lack of research evidence in this area of scholarship. This lack of clarity notwithstanding, the results provide an empirical basis for further research on the helpful or important gender scorecard strategies that are likely to help key college actors ensure gender equality and equity in the CoEs.

Challenges with Using the GRS

The third research question sought to identify the challenges key actors in CoEs faced in implementing the GRS strategies to ensure gender responsiveness and equality. From the study, there was overall valuing of the scorecard and the variety of strategies within it; however, there remained several challenges with using it. As previously discussed, it was clear across the CoE context that there was a lack of familiarity with the scorecard, which is understandable because, although the scorecard was introduced in leadership training, follow-up by T-TEL has been inconsistent, as evidenced by a QA officer from a rural/mixed-sex CoE, who stated:

> We haven't done anything at all. I remember when the gender scorecard was brought in, the thinking was that maybe there will [sic.] some push from T-TEL as to what to do with it, but when we were not getting any indication like that, we just left it.

Even though a self-assessment report based on the GRS was required of every CoE, out of the 10 case study CoEs, only four had prepared such a report and these varied in degree of rigor and reliability. For example, although none of the reports used the actual scorecard template, two of the reports at least outlined each of the competencies and discussed what they had achieved (or not) about each. The other two reports were much vaguer, and the reported responses on strategy achievement were not aligned at all with responses given in this research. This speaks to the need to conduct the self-assessment with a variety of actors from the CoE (i.e., leaders, tutors, students) to triangulate responses, particularly surrounding issues of implementation. Consequently, one challenge with the scorecard was that it had not been used robustly to form the basis for future college improvement planning and development, which was likely due to the "lack of push" from T-TEL on how and when to use it. However, given the respondents' interest in and valuing of the scorecard during this research, it would seem that reintroducing the scorecard with concrete guidelines for use and implementation would bear a great deal of fruit. Given that QA officers and other CoE leaders are in charge of implementation, their responses that the GRS would be helpful seem more a lip service than an action. This aligns with the female tutors and students who would find value in the scorecard if supported top-down.

Another significant challenge in the use of a GRS is that many respondents felt that budgetary constraints would hinder the implementation of strategies. At one rural/mixed-sex CoE, a female tutor stated:

I am looking at the budgeting aspect as a difficult strategy to achieve. This is because the budgetary allocation to the schools and itself has problem [*sic.*] so apportioning part of this budget solely for gender issues I think would be difficult and the willingness of the management to accept to include budget for gender issues is another thing.

At an urban/single-sex female CoE, the vice principal stated:

I think I would look at the budget issues; we are not doing so well because we have not budgeted for issues relating to gender ... I think that once we budget then the college will become gender-responsive.

The vice principal added: "For instance, the gender champion's work has to be budgeted for, then he/she can go about the duty effectively and then the college will become gender-responsive."

From the study, budgets do not pose the only problem about implementing strategies from the gender scorecard. At the same college, the female principal discussed how many of the strategies in the scorecard were also present in the college gender policy that they had developed several months ago. However, due to the recent elections and change in administration, the college's governing Council had yet to be reconstituted and was thus unable to ratify the gender policy that they had developed. The principal stated:

We have tried to have a policy on [gender], though not approved by Council yet; but at least the first Council looked through and has made a few corrections. So at least we have a policy guiding us on gender issues. So, we know that in whatever we do we shouldn't be biased.

This excerpt demonstrates that once a gender policy is in place, deliberate strategies would be pursued and implemented. One way to address this constraint would be for NCTE to provide a national gender policy for CoEs; thus, there would be no need for governing Council ratification and CoEs would be able to start implementing/disseminating policies immediately. The national gender policy could be based on the holistic approach to gender responsiveness as demonstrated in the scorecard and could provide concrete guidelines on how CoEs can go about implementing the strategies outlined in the scorecard. It is, however, noteworthy to say that there appears to be limited or no evidence from the extant literature regarding the challenges that higher education institutions face in using the gender scorecard in CoEs, making it difficult to see how our findings support or contradict earlier findings in this area of study. However, the finding provides an empirical basis for other researchers to examine the challenges of using the GRS in mainstreaming gender equity/equality, not only in CoEs but also in other higher education institutions in Ghana and Africa.

In another vein, insights from the analyses of data suggest that CoE actors had different interpretations of the GRS and its role in promoting and maintaining gender sensitivity and equity/equality in the colleges. In particular, the analysis shows that gender awareness is more likely to be top of mind when the student body and leadership are female, as issues that affect women (such as the need for hygiene bins for sanitary napkins or more substantial accommodation security) are more prominent and can be voiced more easily. In mixed-sex CoEs, cases of "indirect discrimination" were more prevalent, in which policies and protocols were likely developed against standards that were relevant to males and then applied to everyone. This explains why many mixed-sex CoEs had challenges with certain gender-responsive protocols (i.e., chores being assigned along gendered lines), infrastructure (i.e., no hygiene bins), and policy development (i.e., no support for staff/students regarding pregnancy or childcare). This would indicate that the use of the GRS and implementation of its strategies would ensure a gender-responsive CoE, as strategies (and the standards/criteria that underpin them) explicitly mitigate against any indirect discrimination that might unintentionally occur.

From the views and experiences presented in this chapter, all 10 of the case study CoEs had positive outcomes concerning GRS strategies or pedagogy that were fairly intuitive, such as "giving equal chance to females and males." However, there was less consistent implementation of more nuanced scorecard strategies, such as identifying and challenging traditional gender roles in learning materials. This, possibly, was as a result of a lack of exposure to the variety of strategies that constitute gender-responsive pedagogy. It would, therefore, seem fortuitous, in our view, to adapt and/or provide the *Gender Handbook for Teaching Practice Mentors* that T-TEL has developed that provides training on gender-responsive pedagogy for use by tutors in colleges to address this anomaly. Additionally, relevant contexts from this handbook should be incorporated into the new curriculum for ITE that the MoE has recently undertaken to help with the consistent implementation of nuanced gender-responsive strategies in CoEs across the country.

CONCLUSION

The purpose of this chapter was to report on the views and experiences of key actors in 10 CoEs in Ghana regarding their interpretations of a GRS, the scorecard strategies, and challenges faced in implementing the scorecard strategies. In this chapter, we have underscored an aspect of the major reform changes currently taking hold in Ghana's CoEs relative to ITE. While the implications of the findings reported here are many and varied, we privilege two. First, we posit that the fairly intuitive yet vague and/or narrow understanding that respondents have of the GRS could prevent a more holistic approach to GRS strategies from being implemented in the CoEs. Second, and based on our first observation, the intuitive, yet narrow understanding of gender responsiveness appears to pervade college pedagogy. It is our considered view that as the first step toward implementing and maintaining fully gender equality/responsive CoEs, urgent, concerted efforts must be made to ensure that all CoEs actors are sensitized to the GRS and the holistic and action-oriented nature of gender responsiveness. They must also be made to deepen their understanding of the GRS and its use in making their colleges more gender sensitive.

In light of the findings reported in this chapter, we have argued that the elevation of CoEs from pre-tertiary to tertiary status warrants the need for them to reengineer their operations to align with practices of tertiary education institutions, and also to improve the quality of training of preservice teachers, to address poor learning outcomes in pre-tertiary education. One key area to consider, in our view, and in an attempt to achieve the tertiary status bestowed on Ghanaian CoEs, is to research the interpretations, helpful strategies, and challenges of the GRS in CoEs to create the environment that promotes gender sensitivity, equality, and equity, particularly through removing all forms of discrimination against females and those considered to be most marginalized and/or disadvantaged. In line with this thinking, and as an antecedent to more robust research studies to follow in this area, this chapter, drawing on a Gender and Leadership study undertaken by T-TEL and a group of independent researchers, has explored and foregrounded perceptions and experiences of key CoEs actors regarding their contextualized interpretations of a GRS. Based on the findings, it is recommended that the *implementation* of scorecard strategies is imperative to creating a fully gender-responsive CoE. Overseeing and being accountable for the implementation of the gender scorecard could be one responsibility for college gender champions. Besides, CoEs should ensure successful implementation of gender scorecard strategies, as they are specifically designed to mitigate against any indirect discrimination that might unintentionally occur. Thus, the effective use and implementation of the GRS strategies may contribute to promoting female leadership, to teacher development, and girls' success in CoEs, through enhanced gender-responsive practices across the teacher education sector globally. So, although this chapter focuses on Ghana, the findings present useful insights for developing country context. Essentially, the insights have shown the relevance of the GRS in mainstreaming gender in higher education institutions across sub-Saharan Africa.

NOTES

1. The gender-responsive scorecard is a standardized self-assessment of college-level gender mainstreaming practices and performance that is aimed at ensuring accountability of college leadership and improving gender responsiveness (Commonwealth of Learning, 2017). It allows measuring the college's progress toward gender equality and women's empowerment in college leadership and management.

2. The units consisted of (1) setting new directions; (2) systems leadership; (3) operations leadership; (4) leading curriculum, training, and learning; (5) leading and managing change; and (6) strategic leadership. Within each of these units were about six different carefully selected topics to ensure that CoEs leaders were equipped with the necessary skills to lead their colleges to become tertiary institutions. Also embedded in each of these units was the self-assessment of seven quality assurance indicators of Leadership and Management; Training and Learning; Assessment; Student Engagement; Monitoring and Evaluation; Environment and Infrastructure; and Partnership and Cooperation (T-TEL, 2014).

3. St Ambrose and Gambaga CoEs were not included in the Gender and Leadership study on which this article is based because of their delayed entry to the T-TEL program in 2014.

4. Gender focal persons in the colleges of the education.

5. Most case study colleges had a total of eight respondents (i.e., four leaders, two tutors, and two students); however, in the case of two CoEs, researchers extended this pool of respondents to include one male staff and one student, respectively.

6. It is important to note that at the time the Gender and Leadership study was undertaken, only 40 CoEs were duly accredited across the country. As of today, six more CoEs had been added to the fold and fully accredited by NAB making a total of 46 CoEs.

ACKNOWLEDGMENTS

We are grateful to the Government of Ghana and the UK's DFID for funding assistance for the implementation of the project activities on which this article reports. We are also indebted highly to all CoEs leaders, tutors, and students across the country for sharing their insights and experiences with us. Finally, we acknowledge the other members of our research team, namely Yaw Afari Ankomah, Dora Baaba Aidoo, Michael Boakye-Yiadom, and Edward Akomaning who are not designated as authors of this article but whose contributions to the Gender and Leadership research we appreciate immensely.

REFERENCES

Ansah, F., Nudzor, H. P., & Awuku, S. (2018). Rethinking stakeholder engagement in higher education reforms: The case of colleges of education in Ghana. *Ghana Journal of Higher Education*, 4, 1–18.

Apaak, D. (2015). Knowledge level and incidence of sexual harassment in sports: Views of Ghanaian female university athletes. *Journal of Educational and Social Research*, 5(3), 121–123.

Bates, R. H., Greif, A., Levi, M., Rosenthal, J., & Weingast, B. R. (1998). *Analytic narratives*. Princeton, NJ: Princeton University Press.

Berg, B. L. (2004). *Qualitative research methods for social sciences: International students' edition* (5th ed.). Boston, MA: Pearson.

Bloom, B., Owen, B., & Covington, S. (2003). *Gender-responsive strategies: Research, practice and guiding principles for women offenders*. National Institute of Corrections Accession No. 018017. US Department of Justice, National Institute of Corrections, Washington, DC.

Cohen, L., Manion, L., & Morrison, K. (2007). *Research methods in education* (6th ed.). London: Routledge.

Commonwealth of Learning. (2017). *Institutional scorecard for gender mainstreaming*. Burnaby: Commonwealth of Learning.

Creswell, J. W. (2014). *Research design: Qualitative, quantitative, and mixed methods approaches* (4th ed.). London: Sage.

Denzin, N. K., & Lincoln, Y. S. (2000). *Handbook of qualitative research* (2nd ed.). London: Sage.

Esser, A. L. (2017). UNCT SWAP-Scorecard: Assessment results and action plan. Retrieved from https://undg.org/wp-content/uploads/2017/11/UNCT-SWAP-Scorecard-KR-Report-2017_Final-1.pdf

European Institute for Gender Equality. (2018). UNCT performance indicator of gender equality and women's empowerment scorecard. Retrieved from https://eige.europa.eu/gender-mainstreaming/resources/international/unct-performance-indicators-gender-equality-and-womens-empowerment-score-card

Fontana, A., & Frey, J. H. (2000). The interview: From structured questions to negotiated text. In N. K. Denzin & Y. S. Lincoln (Eds.), *Handbook of qualitative research* (2nd ed., pp. 645–672). London: Sage.

Jick, T. D. (1979). Mixing qualitative and quantitative methods: Triangulation in action. *Administrative Science Quarterly*, 24(4), 602–611.

Learn4dev Gender Expert Group. (n.d.). *User's guide for the "gender equality scorecard for trainings."* Retrieved from http://www.learn4dev.net/file/file/download?guid=6e174e23-32fc-40b2-8966-8430ee93b401

Leedy, P. (1995). Research methodology: Qualitative or quantitative. *Practical Research–Planning and Design*, 6, 137–147.

Manuh, T., Gariba, S., & Budu, J. (2007). *Change and transformation in Ghana's publicly funded universities*. Accra: Woeli.

Merriam, S. (1997). *Qualitative research and case study applications in education: Revised and expanded from case study research in education*. Jossey-Bass Education Series. San Francisco, CA: Jossey-Bass.

Ministry of Education (MoE). (2017). *The initial teacher education curriculum writing guide.* Accra: MoE.

Morley, L., Leach, F., & Lugg, R. (2009). Democratizing higher education in Ghana and Tanzania: Opportunity structures and social inequalities. *International Journal of Educational Development, 29*(1), 56–64.

Mulugeta, E. (2012). *Teacher education policies from gender perspective: The case of Ghana, Nigeria and Senegal.* Addis Ababa: UNESCO-IICBA.

Neuman, W. L. (2004). *Basics of social science research: Qualitative and quantitative approaches.* Boston, MA: Pearson Education.

Newman, E. K. (2013). The upgrading of teacher training institutions to colleges of education: Issues and prospects. *African Journal of Teacher Education, 3*(2), 1–13. Retrieved from https://journal. lib.uoguelph.ca/index.php/ajote/article/view/2728

Nudzor, H. P., Dare, A., Oduro, G. K. T., Bosu, R., & Addy, N. (2015). Examining activity-based learning (ABL) practices in public basic schools in the northern region of Ghana. *Educational Research, 57*(4), 437–450.

Nudzor, H. P., Tao, S., Ansah, F., & Agbevanu, W. K. (2019). Examining gendered structures, cultures, and practices of Ghana's colleges of education. *Tertiary Education Series, 9*(1), 25–53.

Pettigrew, A. (1985). *The awakening giant: Continuity and change in imperial chemical industries.* Oxford: Basil Blackwell.

Pettigrew, A. (1990). Longitudinal field research on change: Theory and practice. *Organisation Science, 1*(3), 267–292.

Pettigrew, A. (1997). What is processual analysis? *Scandinavian Journal of Management Studies, 13*(4), 331–503.

Pettigrew, A., Ferlie, E., & McKee, L. (1992). *Shaping strategic change.* London: Sage.

Prah, M. (2002). Gender issues in Ghanaian tertiary institutions: Women academics and administrators at Cape Coast University. *Ghana Studies,* 5, 1–20.

Robson, C. (2002). *Real world research: A resource for social scientists and practitioner-researchers* (2nd ed.). Oxford: Blackwell Publishing.

Saunders, M. N. (2011). *Research methods for business students* (5th ed.). Delhi: Pearson Education India.

Stake, R. E. (2006). *Multiple case study analysis.* New York, NY: The Guilford Press.

Thomas, R. (1995). Interviewing important people in big companies. In R. Hertz & J. Imber (Eds.), *Studying elites using qualitative methods* (pp. 3–7). Thousand Oaks, CA: Sage.

Transforming Teacher Education and Learning. (2014). Systems leadership (UNIT 2): Resources for college leaders. Retrieved from http://www.t-tel.org/about/about-us.html

Transforming Teacher Education and Learning. (2017). What is T-TEL? Retrieved from http://www.t-tel.org/about/about-us.html

Transforming Teacher Education and Learning. (n.d.). Mainstreaming gender responsiveness into Ghana's teacher education system. Retrieved from http://www.t-tel.org

Tsikata, D. (2007). Gender, institutional cultures and the career trajectories of faculty of the University of Ghana. *Feminist Africa,* 8, 26–41.

UNESCO. (2015). *A guide for gender equality in teacher education policy and practices.* Paris: UNESCO. Retrieved from https://unesdoc.unesco.org/ark:/48223/pf0000231646

UNESCO. (2019). *UNESCO gender priority action plan: 2019 revision, 2014–2021.* Paris: UNESCO. Retrieved from https://unesdoc.unesco.org/ark:/48223/pf0000370905

UNESCO Bangkok. (2009). *Gender in education network in Asia-Pacific (GENIA) toolkit: Promoting gender equality in education.* Bangkok: UNESCO Bangkok. Retrieved from https://unesdoc. unesco.org/ark:/48223/pf0000186495

United Nations Development Programme. (2014). *UNDP gender equality strategy 2014–2017.* New York, NY: UNDP.

United Nations Economic Commission of Africa. (2016). *Africa gender scorecard.* Addis Ababa: UNECA. Retrieved from http://repository.uneca.org/bitstream/handle/10855/23036/ b11560113. pdf?sequence=1

Wengraf, T. (2001). *Qualitative research interviewing.* London: Sage.

Yin, R. K. (2003). *Case study research: Design and methods* (3rd ed.) Thousand Oaks, CA: Sage.

Zach, L. (2006). Using a multiple-case studies design to investigate the information-seeking behaviour of Arts administrators. *Library Trends, 55*(1), 4–21.

APPENDIX: INTERVIEW GUIDE AND GENDER-RESPONSIVE SCORECARD

Please note that this is the interview guide for principals, vice principals, QA officers, and gender champions. The guides used for female tutors and students differed only with a reduction of questions that did not pertain to them. This interview guide also includes all the introductory research protocols that were used before interviews commenced.

Introduction of the Research

1. On behalf of NCTE, NTC, and PRINCOF, I would like to thank you for participating in this research study that explores gender issues within the Colleges of Education, and how these can be addressed through programs like T-TEL.
2. This Gender and Leadership study has been commissioned by NCTE, NTC, and PRINCOF and is jointly implemented by T-TEL.
3. Although I normally work on behalf of T-TEL as a College Improvement Adviser, today I am conducting research as an independent researcher for this study.

Explanation of Research

1. This discussion is designed to provide an understanding of the key issues and challenges that occur when trying to implement and maintain a gender-responsive college.
2. I would like to understand your views on gender, what challenges you face, and what think should be done.
3. We hope this information contributes to developing a national gender policy for tertiary institutions in the future.
4. This discussion should last for about one hour and I would like to record it if that is okay with you.

Confidentiality

1. You do not have to talk about sensitive topics if you are not comfortable. You can ask to stop this discussion at any point and I will not be offended.
2. However, I can assure you that all information that I collect during this discussion will be *confidential* and will not be shared with any of your colleagues or students.
3. If anything you say is quoted in a report, your name or college will *not* be used - you will remain completely anonymous.
4. This discussion will be recorded and transcribed. But all the information will be kept in a secure place and only members of our research team will be able to hear it or read it.

Consent

1. I have a consent form that states everything that I've just explained and it will ensure your confidentiality.
2. Although you will sign your signature, this form will be kept in a secure place and not be used to identify you.
3. Do you have any questions concerning this discussion or your rights during this research?
4. Have respondents sign a consent form.

Ground Rules

1. Before we begin, I'd like to say that this is not a test so there are no wrong answers and you will not be judged.
2. I am *not* here to check on whether the college has complied with T-TEL activities - rather, I would like to understand *why* some things have yet to be done.
3. Please feel free to speak about your issues, concerns or opinions, even if they are negative. We need to understand what people are thinking and experiencing so that we can inform future policy and practice to improve things.
4. Do you have any questions?

Please start voice recording now: Kindly record the date, college, and position/role of the respondent

Central Discussion Questions

1. Can you explain what the term "Gender Responsive College" means to you?
2. In your opinion, what specific actions or strategies help to make a college gender-responsive?
3. I am going to read out some gender-responsive strategies that could be implemented in colleges. Please could you provide one of the following answers concerning your college:
   1. Yes - if the strategy has been fully achieved and will be repeated in the coming year.
   2. No/don't know - if the strategy has not yet been started or you don't know if it has (don't worry if this is the case).
   3. Partially - if the strategy is partially complete but improvement is needed.
   4. Not applicable - if the strategy doesn't apply your college because it is single-sex.

Please Read the Statements Below and Mark the Respondent's Answer	Yes	No/Do not know	Partially	Not Applicable	Researcher Comments: (Provide Example/Evidence or Explain Any Issues/Challenges)
1. All tutors have had training on gender-responsive pedagogy					
2. All senior management has had training on gender-responsive management					
3. All nonteaching staff has had training on gender-responsive management					
4. All TP mentors have had training on gender-responsive mentoring strategies					
5. All students have had training or coursework on gender equality and gender-responsive pedagogy					
6. All tutors undergo appraisals/lesson observations for gender-responsive pedagogy regularly					
7. All tutors give equal chance to females and males to participate in activities during class					
8. All tutors assign leadership roles equally to females and males in activities					
9. All tutors are patient with females and males who may be shy or afraid to speak					
10. All tutors point out traditional gender roles that appear in materials and discuss how these limit what females believe they can achieve					
11. All tutors use examples (in exercises or activities) that *challenge or reverse* traditional gender roles (e.g., boys cook, girls are doctors)					
12. All tutors support female students in studying and achieving in subjects like maths and science					
13. CoE cleaning and chores do not reflect or reinforce traditional gender roles (e.g., only females mop)					
14. Class prefect roles are equally assigned to female and male students					
15. There are extra-curricular activities designed to build females' confidence in maths and science					
16. There is a gender club for females/males to discuss equality and challenge traditional gender roles					
17. A guidance counselor is in place to provide support and a safe space for all students					
18. All forms of corporal punishment or intimidating disciplinary measures are banned from use					
19. All female students and staff have safe accommodation that has external light at night, secure doors, security guards, etc.					
20. Female toilets throughout the CoE have water and hygiene bins for sanitary napkins					
21. The CoE has a finalized Sexual Harassment Policy					
22. If so, the policy has an agreed definition of what constitutes sexual harassment					
23. If so, the policy states a transparent reporting system for staff or students experiencing sexual harassment					

24. If so, the policy has an appropriate female staff member to act as the first point for reporting and to act as a counselor

25. If so, the policy has disciplinary measures for those guilty of sexual harassment

26. If so, the Sexual Harassment Policy has been disseminated to all staff, students, and community members

27. A CoE gender focal point/champion has been appointed and is active

28. Female and male staff have completely equal participation and opportunities in discussions, meetings, scheduling, training, promotion, housing.

29. Female and male tutors/staff are paid equally for the same positions/activities

30. Female and male tutors/staff have equal informal duties that do not reinforce traditional gender roles (e.g., females are *not* the only ones to clean up)

31. There are strategies to support female staff with their childcare responsibilities

32. The student admission policy provides dedicated spaces/admission for female students and students from disadvantaged backgrounds

33. The gender policy supports and makes accommodations for female staff/students about pregnancy and childcare

34. The financial management policy provides budgets that provide support to female students/ tutors (e.g., college facilities, scholarships, etc.)

35. The health and safety policy specifies resources for female students/tutors (e.g., hygiene bins for toilets)

36. The tutor professional development policy specifies dedicated training on gender-responsive pedagogy

37. The tutor appraisal policy includes gender-responsive pedagogy in appraisals and/or lesson observations

38. The tutor/student codes of conduct makes reference to a sexual harassment policy

39. The quality assurance policy includes gender-responsive indicators in its monitoring and evaluation strategy

40. The teaching and learning policy includes gender-responsive mentoring guidelines and scorecard

41. The staff recruitment policy aims to actively recruit female tutors/staff

42. The college communication policy includes a gender strategy about topics and/or dissemination

43. The assessment policy includes a gender-responsive appeals and mitigation process

44. The acceptable use policy includes gender-responsive procedures for libraries, ICT, and other facilities

Please Read the Statements Below and Mark the Respondent's Answer	Yes	No/Do not Know	Partially	Not Applicable	Researcher Comments: (Provide Example/Evidence or Explain Any Issues/Challenges)
45. Data on *female student enrollment* are collected/analyzed to understand reasons for disparity with males (if applicable)					
46. Data on *female achievement* are collected/analyzed to understand the reasons for disparity with males (if applicable)					
47. Data on the *number of female tutors* are collected/analyzed to understand reasons for disparity with males (if applicable)					
48. Data on *female senior managers* are collected/analyzed to understand reasons for disparity with males (if applicable)					
49. Data on *female SRC members* are collected/analyzed to understand reasons for disparity with males (if applicable)					
50. There are both *targets* and *strategies* to improve:					
51. Female student enrollment					
52. Female student achievement					
53. Female tutor recruitment					
54. Number of females in senior management positions					
55. Number of female students in the SRC					
56. Number of males involved in gender equality promotion/activities					
57. Budgets are allocated for:					
58. Gender training for CoE staff and students					
59. Gender-responsive infrastructure and resources					
60. Scholarships for female students					
61. Recruitment and promotion of female staff					
62. Implementation of strategies to improve gender targets					
63. CoE gender focal point/champion work					
64. A college self-assessment with the T-TEL gender-responsive scorecard is completed annually					
65. The principal discusses the results of the gender-responsive scorecard with stakeholders and together they decide on follow-up actions					

Thank you for answering those questions. I just have a few final follow-up questions for you.

4. Which of the gender-responsive strategies do you think are the most important or valuable?
5. In your opinion, which ones are the most difficult to achieve? Why? (probe for answers beyond "funding")
6. What could be done to help support college leaders to achieve all the strategies we discussed? (probe for answers beyond "funding")
7. Are there any strategies that you do not agree with? Why?
8. Has anyone at the college done a self-assessment with the gender-responsive scorecard from the T-TEL Leadership and Management Unit 2? If so, what did they do with the assessment? Were any actions taken?
9. Do you think it makes a difference if there is a gender balance among tutors and college leaders? If so/not, why?
10. From your understanding, how many female and male tutors are there, and how many female and male managers are there?
11. In your opinion, what are the *barriers* to achieving a gender balance among tutors?
12. In your opinion, what are the *barriers* to achieving a gender balance among college leaders?
13. In your opinion, what strategies could be taken to improve the gender balance among tutors?
14. In your opinion, what strategies could be taken to improve the gender balance among college leaders?
15. From your understanding, what are the roles and responsibilities of the college "Gender Champion"?

CHAPTER 11

ETHICAL ISSUES AND THE NORDIC EDUCATION MODEL: LEARNING-DRIVEN ECOSYSTEMS APPLIED TO INTERNATIONAL COHORTS

Bruno F. Abrantes, Thomas D. Eatmon and Charlotte Forsberg

ABSTRACT

The societal role of universities (u-pillar) is a long-standing discussion dividing the education researchers worldwide. Entering the sphere of the eminent Nordic education model (NEM), we aim at grasping its contemporaneity with regard to social value creation (SVC) and to the promotion of equality in education (EiE).

A theoretical review of literature revisits the foundations of the NEM in the light of the postmodern education challenges and the inherent governance practices of higher education institutions (HEIs) in the global eduscape.

One of the oldest HEIs in Denmark, Niels Brock Copenhagen Business College (NBCBC), is here instrumentalized as the target case research. The latter exhibited a sophisticated educational design, oriented toward digital apprenticeship and cumulative proximity to the students' population of both national and international cohorts.

International Perspectives in Social Justice Programs at the Institutional and Community Levels
Innovations in Higher Education Teaching and Learning, Volume 37, 177–195
Copyright © 2021 by Emerald Publishing Limited
All rights of reproduction in any form reserved
ISSN: 2055-3641/doi:10.1108/S2055-364120210000037011

Keywords: Active pedagogy; collaborative learning environments; contemporary Nordic education model; course management systems; educational progressivism; equality in education; excellency; higher education institutions; instructional development and effectiveness assessment; intelligent tutoring systems

1. INTRODUCTION

Prior studies have associated further adult education with economic growth and higher living standards (Chisolm, Larson, & Mossoux, 2004; Rubenson & Desjardins, 2009). Nevertheless, the fostering of supranational educational policies seems dependent on the articulation of a *triple helix* of governments (G), industries (I) and universities (U) (Etzkowitz & Leyesdorff, 2000). Despite interconnected, their actions of these parts signal disarticulation, divergence and antagonisms. Within the u-pillar (universities), opposing views held by educational theorists on the role of institutions and their instructing paths is perceived as a postmodern philosophical education crisis with direct interference upon the subsequent role of governments and industries (Greenberg et al., 2003; Soëtard & Fabre, 2007). In addition, some governance practices of higher education institutions (HEIs) distance themselves from other institutions, being characterized by conflicts of interests, and furthermore, a lack of universal consensus dominates the global eduscape with regard to the practice of a best teaching model for effectively activating competences. Such conflict is demonstrated in the disagreement to questions such as how to educate for sustainable development or how to build "action competences" in the learners' population (Bell & Bryman, 2007; Lundegård & Wickman, 2007).

As the neoclassical Nordic education model (NEM) advocates the universality and equalitarianism of education, global excellence, community fellowship and student involvement within the apprenticeship process, this chapter observes the NEM to grasp its contribution to social value creation (SVC) and to the promotion of equality in education (EiE) (Elken, Hovdhaugen, & Stensaker, 2016; Kolm & Tonin, 2015; Telhaug, Mediås, & Aasen, 2006). A theoretical review of literature revisits its microfoundations and draws its pathway to current times. Moreover, the investigation focuses on the business administration and law programs in the country of Denmark, which attracts more than one fourth of the overall international students (ISs) enrolled at the bachelor- and master's-degree levels (Antikainen, 2006; Organization for Economic Co-operation and Development (OECD), n.d.).

Niels Brock Copenhagen Business College (NBCBC) being one of the oldest HEIs in Denmark is purposively sampled for this research, from which data were collected with regard to the current learning methods. The aims of the investigation included (1) to explore the traits of Nordism and describe the contemporary Nordic educational model (CNEM) in the twenty-first century; (2) to grasp the current contribution of Nordic HEIs to SVC; and (3) to determine the

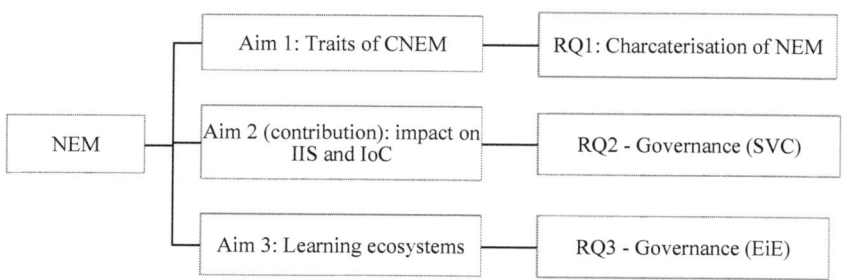

Fig. 1. Modeling Components of CNEM Including NEM, CNEM, SVC, EiE, IIS and IoC.

contribution of NBCBC to EiE. Each of these aims was linked to corresponding research questions (RQs) as follows: (RQ1) What's the current interpretation of the HEIs of "Nordic education"? (RQ2) How do HEI policies promote equality and further value for societies?; and (RQ3) What's the current reality of learning and communication mechanisms, inside and outside the classroom? A basic diagrammatic representation of the CNEM exhibited in Fig. 1 models the interrelations of these two components (A*n*; RQ*n*).

Aim 1 (further developed theoretically in Section *2.3. The contemporaneity of the NEM*) assumes a generalist design describing the CNEM, or what it has been labeled as "contemporary Nordism." Aims 2 and 3, respectively, addressed in Sections 2.3 and 3 address the aspects of governance including the contribution to society manifested in the dual notion of SVC and EiE, educational methods and learning ecosystems, taken together with the characteristics of the NEM for describing the CNEM.

2. THE NORDIC MODEL AND THE DEMOCRATIZATION OF EDUCATION

2.1. The Microfoundations of the NEM

Emerging during the second-half of the twentieth century in northern Europe (Denmark, Finland, Iceland, Norway and Sweden), the model is based upon values held independently but shared across nations (Lundahl, 2016). This model proclaimed a clear progression of values dominated by bold philosophical assumptions and a doctrine summarized in Table 1.

Positing a universal participation, the NEM configures itself as a form of educational progressivism and active pedagogy (progressivistic thinking) blended with an esthetic and practical learning where space was given to local aspects, as with the notion of *Heimstadlære* as to the "giving space for local knowledge areas in the school curricula" (Carlgren, Klette, Mýrdal, Schnack, & Simola, 2006, p. 302). Moreover, based on psychological thinking, the progressivism places the pupil in the center of learning, building the road for individualization and

Table. 1.   NEM Basic Description.

Values	Philosophy	Doctrine
Social justice Equality Cohesion	Universality Excellency	Identical access to education opportunities (including the conditions of apprenticeship) Community's cooperation and fellowship Multiple approaches and resources toward learning Pupil-centered learning through experimentalism and self-education Progressiveness/openness to change and international influences

Source: Own elaboration.

activating the role of pedagogy and tutor's guidance. This neoliberal individualization logic, also denoted in an added *strictum sensum* as "classroom flip" or
"inverted classroom," does not fully portray individualization (Baker, 2016; Lage,
Platt, & Treglia, 2000). Thus, the NEM extended the traditional laws of neo-
classic education (e.g., lecture-based, tutor-centric, one-way communication and
assessment, focus on technical competences) pillared in aspects such as conducting international teachers' seminars, revising textbooks, evaluating curricula and
syllabi and participating in international conferences (Elmersjö, 2015). Moreover,
it instrumentalizes the learner as an active resource exploitable in terms of action
competences to conduct self-studying, further searching and own knowledge-
building (Lundegård & Wickman, 2007).

Anchored in neoliberal foundations, its philosophy revolves around the universality and excellence of education encompassing a social-political aspiration
to provide equal accessibility and conditions of apprenticeship (universality) to
all students and fixing high standards in the quality of instruction, regardless
of the pupil's background (Antikainen, 2006). The attainment of these goals is
based on its values: social justice, equality and cohesion, in which the context of
social-education policies and educational governance is tied to a welfare system
and geared by high technological and social development (Kolm & Tonin, 2015).

As the NEM doctrine and frame grounds itself upon a progressive neoliberal
ideology, it accounts democratic values of equalitarianism in the access to education opportunities, global excellence, community fellowship and student eman-
cipation within the apprenticeship process (Elken et al., 2016; Kolm, & Tonin,
2015; Telhaug et al., 2006). Moreover, the model perceives education as a social
institution with two facets, a local and global one (Antikainen, 2006). The first
refers to the relation to its close surroundings, aiming at adjust to the local agents
and the state, attentive to local values and practices, while the latter advocates
the openness and exposure to international conditions and influences in order to
attain societal progressiveness as an outcome and/or as a mean to evolve through
the finding of new unprejudiced solutions. Its vision follows Husén's (1986) ideal
of a "learning society" at both local and international levels, which is believed to
be fulfilled by four criteria including lifelong learning opportunities, formal education to all ages, informal and self-learning and institutional support of learning.

2.2. International Education Systems - The "Nordization" Path

During the 1990s and 2000s, the echoes of the NEM have spread across the globe as several countries adopted new public management (NPM) reforms toward the pursuit of a new liberal ideology. Such a change came through an increase in the flexibility of the prior rigid and obsolete educational systems and comprised the decentralization of school management through the empowering and freedom given to municipalities to administrate infrastructures and resources according to local requirements (Lundahl, 2016).

Since the trailblazer reforms initiated in Sweden in the 1960s (the Swedish model) comprise the decentralization of education management and compulsory English language in school curriculum, rapid cultural changes occurred jointly with rapid policy changes in education; nowadays, the impact of the latter on the national cultures seems to have slowed down significantly in the Nordic region (Antikainen, 2010; Bigsten, 2001). However, Nordic countries maintain the NEM roots, namely the principle of relative equal education at all levels. Nevertheless, a clear distancing between countries is noted (Antikainen, 2010). For instance, Sweden has liberalized the educational system, registering in the last 15 years a rapid increase of fully tax funded free schools owned by private-equity firms, currently registering one in every two students at the upper-secondary level. Thus, free schools become a dominant phenomenon in the country. On the other hand, in Denmark, it is still marginal, since only 1%–2% of students in compulsory school attend a free school (Lundahl, Erixon, & Holm, 2013).

The case of Denmark seems quite *sui generis*. A twofold track coexist, academic and vocational learning, with private schools adopting a voucher system where their subsidization is combined with substantial autonomy in teaching methods with an ongoing focus on quality of the education rather than social inclusion, as the educational system incorporates already mature policies for equitable and inclusive participation since early childhood and care (ECEC), throughout the whole comprehensive school system until an higher education level (Rangvid, 2008). However, if policy-makers and educators are rather focused on the quality of the education, social inclusion in the country is not disregarded in schooling programs (Rasmussen & Moos, 2014).

Conversely, Norway's rising figures of children and youngsters with special needs led the Norwegian Directorate for Education to institute individual and small group's instruction aside the regular classroom. Arnesen and Lundahl (1996) argue that the idea of inclusion varies from the equality driver of the NEM, so children regardless of background or disability are entitled to attend a regular school and pursue a mainstream education, unless they require special needs or treatments (Frímannsson, 2006). Several other European countries have more recently undertaken similar reforms in terms of decentralization and individualization, despite the financing model of education systems remains though with substantial differences from Nordic countries, which still keep the original principle that parental resources should not restrain children from getting (quality) education. Thus, education remains free (no tuition fees) from primary level to tertiary level. However, ISs from non-European Union or European Economic

Area (EU/EEA) are since 2006 applicable to a tuition-fee policy (Wilken & Dahlberg, 2017). According to Frímannsson (2006) and Lister (2009), such policy functioned as a "social equalizer," with positive outcomes on higher economic contribution from women and with a rapid upbringing of social knowledge.

2.3. The Contemporaneity of the NEM

An initial question concerning primarily Pan-Scandinavian scholars is, to what extent can we still refer to a "Nordic education model"? A forthright answer is, studies in Nordic education policies are scarce, despite the contribution of Blossing, Imsen, and Moos (2014) on Nordic-comparative studies of the tensions between older/newer education, hitherto marked by the belief of other scholars that the virtues one education is the prevention of unemployment, social exclusion and ill health (Lundahl, 2016). Such absence constitutes a gap mainly due to the advancements of the education policy research (EPR) in Nordic countries in other directions. The EPR has devoted rather attention to the ideological roots of education (e.g., the democratic-participatory vs. neoliberal education) but also to the education governance side, covering themes such as NPM, school choice, marketization/privatization and academic performance. Hence, Arnesen and Lundahl (2006) advert for the fading utility of education in postmodernity to whom Frímannsson (2006, p. 227) has counter-argued by directly answering to the question, "Is there a Nordic model of education? I think the answer to this question is positive: there does seem to be a Nordic model of education." The enduring condition lays on its fundamental aims: opportunity-equalization and the upskilling of children and youngsters for a professional and social existence.

Likewise, Carlgren et al. (2006) argue that progressivistic and individualistic educational ideology is not losing traction at all, while advocating the frank expansion in the Nordics of the comprehensive school system (for the primary and lower secondary levels). Contrary to what Arnesen and Lundahl (2006) have claimed, these authors argue that the virtue of education is no longer having just "educated citizens" but "individuals responsible for his/her own life," despite the nuances noticed across the Nordics (Carlgren et al., 2006).

In Sweden, the national curriculum accompanied by a new marking system introduced in the 1990s increased the responsibility and pressure of both teachers and students on individual learning, opened the need for self-regulative methods and student's ability to self-evaluation. Norway registers a less progressive reality, as although lecturing is balanced with seatwork in the classroom, the plenary teaching and teacher-centered interaction is still dominant and determined by tutors on an individual basis. Denmark reports heterogenic pedagogical practices of great experimental work and school development, and an ongoing debate is centered on the progression of individualized education (pupil differentiation) toward "teaching differentiation," and on the virtues of advancing individualization by balancing it with community learning and solidarity learning (Nielsen, 1995, as cited in Carlgren et al., 2006). In the Danish educational context, the social constructivist learning theories reframed the meaning of individualization quite a while, which was associated with neoliberal individualism. The teaching integration logic started, at the Danish HEIs, in middle 1970s and extended itself to *Folkeskolen* later, in which the component of project work became likely the most visible mark of teaching/learning variations. Here, a "hidden curriculum" symbolizes later modern development of new teaching which accounts for soft components of non-technical learning as organization and self-discipline (e.g., dutifulness, patience, punctuality or subordination).

According to Simola (2005), this "hidden" agenda observed in Denmark seems to be also the secret for the Finnish "PISA shock," since the results of the PISA 2000 report are attributed not solely to high quality of comprehensive schooling but also to social cultural and historical factors, that is, the collective mentality; the popularity of teaching profession; and the pedagogical dialogue, placing the teacher at a high social strata interacting with students and parents not in a personal and confident manner as in other Nordic countries but as an adult model acting as gatekeeper of discipline, order and safety.

3. LEARNING ECOSYSTEMS OF THE TWENTY-FIRST CENTURY

3.1. Disruption of Postmodern Education Through Technology: Learning-driven Environments

Kolm and Tonin (2015) argue that technological development, intertwined with substantial societal changes (e.g., multilingualism, multiculturalism, cross-borders education, globalization of education and technological advancements), conveys global challenges, undermining Nordics disparities but opening a new era as to the internationalization of education and student mobility (Abrantes, 2020; Giles & Eyler, 1994; Restivo, Carvalho, Mendes, Magalhães, & Gróf, 2006). The latter is confirmed in Table 2 by the significantly increasing numbers, of foreign (prospective and effective) students enrolled in post-secondary and tertiary education, cross-border academic programs and global competition for quality and recognition world-class status both within public/private universities (Abdullah, Aziz, & Ibrahim, 2014; Altbach, Reisberg, & Rumbley, 2009). According to the Global Migration Data Analysis Centre (GMDAC) report for 2018, of the International Organization for Migration (IOM), the current figures of international student's mobility (ISM) in 2018 reached the 4.9 million, with a rise of 36.11% compared to 2017 (3.6 million), unveiling a pronounced tendency for the growth of this phenomenon (IOM, 2018). Thus, we have compared the ISM data at the HE level from the last five years using official datasets on large IS receiving centers: the European-American-Australian block (Madge, Raghuram, & Noxolo, 2015) (Table 2).

The data from OECD and NCEs, from the US Department of Education, uncover a stunningly low numbers in IS enrollment in the Nordic region. The figures for the last year of Denmark, Norway and Finland with positive growth rates (8.69%, 10.83% and 12.28%, respectively) unveil though a lowering growth trend when compared with the global average. Iceland and Sweden exhibit negative

Table. 2.   Foreign/IS' Enrollment at a HEI per Year and Country.

IS-Receivers	Year[b]				
	2008	2009	2010	2011	2012
Nordic countries					
Denmark	19.121	22.556	26.181	29.708	32.291
Finland	11.303	12.596	14.097	15.707	17.636
Iceland	815	930	1.080	1.239	1.186
Norway	16.104	17.507	15.737	16.628	18.428
Sweden	34.556	39.514	44.849	50.078	42.296
Other EU countries					
France	243.436	249.143	259.935	268.212	271.399
Germany	245.522	256.719	263.972	272.797	287.353
Italy	60.448	65.873	69.905	73.461	77.732
Netherlands	40.795	44.409	49.137	57.379	62.497
UK	462.609	498.998	534.555	559.948	568.816
Other top hosts					
Australia	264.205	292.545	307.653	301.643	291.889
Canada	185.781	191.202	195.550	203.823	221.406
United States[a]	–	–	707.700	–	783.600

Sources: Organization for Economic Co-operation and Development (OECD, 2017) and National Center for Education Statistics (2018).
[a]Rounding of the number to hundreds.
[b]Based on OECD's variable "Non-citizen students of reporting country."

ratios. In Sweden, a significant reduction since 2012 of ISs' inflow is observed. These figures certainly leave the door open for a debate on the attractiveness of these countries and related public policies as to the openness to receive foreign tertiary students.

Undoubtedly, these figures of ISM are certainly geared by the rapid *techno-logical development* in the last decades (one of the pillars of the NEM) which has revolutionized the education in terms of the democratization of its accessibility, proliferation of methods and bringing other societies closer to the NEM. First, the emergence of communication technologies has shaped the way children, youngsters and adults learn since the last three decades of the twentieth century (Alavi, 1994). Second, the upsurge of computer-supported learning added more than a myriad of learning possibilities from the traditional classroom instruction to a blast in number of online programs taught either partially (blended-learning) or fully online, disrupting the two-century moribund distance education sector (Moore, Dickson-Deane, & Galyen, 2011). Thus, distance education has increased drastically with the advent of internet technologies and with the rapid growth in the number of users worldwide, paving the way for the generalization of (in)formal distance education as internet assumed among others the epithet of learning technology, associating itself with the advent of online collaborative learning, web-based learning, electronic-learning (e-learning), mobile learning, virtual learning and technology-mediated learning (Conrad, 2006). Despite differences in these concepts, one commonality is perceived among these, the instruction occurs between two parties (*learners* and *instructor*), and it is held at different times and places using various forms of learning materials (Moore et al., 2011).

The mediation of internet and electronic instructional materials democratized the Nordic model as global learning environment, widening the student-centric learning (SCL) tool box outside in complementary to the classroom seatwork, promoting an evolution toward competency-based curricula, centered on learning outcomes, in turn, enhancing the involvement and knowledgeability of learners (Ruiz, Mintzer, & Leipzig, 2006).

The notion of internet-mediated learning environment or online learning environment (OLE) encompasses though a plethora of features, such as learning management system (LMS), course management systems (CMSs) also referred to as collaborative learning environments (CLEs), or a virtual learning environments (VLE), intelligent tutoring systems (ITSs) and knowledge content distributors (KCD) (Moore et al., 2011). These typologies of learning environments (e.g., courses, programs and learning objects) may be described as to its mechanics of adoption as being self-paced, self-directed or instructor-led, demonstrating an evolution from the most common form of distance-related course design, that is, the synchronous one (instruction-led) toward a division of collaborative versus personal learning (synchrony/asynchrony) (Moore et al., 2011). Here, it should be mentioned that the latter division between personal learning environment (PLE) versus the CLE crosses the philosophical discussion undertaken at the Nordic countries (particularly among Danish educators) concerning the education progressivism, as it should point in one direction or the other (Chen & Lo, 2004; Harmelen, 2006; Sclater, 2008). The NEM debate surrounding the neoliberal ideology among educational progressivists/social constructivists, as to the rupture between the neoliberal individualization ideology and the neoliberal collaborative ideology, is in the authors' point of view not an incompatible issue. These two OLEs (PLE/CLE) are clearly distinct; however, as mentioned by Ruiz et al. (2006), the utility of OLEs resides in the enhancing of learning outcomes rather than processes of education (as it seems to be plenary teaching), which means that an online instructional design may, according to our interpretation of the utility of internet technologies and OLEs, be combined to achieve more effective instructional designs. Nevertheless, this discussion is not a simplistic one, as the barriers between both PLE/CLE are tenuous and the benefits of their underlying methods are fuzzy (e.g., self-paced learning, self-directed learning, instructor-led learning, feedback, scaffolding, streaming, webinars, video-conferencing and so forth).

Hitherto, OLEs are focused rather on the interface with the learners (front-end development). Here, technology-mediated learning has advanced rapidly in terms of instructional environments per se (e.g., automated tutoring, collaborative learning boundary objects and on the availability of electronic contents) (Fominykh, Prasolova-Førland, Divitini, & Petersen, 2016). However, advancements on LMS have also covered the back end, evolving also the administration process of the e-learning offer, either as a hybrid (e.g., discussion threads) or pure administrating components (e.g., courseware and spyware). Some of the most renowned LMSs with a holistic architecture are shared by several HEIs, such as Blackboard, Canvas, Moodle or Phoenix. Additionally, specific applications are growing, such as the group decision support systems (GDSSs) such as *ThinkTank* or *Spilter* focused on the communicational process (e.g., group-thinking enhancers; miscommunication/conflict solving; unifying foreign language learners and hearing-impaired classes) or the student evaluation of teaching effectiveness (SETE) evolving toward student description of teaching (SDT) questionnaire; the student's evaluation of education quality (SEEQ) instrument; and the instructional development and effectiveness assessment (IDEA) (Aiken, Martin, Vanjani, & Sexton, 1994; Wang, 2003; Živkovic, Nikolic, Savic, Djordjevic, & Mihajlovic, 2017).

3.2. *Learning Environments: Student-centric and International Cohorts' Challenges*

The conventional instructional approaches oppose clearly the SCL advocated by the NEM, which according to Cannon and Newble (2000) emphasizes the responsibility and activity learning. The first follows a positivistic rationale where the information and concepts are acknowledgeable though residing on an independent dimension from its observers, which means it naturally exists separately from the perception of the apprentices, follows a more rigid design and is not subject to the determinism of contextual variations or changes. On the other hand, the SCL touts a social constructivism, arguing the virtues of practice, interaction and experimentalism of learning objects, claiming besides that the problems and limitation are challenges for deepening learning and attaining solution-oriented experiences and knowledge-development (Lea et al., 2003).

Immersing into the SCL, a clear dual path it poses in front of educators, whether to adhere to individualized or to a collective learning approach. The NEM corroborates the latter one, as individualization is reductive perspective to what learning, neglecting the relations. The Nordic model adopts thus a relational view acknowledging that the learning comprises both content and context. The context is a network of interacting variables surrounding the effectiveness of learning, such as the *individual network learning structure* (INLS), and it is perceived as a holistic view of students' needs upon personal development. Here, the *network* learning accounts a triad of relations: (i) among students; (ii) student with tutors; and (iii) student with the learning resources (Jones, Ferreday, & Hodgson, 2008). However, substantial differences separate relational learning (RL) and networking learning (NL). RL refers to the general learning process (i.e., the apprehended content regarding of the context), while network learning refers to the specific learning of the surrounding conditions of a complex set of relations. Thus, the RL in the context of international cohorts implies the widening of the idea of *student experience* (i.e., the learning context of local relations) to a *total experience*, as their staying abroad (i.e., *the international sojourn*) represents a full immersion into a culture that requires some extent of societal adjustment, in which the social interaction impacts directly on the absorptive capacity of the individual and his/her overall learning performance (Abdullah et al., 2014). Thus, the challenges of RL are amplified in international cohorts, and their external interaction, network relations and ties is beyond the teacher's span of action, even though it has a direct impact on the student's ability to assimilate content and subsequently on his/her learning outcomes. Such a condition requires further attention of the HEI's governance and supportive structure (e.g., administration, counseling, rectory) to improve the total experience in the country, or international sojourn, as an instrument to optimize learning outcomes. This poses itself as a pedagogical, managerial and ethical-moral challenge, aggravated within private HEIs by an extended customer-provider perspective.

Conversely, the effort required to allocate additional resources for a "total experience" is normally channeled to research activities due to the prevailing logic among entrepreneurial universities to publish or perish, mediated by industry forces claiming the primacy of investment on research for further scientific advancements (Guerrero, Cunningham, & Urbano, 2015). This dichotomy of knowledge-dissemination (education) versus knowledge-development (research) on whether to allocate resources to create optimal conditions, either to learning ecosystems or research projects, is here dubbed as the *knowledgeness paradox* and perceived in literature as an internal and intra-organizational confrontation obstructing the ability to search for appropriate answers to both issues, teaching-driven and research-driven practices (Waitoller & Kozleski, 2013).

Kondacki, van der Broeck, and Yildrim (2008) posit that studies on IS' hosting, such as the receiving of someone holding a foreign nationality while pursuing post-secondary/tertiary education outside of his/her country of origin, are still on an early progressive stage, and regrettably, the IS seems an invisible part of the equation (Abdullah et al., 2014). Some theorists assert that this so-called social conditions of interaction outside campus is as relevant as the "academic conditions" (Gu & Schweisfurth, 2006). Therefore, these authors advocate that the solution for higher results within this RL view of NEM perspective within international cohorts is to place ISs into the center of the solution. They claim that HEIs urge to invest upon the IS' *intercultural competences* building, as the willingness to embrace another cultures while retaining own ethnic identity, which implies the adoption of a *multicultural interaction strategy* which ought to be modeled within the HEIs' sphere (Brown, 2009). The solution seems to improve the total experience, at three separate levels: adaptation, change and development, in which the first (adaptation) is a critical one, comprising the support to both psychological adjustment and sociocultural adaptation, which are recognized as causes of great distress to newcomers (Gu & Schweisfurth, 2006).

3.3. The Nordic Learning-driven Ecosystems of the Twenty-first Century

The late/postmodern educational ground is occupied nowadays, at the Nordic region, by two main discourses with a contrary nature. The first is a culturalist discourse with a conservative tone that supports the public policies that safeguard the interests of the country in terms of national cultural and protection of the welfare state system (Hultgren, Gregersen, & Thøgersen, 2014). The second is the internationalist discourse populating some universities with a far more progressivistic mark, in which the Englishization of teaching instrumentalizes the openness to foreign influences (Hultgren et al., 2014). The latter (internationalist discourse) goes back to the neoliberal ideology on the roots of the NEM related to foreign influences, openness, progression and global excellency (Antikainen, 2006; Arnesen & Lundahl, 2006). However, revisiting recent data of international students' enrollment, it is evident both a moderate growth of this phenomenon and a decline in the number of inward flows. In fact, the European Commission's (EC) brief report (EMN FLASH #7–2019) issued in 2019 by the European Migration Network's (EMN) reinforces that peripheral condition of Nordic countries in IS' intake, being absent of the list of top-five countries in EU for capturing ISs. Actually, the Nordic policies reveal increasing restrictions to international mobility. For instance, the reforms introduced in Sweden comprised of the introduction of tuition fees have decreased substantially the number of free-mover students in the country from outside the EU (EMN, 2016). As to the case of Denmark, the Ministry for Higher Education and Research capped the number of English-taught programs and IS' admissions by one fourth and focused on a regionalization program for the higher education area discouraging international prospective students and which harvested timid figures of employability of national recent graduates in the country (*Arbejderbevægelsens Erhvervsråd*, 2018). The contribution of Blossing et al. (2014) for the comprehension of the contemporaneity of the NEM in Denmark, Norway and Sweden corroborates with the aforementioned assertion of the existence of recent public policies obstructing the progressive ideological practices of the original model. The authors claim that this ideology has been toned down in the latest school reforms, and pedagogical thinking muffled, as public policies seem to value currently the individualization of teaching through the complexification of group work and test-based equalization, in which pedagogical communication is reduced, and the variation in curricula is more limited, even though the NEM argues those to be paramount for having a democratic school, open to all, offering meaningful education regardless of the social background, ethnicity and personal competences.

In this context, an ideological confrontation is found recently between neo-conservative policies and the non-affirmative approach. Recent neo-conservative actions of policy-makers, as above exemplified in the previous paragraph, highlight a sense of national cultural homogenization contrasting to a trend of global homogenization portrayed by the growing pluralization of many countries (and their natural economic differentiation or specialization) (Moos, 2017). The non-affirmative theories on educational leadership argue that the complexification of postmodern education does not require evasive palliative actions of politicians and solo-playing actions of HEIs, but instead it calls for a rethinking of the modern-state policies of education. This non-affirmative approach evokes the roots of the NEM, envisioning education as a relational and hermeneutical model, summoning to self-activity and meritocracy-recognition. Thus, non-affirmative thinking as a widespread view upon education ought to be achieved by the creation of a conceptual system capable of coordinating the virtues of contributory curricula and didactic to current education, with a heterarchical design, where education policies are weighted with economic and cultural influences.

Educational policies in the Nordic states are then appealed for both a policy redefinition and the rethinking of pedagogical practices. Jónsson (2016) pinpoints an anachronism in the roots of the NEM. Despite the values of the model pointed out an inclusive and democratic education system, the boundaries of this plurality are left blurred. Here, this refers to the establishing of transgressive boundaries as central for the building of order and subsequent exercise of self-learning. In fact, the Deweyan conception of democracy that constituted the foundation for the NEM is supportive of the Foucault's notion of *transgression*, since it argues that self-learning is pillared in experimentalism, learning-by-doing and empirical practice (Carr & Kemmis, 2003; Noddings, 2010). According to Jónsson (2016), educators have the intellectual authority to institutionalize these principles of democratic education and to empower the learner with the individual freedom to use transgression not as a marginal practice but as a mainstream pedagogic tool of learning, which clearly opposes to the neo-conservative discourse. For instance, the Icelandic education model is clouded by practices of (i) individual understanding, (ii) adoption of a "medical model," (iii) supremacy of a technical approach, and (iv) market-commodity view of education (Jónsson, 2016). These practices refer to, first, a lack of comprehension that individualized difficulties are a font for collective learning (not individualization). Then, second, learning implies the de-codification of terminologies, concepts and ideas which are not crystal clear to the learner. A medical model has to be an inclusive one operating at the level of individualistic learning difficulties but rather focused in diagnosing these (learning difficulties), as the Foucault's notion of *medical gaze*, since the production of symptoms and signs on the individual determines the frameworks of signification of a certain struggle. Third, a technical approach appropriating the use of technology, as a mere instrument of diagnosis of individual quandaries, is reductive of the technical potential for extending the students experience and skills.. Finally, the commoditization underlying at the perception of upper-secondary school and higher education as an investment for increasing market value is a logic of competition where graduates compete against each other in the market. This directive approach, contrary to the ideas of democratic education, puts the student's preferences at the bottom of the scholar's value scale, as educators entrench themselves into technical practices avid for student's success.

4. THE CASE OF NBCBC

4.1. Description of NBCBC

On the etymology of the NEM lays NBCBC, a Danish HEI established in the nineteenth century with a multigenerational contribution to upper-secondary and higher education as one of the first business schools ("handelsskole") in the country. This constitutes itself a heavy-weighting motive for considering it as a case study. Moreover, NBCBC´s progressive thinking has positioned this institution at the forefront of international education in Denmark, with programs for national/ISs established in the country and programs in America and Asia. NBCBC as a global education institution follows the twofold facets of the NEM, general (or local) and global, with a clear focus upon businesses and management sciences ("erhvervsuddannelse") at academic and vocational training from upper-secondary school (or "gymnasium") until higher education (master level: "candidate").

The institution has long ago established international educational partnerships and offers currently several programs at bachelor- and master's-degree levels in the country and overseas. As a groundbreaking event in Denmark, NBCBC established in 1995 the first international joint program with the School of Computing Sciences, of De Montfort University (DMU) in the United Kingdom. Nowadays, NBCBC with an accentuated international mark as a spinout of DMU, Leicester Castle Business School and Middlesex University offers ISs programs fully taught in English language ranging from international business, management sciences, international hospitality and tourism. As a result of a long-lasting partnership with DMU, currently, a wide cross-collaboration between parts comprises staff exchanges, joint research and publication, joint module development and consultancy work. Moreover, within the Niels Brock (NB) realm, a cross-collaboration with the *gymnasiums*, particularly with the *International Business Baccalaureate* (IBB), is noticeable on the engaging of students from both sides in each other's academic events and establishing crossed-coursework dynamics for formative evaluation.

4.2. A Peripatetic Approach Toward Learning

This single-case research encompassed the collection of data occurred at the *Bispetorvet* campus in Copenhagen, in the context of the first edition of the International Teaching and Learning Conference (ITLC) held at NBCBC on June 14, 2019. Here, integrated in the regular agenda of the event, the participants were invited to gather in smaller groups blended with the faculty staff of NBCBC to debate a single theme: the present-day student-oriented learning methodologies and the future at NBCBC.

From the outputs of this session, it is perceived that students are in multiple ways encouraged to an extended relational/experiential learning, embedded in the stimuli to engage in additional academic and social activities, in and outside campus, such as, master classes, guest lectures, company visits, case competitions, thematic workshops, study halls, conferences, academic writing sessions or, even, in simply hanging out, in Danish "hygge cafes." In fact, it may be claimed that NBCBC is one of the neoliberal HEIs surfing the wave of the progressivistic thinking. It follows the Greek peripatetic philosophy adapted to modern times, as to the notion of walking the students through a path of personal development, where "walking through" means, among other endeavors, to literally undertake on-motion lectures or "walking lectures." The underlying principle to this is the intellectual stimulation of thinking and further participation, since the march of apprenticeship and knowledge-building and dissemination is socially constructed; therefore, inertia and isomorphism is seriously fought and refuted. In fact, practical components (tutorials) of all modules are balanced in a way that the theoretical component (lectures) are fairly equally distributed, as clearly stated at the syllabus of the courses. But entering the lectures, students are not just dumped into piles of theoretical contents, as lectures are anchored in background contextualization and case analysis, since learning has a problem-solving orientation.

Technical-enhanced learning plus research and transversal competences are developed under the direct interaction with the tutors' intervention, where students are exposed to a plethora of mechanisms of apprenticeship such as presentations, group work, peer reviewing, peer assessment, case analysis, essay and report writing, video and podcast production, project development, data analysis, questionnaires, gaming, article reading/summarizing, surgery time, questions and answers (Q&A) sessions, *alumni* presentations, open lectures, library classes and so forth. In this sense, the flexibilization of learning also implies an effort to make multidisciplinary content available whether in digital or non-digital format, presential or non-presential, synchronous or asynchronous. Technology plays a decisive role on enhancing and accelerating the students' experience. Students use mostly e-books in classroom and have a broad access to different academic platforms either belonging to NBCBC or to its partner institutions, which comprises physical and online library contents, academic and professional databases, software, online recorded lectures, additional reading sources, past assignments, mock tests, quizzes and webinars. Other supporting systems ensure the IS' self-management of own accessibility, attendance and assessment of the institutional programs, modules, tutors, contents, methods and practices. A manifest digitalization path is clearly guiding the past agenda of mainstream module teaching and evaluation through a chain of online working, online submission online marking, with underlying benefits in terms of traceability and transparency of the student coursework track, furthermore, establishing quality and ethical standards and ensuring the compliance with norms, rules and regulations.

5. CONCLUSION

Considering the aims of this research, the case reveals a sophisticated educational design, and learning methods and practices adopted, as to the domains of digitalization and IS' proximity. Furthermore, an equalization of the accessibility and conditions to students regardless of its background was observed. The societal contribution of NBCBC in the instruction of IS seems to go beyond the breadth of theoretical contents, into real transversal competence-building with particular focus upon the building of digital technologies/communicational literacy and problem solving.

Methods are applied multivariably among tutors, according to their free discretion, which, in turn, is connoted with a wider discussion within the EPR to whether to follow standardization or flexibilization path and to what extent a hybrid model. Methodological practices reveal no substantial predeterminations and/or managerial impositions, although a common basis of action guides lectures/tutors and aligns them within a marked "NBCBC educational culture" (e.g., in terms of feedback time or standard number of articles for reading or guest speakers/company visits or conference participation). However, a contiguous issue remains fairly unexplored across Nordic-HEIs, including the case-HEI: *How do HEIs deal with the psychological adjustment, and socio-cultural adaptation of new-arriving international students?* A lack of a formal design is noticed, a multicultural international strategy (MIS), as suggested by Brown (2009).

Moreover, the CNEM demonstrates congruence to the original values and philosophies, despite an evolving rationale from the developing students' competences to the building of citizenship (Arnesen & Lundahl, 2006; Carlgren et al., 2006). Second, the integration of transgressive practices of self-learning seems not consolidated in the CNEM, which requires a further maturation as to the principles of inclusion and democratic education. Third, the global orientation, one of the facets of the NEM, seems inadequate to the current needs of ISs abroad. Here, the HEIs are expected to act upon cross-cultural differences, by softening their impact through the adoption of multicultural interaction strategies (MIS), particularly emphasized upon the actions to take place on the initial phase (adaptation) where newcomers require further accompaniment toward psychological adjustment and sociocultural adaptation. Finally, current educational policies seem to be rowing conversely on the direction of cultural homogenization drawing forthcoming policies toward neo-conservative path, that is, antagonistic to the NEM philosophy with underlying risks of deviation toward individualization and/or misuse of technology.

REFERENCES

Abdullah, D., Aziz, M. I. A., & Ibrahim, A. L. M. (2014). A "research" into international student-related research: (Re) Visualising our stand? *Higher Education, 67*(3), 235–253.

Abrantes, B. F. (2020). Governance of academic laboratories (AL) and the capabilisation of higher education students (HES). *International Journal of Management in Education, 14*(2), 135–158.

Aiken, M., Martin, J., Vanjani, M., & Sexton, R. (1994). Group decision support systems in higher education. *Journal of Educational Technology Systems, 23*(1), 3–12.

Alavi, M. (1994). Computer-mediated collaborative learning: An empirical evaluation. *MIS Quarterly, 18*, 159–174.

Altbach, P. G., Reisberg, L., & Rumbley, L. E. (2009). *Trends in global higher education: Tracking an academic revolution.* A report prepared for the UNESCO 2009 World Conference on Higher Education. UNESCO Publishing, Paris.

Antikainen, A. (2010). The capitalist state and education: The case of restructuring the Nordic model. *Current Sociology, 58*(4), 530-550.

Antikainen, A. (2006). In search of the Nordic model in education. *Scandinavian Journal of Educational Research, 50*(3), 229–243.

Arbejderbevægelsens Erhvervsråd. (2018). Beskæftigelse – Beskeden fremgang i dansk økonomi. Retrieved from https://www.ae.dk/emne/beskaeftigelse-0

Arnesen, A. L., & Lundahl, L. (2006). Still social and democratic? Inclusive education policies in the Nordic welfare states. *Scandinavian Journal of Educational Research, 50*(3), 285–300.

Baker, J. W. (2016). The origins of "the classroom flip." In *Proceedings of the 1st annual higher education flipped learning conference*, Greeley, Colorado.

Bell, E., & Bryman, A. (2007). The ethics of management research: An exploratory content analysis. *British Journal of Management, 18*(1), 63–77.

Bigsten, A. (2001). *Relevance of the Nordic model for African development.* No. 2001/131. WIDER Discussion Papers/World Institute for Development Economics (UNU-WIDER).

Blossing, U., Imsen, G., & Moos, L. (2014). Progressive education and new governance in Denmark, Norway, and Sweden. In *The Nordic education model* (pp. 133–154). Dordrecht: Springer.

Brown, L. (2009). The transformative power of the international sojourn: An ethnographic study of the international student experience. *Annals of Tourism Research, 36*(3), 502–521.

Carlgren, I., Klette, K., Mýrdal, S., Schnack, K., & Simola, H. (2006). Changes in Nordic teaching practices: From individualised teaching to the teaching of individuals. *Scandinavian Journal of Educational Research, 50*(3), 301–326.

Cannon, R., & Newble, D. (2000). *A guide to improving teaching methods: A handbook for teachers in university and colleges.* London: Kogan Page.

Carr, W., & Kemmis, S. (2003). *Becoming critical: Education knowledge and action research.* New York, NY: Routledge.

Chen, C. Y., & Lo, W. S. (2004). An agent e-learning system for interactive and collaborative communication. *WSEAS Transactions on Computers, 3*(4), 1013–1017.

Chisolm, L., Larson, A., & Mossoux, A. F. (2004). *Lifelong learning: Citizens' views in close-up. Findings from a dedicated Eurobarometer survey.* Cedefop, Luxembourg.

Conrad, D. (2006). E-learning and social change: An apparent contradiction. In M. Beaudoin (Ed.), *Perspectives on higher education in the digital age* (pp. 21–33). New York, NY: Nova Science Publishers.

Elken, M., Hovdhaugen, E., & Stensaker, B. (2016). Global rankings in the Nordic region: Challenging the identity of research-intensive universities? *Higher Education, 72*(6), 781–795. http://dx.doi.org.proxy.library.dmu.ac.uk/10.1007/s10734-015-9975-6

Elmersjö, H. A. (2015). The Norden Associations and international efforts to change history education, 1919–1970: International organisations, education, and hegemonic nationalism. *Paedagogica Historica, 51*(6), 727–743. https://doi-org.proxy.library.dmu.ac.uk/10.1080/00309230.2015.1013560

Etzkowitz, H., & Leyesdorff, L. (2000). The dynamics of innovation: From national systems and "Mode 2" to a triple helix of university-industry-government relations. *Research Policy, 29*(1), 109–123.

European Migration Network. (2016). EMN policy report 2015 – Sweden. Migrationsverket (Swedish Migration Agency). Norrköping. Retrieved from https://ec.europa.eu/home-affairs/sites/homeaffairs/files/what-we-do/networks/european_migration_network/reports/docs/annual-policy/annual-policy-27a_sweden_apr_2015_part2_en.pdf

Fominykh, M., Prasolova-Førland, E., Divitini, M., & Petersen, S. A. (2016). Boundary objects in collaborative work and learning. *Information Systems Frontiers, 18*(1), 85–102.

Giles, D., Jr, & Eyler, J. (1994). The impact of a college community service laboratory on students' personal, social, and cognitive outcomes. *Journal of Adolescence, 17*, 327.

Frímannsson, G. H. (2006). Introduction: Is there a Nordic model in education? *Scandinavian Journal of Educational Research, 50*(3), 223–228.

Guerrero, M., Cunningham, J. A., & Urbano, D. (2015). Economic impact of entrepreneurial universities' activities: An exploratory study of the United Kingdom. *Research Policy, 44*(3), 748–764.

Greenberg, M. T., Weissberg, R. P., O'brien, M. U., Zins, J. E., Fredericks, L., Resnik, H., & Elias, M. J. (2003). Enhancing school-based prevention and youth development through coordinated social, emotional, and academic learning. *American Psychologist, 58*(6–7), 466.

Gu, Q., & Schweisfurth, M. (2006). Who adapts? Beyond cultural models of 'the' Chinese learner. *Language, Culture and Curriculum, 19*(1), 74–89.

Gu, Q., Schweisfurth, M., & Day, C. (2010). Learning and growing in a 'foreign'context: Intercultural experiences of international students. *Compare, 40*(1), 7–23.

Harmelen, M. (2006, July). Personal learning environments. *ICALT, 6*, 815–816.

Hultgren, A. K., Gregersen, F., & Thøgersen, J. (2014). *English in Nordic universities: Ideologies and practices.* In A. K. Hultgren, F. Gregersen, & Thøgersen, J. (Eds.), *English in Nordic universities: Ideologies and practices* (pp. 1–26). Studies in World Language Problems (5). Amsterdam: John Benjamins.

Husén, T. (1986). *Learning society revised.* Oxford: Pergamon Press.

Kolm, A. S., & Tonin, M. (2015). Benefits conditional on work and the Nordic model. *Journal of Public Economics, 127*, 115–126.

Kondacki, Y., van der Broeck, H., & Yildrim, A. (2008). The challenges of internationalisation from foreign and local students' perspective: The case of management school. *Asia Pacific Education Review, 9*(4), 448–463.

IOM. (2018). *Global migration indicators 2018.* Berlin: Global Migration Data Analysis Centre (GMDAC). Retrieved from https://publications.iom.int/system/files/pdf/global_migration_indicators_2018.pdf

Jones, C. R., Ferreday, D., & Hodgson, V. (2008). Networked learning a relational approach: Weak and strong ties. *Journal of Computer Assisted Learning, 24*(2), 90–102.

Jónsson, Ó. P. (2016). Democratic and inclusive education in Iceland: Transgression and the medical gaze. *Nordic Journal of Social Research, 7*(1), 78–92.

Lage, M. J., Platt, G. J., & Treglia, M. (2000). Inverting the classroom: A gateway to creating an inclusive learning environment. *Journal of Economic Education, 31*(1), 30–43.

Lea, S. J., Stephenson, D., & Troy, J. (2003). Higher education students´ attitudes to student-centred learning: beyond educational bulimia?. *Studies in higher education, 28*(3), 321-334.

Lister, R. (2009). A Nordic nirvana? Gender, citizenship, and social justice in the Nordic welfare states. *Social Politics: International Studies in Gender, State & Society, 16*(2), 242–278.

Lundahl, L. (2016). Equality, inclusion and marketization of Nordic education: Introductory notes. *Research in Comparative and International Education, 11*(1), 3–12.

Lundahl, L., Erixon, A. I., & Holm, A. (2013). Educational marketization the Swedish way. *Education Inquiry, 4*(3), 497–517.

Lundegård, I., & Wickman, P. O. (2007). Conflicts of interest: An indispensable element of education for sustainable development. *Environmental Education Research, 13*(1), 1–15.

Madge, C., Raghuram, P., & Noxolo, P. (2015). Conceptualizing international education: From international student to international study. *Progress in Human Geography, 39*(6), 681–701.

Ministry of Education and Science. (n.d.) European tools for mobility and transparency. Retrieved from https://ufm.dk/en/education/internationalisation-and-cooperation/international-cooperation-on-guidance/euroguidance-denmark/european-tools-for-mobility-and-transparency

Moore, J. L., Dickson-Deane, C., & Galyen, K. (2011). e-Learning, online learning, and distance learning environments: Are they the same?. *The Internet and Higher Education, 14*(2), 129–135.

Moos, L. (2017). Neo-liberal governance leads education and educational leadership astray. In M. Uljen, R. Ylimaki (Eds.), *Bridging educational leadership, curriculum theory and didaktik* (Educational Governance Research, Vol. 5, pp. 151–180). Cham: Springer.

National Center for Education Statistics. (2018). Total fall enrollment in degree-granting postsecondary institutions, by level of enrollment, sex, attendance status, and race/ethnicity or nonresident alien status of student: Selected years, 1976 through 2017. Retrieved from https://nces.ed.gov/programs/digest/d18/tables/dt18_306.10.asp

Nielsen, V. O. (1995). *Folkeskolen i 90'erne – loven og samfundet* [*The folk school in the nineties – the education act and the society; in Danish*]. Vejle, Denmark: Kroghs Forlag.

Noddings, N. (2010). *Dewey's philosophy of education: A critique from the perspective of care theory*. Cambridge: Cambridge University Press.

Organization for Economic Co-operation and Development (OECD). (2017). *Education at glance 2017*. Paris: OECD. https://doi.org/10.1787/eag-2017-en

Organization for Economic Co-operation and Development (OECD) (n.d.) *Education at Glance 2017*. Retrieved from https://www.oecd-ilibrary.org/education/education-at-a-glance2017_eag-2017-en;jsessionid=2fsdkda6kh3eb.x-oecd-live-02. Accessed on July 9, 2018.

Rangvid, B. S. (2008). Private school diversity in Denmark's national voucher system. *Scandinavian Journal of Educational Research, 52*(4), 331–354.

Rasmussen, A., & Moos, L. (2014). A school for less than all in Denmark. In U. Blossing, G. Imsen, & L. Moos (Eds.), *The Nordic education model. A school for all encounters neo liberal policy* (pp. 35–55). Dordrecht: Springer.

Restivo, M. T., Carvalho, I., Mendes, J., Magalhães, R., & Gróf, G. (2006). Remotely visiting academic labs using ICTs. In *Proceedings of SEFI 34th annual conference – Engineering and education active students*, Uppsala, Sweden, Session 4, pp. 64.

Rubenson, K., & Desjardins, R. (2009). The impact of welfare state regimes on barriers to participation in adult education: A bounded agency model. *Adult Education Quarterly, 59*(3), 187–207.

Ruiz, J. G., Mintzer, M. J., & Leipzig, R. M. (2006). The impact of e-learning in medical education. *Academic Medicine, 81*(3), 207–212.

Sclater, N. (2008). Web 2.0, personal learning environments, and the future of learning management systems. *Research Bulletin, 13*(13), 1–13.

Simola, H. (2005). The Finnish miracle of PISA: Historical and sociological remarks on teaching and teacher education. *Comparative Education, 41*(4), 455–470.

Soëtard, M., & Fabre, M. (2007). Crise de la modernité (de la post-modernité?), ressort de l'éducation. Rousseau, Pestalozzi et les autres. *Recherches en Éducation, 2*(1), 9–16.

Telhaug, A. O., Mediås, O. A., & Aasen, P. (2006). The Nordic model in education: Education as part of the political system in the last 50 years. *Scandinavian Journal of Educational Research, 50*(3), 245–283.

Waitoller, F. R., & Kozleski, E. B. (2013). Working in boundary practices: Identity development and learning in partnerships for inclusive education. *Teaching and Teacher Education, 31*, 35–45.

Wang, Y. (2003). Assessment of learner satisfaction with asynchronous electronic learning systems. *Information and Management, 41*(1), 75–86.

Wilken, L., & Dahlberg, M. G. (2017). Between international student mobility and work migration: Experiences of students from EU's newer member states in Denmark. *Journal of Ethnic and Migration Studies, 43*(8), 1347–1361.

Živković, Ž., Nikolić, D., Savić, M., Djordjević, P., & Mihajlović, I. (2017). Prioritizing strategic goals in higher education organizations by using a SWOT–PROMETHEE/GAIA–GDSS model. *Group Decision and Negotiation, 26*(4), 829–846.

ABOUT THE AUTHORS

Bruno F. Abrantes holds a PhD in Management with specialization in strategy and entrepreneurship from ISCTE-IUL University Institute of Lisbon (Portugal). He is an Associate Professor in Strategic Management from Niels Brock Copenhagen Business College, and his research interests encompass the fields internationalization, business networks, and capabilization models.

Wisdom Kwaku Agbevanu is a Research Fellow in educational planning and research at the Institute for Educational Planning and Administration, University of Cape Coast, Ghana, and the Editor of Journal of Educational Management. He holds a PhD in Education with emphasis on Qualitative Research, an MPhil (Educational Planning), and a PGDE from the University of Cape Coast and a BA (Economics) from the University of Ghana. As part of his PhD education, he was a Visiting Research Scholar on Split-site Commonwealth Scholarship at the University of Bath, UK, in 2011–2012. He teaches courses in educational planning, administration, leadership, and research methods. He worked as a College Improvement Advisor and College Gender Advisor for Transforming Teacher Education and Learning, Ghana, and as an Independent Researcher for Ghana Education Service and UNICEF Ghana. He is currently working on an EQUAL Global Network funded research project on "Measuring quality in non-formal education and youth skills training" and on a Girls' Education Unit-UNICEF Ghana supported research project on "Adolescent girls' school attendance and completion in deprived districts" in Ghana. His research interests include educational resource planning and management, school-built environments, education sector-wide planning and policy, quality education, and gender equality issues.

Francis Ansah is a Research Fellow in higher education policy and quality assurance at the Institute for Educational Planning and Administration (IEPA) of the University of Cape Coast, Ghana. He is an Academic Quality Auditor of the National Accreditation Board (NAB) of Ghana and a quality assurance consultant to Garden City University College in Kumasi, Ghana. In 2018, he was Carnegie Corporation of New York Visiting Scholar at Institute for Post School Studies, University of the Western Cape, Cape Town, South Africa. In addition, he has been a College Improvement Advisor (CIA) to more than eight Colleges of Education in Ghana. He holds a Doctor of Philosophy in Education with specialization in Higher Education Quality Assurance from La Trobe University in Melbourne, Australia. He also holds a Master of Science in Educational Policy and Management Studies from University of Twente in the Netherlands and a Bachelor of Management Studies from University of Cape Coast in Ghana. His research interests are in Higher Education Policy and Quality Assurance. He is a

Member of American Society for Quality (ASQ) and Golden Key International Honour Society (GKIHS).

Irene Antonopoulos is a Senior Lecturer in Law at De Montfort University, Leicester. She holds a PhD in Human Rights and the Environment from the University of Aberdeen. She is a Fellow of the Higher Education Academy. Prior to entering academia, she was a Trainee at the Council of Europe. Her research focuses on human rights and sustainability, including embedding the Sustainable Development Goals into the Law curriculum.

Bridget Backhaus is a Lecturer in the School of Humanities, Languages, and Social Science at Griffith University. Her research focuses on issues of voice, listening, and social change in community media. She lectures in media and communications and has contributed to research projects exploring work-integrated learning and service learning across a range of disciplines. She holds a PhD from Loughborough University London.

Paul Beehler is an Associate Director of the University Writing Program (UWP) and Director of the Entry Level Writing Requirement (ELWR) for the University of California at Riverside. Currently serving as an Associate Professor of Teaching in the Department of English, he has authored over a dozen articles including "Change and Sexuality: Ursula and Ariel as Markers of Metamorphosis in The Little Mermaid" (2017), "Training International Teaching Assistants Through a Writing Across the Curriculum Course" (2016), and "Macduff's Amorphous Identity: Equivocation and Uncertainty as Defining Markers in Shakespeare's Macbeth" (2009). Another article, "Historical Nexus: Bewitching Nurses in Rupert Goold's Visual Medium of Macbeth," is forthcoming in *The Southern African Journal of Medieval and Renaissance Studies*. His research interests include Shakespeare, composition theory, and writing program administration. He serves as Ex Officio on the Committee on Preparatory Education at the University of California, Riverside, and Chairs the University of California system-wide committee on English for Multilingual Students. Additionally, he is Co-editor of the *Instructor's Manual for Write It*. Of particular note is his role as the Co-founder and Co-director of the Writing and Foster Youth Alliance (WAFYA).

Patrick Blessinger, EdD, is an Adjunct Associate Professor of Education at St. John's University, a Math and Science Teacher with the New York State Education Department, and Chief Research Scientist of the International Higher Education Teaching and Learning Association (in consultative status with the United Nations). He is the Editor and Author of many books and articles, and he is an Educational Policy Analyst and Contributing Writer with UNESCO's Inclusive Policy Lab, University World News, The Hechinger Report, The Guardian, and Higher Education Tomorrow, among others. He teaches courses in education, leadership, and research methods, and he serves on doctoral dissertation committees. He founded and leads a global network of educators focused on teaching and learning, and he is an Expert in inclusion, equity, leadership, policy, democracy, human rights, and sustainable development. He provides professional development workshops to teachers and professors and regularly gives presentations and keynote addresses at academic conferences around the world. He has received several educational awards, including Fulbright Senior Scholar to Denmark (Department of State, USA), Governor's Teaching Fellow (Institute of Higher Education, University of Georgia, USA), and Certified Educator (National Geographic Society, USA).

Thomas D. Eatmon received his PhD in Public Policy from Southern University and A&M College in 2008. He joined Niels Brock Copenhagen Business College in 2015 and is currently Dean of Academic Affairs for Postgraduate Programmes and Research. His teaching and research activities examine the technological, economic, and social dimensions of innovation and entrepreneurship.

Charlotte Forsberg has an MSc (Econ) in International Business Administration and Modern Languages from Copenhagen Business School. She also holds a Master in Adult Education and Human Resource Management from Roskilde University and a Master in European Studies from Universidad Nebrija, Spain. Her research interests are the international student experience and institutional and national framing thereof. She studies educational mobility, the sense-making process of international students and how institutional policies affect this. Alongside a career in international teaching, she is currently doing her PhD at De Montfort University on the transformative effect of studying abroad.

Omar Madhloom is Senior Lecturer at the University of Bristol. He is a qualified Solicitor and specializes in Clinical Legal Education. He is a Senior Fellow of the Higher Education Academy. He has established two university law clinics prior to joining the University of Bristol. His research focuses on reflective practice and moral autonomy.

Erin McLaughlin, PhD, is a Professor of Business at Cabrini University. She is a certified member of the National Association of Small Business International Trade Educators (NASBITE) Global Business Professionals. Her areas of interest focus on international corruption, economic development, and international culture. By incorporating her research into coursework, she inspires students to think beyond the "bottom line." She provides students with real-life examples to better understand the economic issues and their implications. This can be seen in coursework that includes advocating on behalf of orphans and vulnerable children in Zambia and Swaziland to start a craft business by developing a social business strategy.

Rory Moore is a Lecturer in the University Writing Program (UWP) at the University of California, Riverside campus (UCR). Previously, she was Associate Director of Academics and Assessment for Long Island University's Higher Education Opportunity Program in Brooklyn, New York; GradSuccess Coordinator for Graduate Division at UCR; and Lecturer in the Department of English at UCR.

She has published scholarship in the field of nineteenth century British literature in *Women's Writing* (2013) and *Nineteenth-Century Contexts* (2011), representing her interests in the intersections of literature, gender, and popular culture during that period. Current research and professional interests focus on composition pedagogy, program administration, accessibility, and student success. She has presented in these areas at a number of conferences, including the Long Island Council of Student Personnel Administrators Annual Conference (2016), UC Writing Conference (2017), and Conference on College Composition and Communication's Annual Convention (2019). She is a committed advocate for inclusive teaching practices as well as for marginalized student populations. This is most apparent in her 2018 co-founding of the Writing and Foster Youth Alliance (WAFYA), a faculty-led academic mentoring program within the UWP at UCR, which she also co-directs.

Hope Pius Nudzor is a Researcher and a Critical Education Policy Analyst. He was formerly UK's Economic and Social Research Council's (ESRC) Postdoctoral Research Fellow with the University of Strathclyde, and before that a Postdoctoral Teaching Fellow with Liverpool Hope University in 2009 and 2008, respectively. He obtained his bachelor's degree in Linguistics and Swahili from the University of Ghana in 2001. Thereafter in 2003, he proceeded to the University of Strathclyde in Glasgow for his MSc degree in Management and Leadership in Education in 2004, and after this his PhD in Educational and Professional Studies in 2007. Currently, he works as a Senior Research Fellow for/ at the Institute for Educational Planning and Administration of the University of Cape Coast, Ghana. His research interests and expertise relate to policy success and failure, management and leadership issues in education, educational decentralization, critical discourse analysis, higher education institutions and their governance systems, transnational higher education partnerships, and educational research methods. He has written widely in education policy, qualitative research methods, educational decentralization in Ghana, activity-based learning practices in Ghanaian schools, and on the group of young people referred to in policy terms as not in education, employment, or training (NEET).

Kshama Pandey is working as Associate Professor in the Department of BEd/ MEd, MJP Rohilkhand University, Bareilly. She has more than 12 years of teaching experience with various administrative capacities. Her research interests include ICT-based Innovative Pedagogy and Human Rights and Peace Education. An international edited book *Handbook of Research on Promoting Global Peace and Civic Engagement through Education* has been published by IGI Publication, USA. She is Section Editor of an edited reference book *Handbook on Mobile Teaching and Learning* published by Springer, New York. She is Editorial Board Member and Reviewer of various international journals, that is, *Computers & Education*, Elsevier; *Independent Journal of Management & Production*, Brazil; and *Sukimat Multidisciplinary Research Journal*, University of Bauie, Philippines. Various research papers have been published in *National and International Journals*. Her various chapters have been published in edited books with national and international repute like Springer, IGI Global Publication, and International

Book Series, USA, and Infotech, England, etc. Recently, she has completed a Project "Effect of design thinking on reflective engagement and innovation of pupil teachers in blended learning environment" by IUCTE, CASE (MHRD).

Umesh Chandra Pandey holds an MPhil in Environmental Science and a PhD in Physics. Presently, he works as Regional Director of Indira Gandhi National Open University (IGNOU) at Bhopal (India). During nearly three decades of professional career, he has performed several academic and administrative responsibilities in IGNOU where he joined initially as Lecturer in Physics in 1990 and subsequently rose to the level of Dy Director and Regional Director. He also worked as Director (Knowledge Management) in School of Good Governance and Policy Analysis (Bhopal, India), where he significantly contributed for the identification, compilation, and dissemination of best practices in governance. His current research interests include the Open and Distance Learning and Sustainable Development.

Susan Jacques Pierson is an Associate Professor of Education at Cabrini University. Her interests include social justice and human rights education. She serves on the Board of Volunteer English of Chester County, an organization dedicated to working with immigrants and refugees. She shares her experiences working internationally with teachers and students in Argentina, Zambia, and Swaziland with her graduate and undergraduate students as one means of inspiring them to serve as advocates for young people and agents for change. She has developed course work for immersion experiences to Argentina, Swaziland, and Zambia focused on human rights education.

Enakshi Sengupta, PhD, serves as Associate Director of HETL and is responsible for the advancement of HETL in Asia, Middle East, and Africa. The Associate Director works closely with the executive director to fulfil the mission of HETL. She is also the Director of the Center for Advanced Research in Education (CARE), Associate Series Editor of the book series, Innovations in Higher Education Teaching and Learning, Emerald Group Publishing. She is the Managing Editor of the *Journal of Applied Research in Higher Education*, Emerald Publishing, and serves as the Vice Chair of the Editorial Advisory Board of the Innovations in Higher Education Teaching and Learning book series, Emerald Publishing. She is Senior Manager of the Research, Methodology, and Statistics in the Social Sciences forums on LinkedIn and Facebook responsible for managing all aspects of those forums. She is a PhD holder from the University of Nottingham in research in higher education, prior to which she completed her MBA with merit from the University of Nottingham and master's degree in English Literature from the Calcutta University, India. She has previously held leadership positions in higher education institutions.

Alia Sheety, PhD, is an Associate Professor of Education at Cabrini University. Living and working in a diverse society, She believes that through education, we can build a better world. Social justice, human rights, and restorative practices are central to her teaching and scholarship with an effort to ensure marginalized groups' voices are heard. She took part in various initiatives that dealt with education for peace, interfaith, and implementation of restorative practices. She is an Author and Co-author of various publications and has presented her work in national and international conferences.

Anil Shukla is presently working as Vice Chancellor in MJP Rohilkhand University, Bareilly. He has more than 33 years of teaching experience with various administrative capacities. As a teacher, many innovative approaches in teaching like PATE, SMART, and Hybrid were introduced by him and successfully executed in the classroom. He is the Recipient of various prestigious fellowship, viz., Fulbright Fellow, US; Commonwealth Fellow, Oxford University, UK; and Korea Foundation Fellow, South Korea, which helped him a lot in making his vision of higher education global in outlook, on the one hand, and rooted to culture, on the other hand. He is the Member of different national apex bodies, that is, NCTE, MHRD, UGC, ICSSR, etc. He was also the President and General Secretary of Teacher Association of Lucknow University. He has worked for various international Research Projects funded from World Bank and several National Agencies. He has authored more than nine books. He has about 45 publications in referred journals and edited books. He has also attended and pioneered several national and international webinars, seminars, conferences, campaigns, and exhibitions on contemporary issues. His research interests include Quality Education, Teacher Education, and Internationalization of Higher Education.

Sharon Tao is a Senior Education and Gender Adviser for Cambridge Education and is currently part of DFID's Girls Education Challenge, which supports 41 projects in 17 countries. She has implemented several large-scale education programmes, having worked as a Key Adviser for technical areas that include Teacher Development, Gender & Inclusion, and M&E/Research on DFID-funded programmes in Tanzania, Ghana, Nigeria, Sierra Leone, Uganda, and India. Her work on systems strengthening, intervention/programme design, and policy development within these programmes has been underpinned by PhD research and engagement with a wide evidence base; as well as experience in teaching classes of 100+ students in government schools in Tanzania and Rwanda. Her academic rigor and programme experience in nurturing government relationships, managing teams, and overseeing budgets/work planning has resulted in an ability to shape and deliver innovative and successful education programs.

Faith Valencia-Forrester is a Senior Lecturer and the Director of the Service-Learning Unit, delivering Griffith University's Community Internships program. Her research into work-integrated learning (WIL) has been instrumental in developing engaged connections between the university's journalism program and the community. She has led pioneering WIL research projects – Project Safe Space and Project Open Doors – which have raised the benchmarks for inclusive journalism and media education. In addition, she leads the university large-scale collaboration with Nine/Fairfax Media for the 2014 G20 Leaders Summit and the 2018 Commonwealth Games in Brisbane, Australia. She has degrees in Arts, Law, and Business and holds a PhD from Griffith University, Australia.

Alan Vogelfanger is a Lawyer (University of Buenos Aires, School of Law), Fulbright Scholar for a Master of Laws in International Legal Studies, with a specialization in Human Rights (American University Washington College of Law), postgraduate degree on Pedagogy and the Teaching of Law (University of Buenos Aires), Legal Advisor at the Ombudsperson's Office of the City of Buenos Aires, Lecturer of the courses "Human Rights and Guarantees" (University of Buenos Aires) and "Environmental Law" (University of Business and Social Sciences), Consultant for the Danish Institute for Human Rights and UN Argentina, and Former Visiting Professional at the Inter-American Court of Human Rights. Other previous employers include the Legislature of the City of Buenos Aires, the Attorney General's Office, the Judiciary of the City of Buenos Aires, and national NGOs. Representative of the University of Buenos Aires at the Nelson Mandela World Human Rights Moot Court Competition, the Philip C. Jessup International Law Moot Court Competition, the Jean-Pictet Competition on International Humanitarian Law, and the Inter-American Human Rights Moot Court Competition.

NAME INDEX

SUBJECT INDEX

Note: Page numbers followed by *"n"* indicate endnotes.